READINGS IN LANGUAGE STUDIES

VOLUME 6

A CRITICAL EXAMINATION OF LANGUAGE AND COMMUNITY

INTERNATIONAL SOCIETY FOR LANGUAGE STUDIES

READINGS IN LANGUAGE STUDIES

VOLUME 6

A CRITICAL EXAMINATION OF LANGUAGE AND COMMUNITY

EDITED BY
PAUL CHAMNESS MILLER
BRIAN G. RUBRECHT
ERIN A. MIKULEC
CU-HULLAN TSUYOSHI McGIVERN

A PUBLICATION OF THE
INTERNATIONAL SOCIETY FOR LANGUAGE STUDIES, INC.

Copyright © 2016

International Society for Language Studies, Inc.
1968 S. Coast Hwy #142
Laguna Beach, CA, 92651
USA

All rights reserved.

ISBN 978-0-9964820-1-1
Library of Congress Control Number: 2008927091

Text layout by Julie Wernick Dallavis

Cover art comes from the original painting of mixed media and acrylic on canvas, *Las Tres Almas*, by Hector Rolando Garza. Cover art reproduction of the painting used with permission from the artist. Those interested in his work may reach him at hgarza26@gmail.com.

This book was printed on acid-free paper.

Printed in the United States of America.

For all those who struggle to find a sense of community – PCM

To Lisa and Rick, who constantly remind me that love cannot be restricted by either time or space – BGR

This volume dedicated to those who are committed to building community – EAM

Dedicated to my two-year-old daughter, Leah – CTM

CONTENTS

Introduction ix

1 Language Rights for Minorities and the Right to Code-Switch in the United States Workplace 1
Eduardo D. Faingold

2 Do Experiences of Teaching Abroad Impact Identity Transformation in Second Language Teachers? 15
Keiko Kitade

3 Language Engineering in Totalitarian Régimes: Controlling Belief and Behavior Through Language 39
Timothy G. Reagan

4 Dramaturgical Critical Analysis: A Case for Performance Plays to Stage Critical Multicultural Analysis of Literature 57
Paulo Andreas Oemig

5 Critical Sociolinguistics and Commodification: Studying English as a Foreign Language in Mexico 83
Gerrard Mugford

6 (Mis)understanding in the Language Classroom: The Case of a Japanese Student and a Brazilian English Language Teacher 103
Priscila Leal

7 Researching College Community Services Engages Isolated Foreign-Born English Language Learners in Campus Life 125
Bettina P. Murray

8 Testing the Grounds of Reciprocity and Multilingualism: Forays into Writing Collaborations among L2 and L1 Writers 143
Mary Jeannot and John Eliason

9 Hispanic Settlement in Rural Settings: The Role of Language in Adaptation 167
María Cristina Montoya and Ho Hon Leung

10 Critical Analysis of Nation-Building and Maintenance Through Discourse: Transition in Slovenia 197
Anton Vegel

11 The Benefits of Play-Based Learning in a Native American Community 215
Thomas M. Hill, Jr.

12	Discourse, Globalization, and the Translocalization of Gangspeak: Evidence from Trinidad	233
	Renée Figuera and Wendell C. Wallace	
13	Reaching Outside the Classroom: A Qualitative Look at the Effects of Community on the Heritage Language Development of University Students	265
	N. Ariana Mrak	
14	Literacy Practices and Identity Construct: A Critical Discourse Analysis with an SFL Perspective	281
	Leonor Juárez García	

Index	297
About the Editors	301
About the Contributors	303

INTRODUCTION

The International Society for Language Studies has its origins in a grassroots effort to bring together multiple disciplines around issues of language, power, and identity. In 2002, a group of international scholars began planning a conference that would eventually grow to forty papers, representing such diverse fields as medicine, law, education, and linguistics, presented the following year in St. Thomas, U.S. Virgin Islands. This fledging "society" was further advanced through its incorporation as a 501c(6) non-profit with the vision of founding a volunteer-based organization of scholars and practitioners committed to critical, interdisciplinary, and emergent approaches to language studies. Fast forward to 2016. We are well into our second decade as an organization, as well as wrapping up the thirteenth volume of the society's official journal, *Critical Inquiry in Language Studies*, published by Routledge/Taylor and Francis. Our first conference in Asia was successfully organized two years ago in Akita, Japan, and we are currently planning our tenth conference to be held at the University of Hawai'i - Manoa in 2017. We have also been experimenting with recruiting universities to host our conferences in an effort to involve more local scholars in the planning process, as well as to offer greater savings to presenters and attendees facing ever-decreasing travel budgets. This year we are also delighted to have a formal travel grant competition available to support scholars who would otherwise be unable to afford conference participation.

International membership continues to grow, and throughout this period of growth the society has remained focused on providing a means to disseminate the important scholarship of its membership. This sixth volume of the *Readings in Language Studies* series, focusing on language and community, represents ISLS's continued efforts to provide peer-reviewed fora as a reflection of its mission.

Readings in Language Studies, Volume 6: A Critical Examination of Language and Community features international contributions that represent state-of-the-field reviews, multi-disciplinary perspectives, theory-driven syntheses of current scholarship, reports of new empirical research, and critical discussions of major topics centered on the intersection of language and community. Consistent with the mission of ISLS, the collection of 14 chapters in this volume seeks to "bridge these arbitrary disciplinary territories and provide a forum for both theoretical and empirical research, from existing and emergent research methodologies, for exploring the relationships among language, power, discourses, and social practices."

In Chapter 1, Faingold initiates the volume with a chapter based on an expert witness report produced for a minority language discrimination case brought by Mexican Americans against the City of Altus in Oklahoma (*Maldonado v. City of Altus*, 2006). Using well-established theories of bilingualism as evidence, as well as the details of this legal case, Faingold argues that the use of minority languages in the workplace not only constitutes an unconscious and automatic linguistic behavior but is also a crucial marker of social and cultural identity. He maintains that a work environment that establishes official language rules prevents minority-language speakers from doing something natural and culturally relevant to them. Furthermore, prohibiting the use of minority languages at work is a violation of the civil rights of bilinguals.

Kitade turns the focus in Chapter 2 to the classroom with a study that addresses how novice language teachers' experiences of teaching abroad impact their identities and their later teaching practices. Narrative inquiry data of two Japanese native-speaking teachers are analyzed using the Trajectory Equifinality Approach to capture the critical points of the teachers' development, along with the social affordances and constraints that accompany this development, during and after their experiences teaching abroad. The findings show whether the teacher is admitted as a legitimate member of the local teachers' community impacts the teachers' appreciation of contextual aspects. Kitade's study reveals that such border-crossing experiences shape teachers' awareness of culturally critical matters later in their careers.

Language, as Reagan reminds us in Chapter 3, is profoundly important in terms of how we construct our daily activities, as well as in developing and articulating our understanding of society, politics, ideology, and culture. This chapter explores language in two totalitarian societies as it was utilized to promote social control and ideological hegemony, namely the USSR in the years immediately following the 1917 Revolution and Nazi Germany. Lastly, Reagan discusses the implications of these cases, both for understanding an important aspect of totalitarian régimes more generally and for citizens of modern democratic countries, especially the United States.

Chapter 4, contributed by Oemig, explores the applicability of critical multicultural analysis as constructed by Botelho and Rudman (2009) in the field of performance plays. In this study, a high school theater class was chosen to examine how students engage with and read plays. Whereas Botelho and Rudman analyze book sets arranged by themes and genres, Oemig presents recommendations for classroom instruction to reach deeper levels of critical literacy. In combining critical multicultural analysis and Goffman's (1959) dramaturgical analysis, he illustrates how a critical engagement of all dimensions of text and language is possible through dramaturgical critical analysis.

Mugford examines one group of Mexican adult learners' aspirations and realities in studying English as a Foreign Language (EFL) in Chapter 5. He argues that current critical research strongly focuses on larger issues such as linguistic imperialism, resistance perspectives, and the politics of pedagogy, but the body of literature has largely ignored real-life classroom concerns, such as adults' goals in studying English and their likelihood of achieving success. From a critical sociolinguistic stance, Mugford argues that the packaging or commodification of EFL often builds up false expectations. Based on the data collected from 70 beginner adult students who responded to written questionnaires about their goals, the analysis indicates that learners may be disappointed with what they can really achieve.

Continuing with a focus on the classroom, in Chapter 6 Leal addresses another area that is largely under-researched in language education: misunderstanding. She maintains that this topic is significant because, as teachers describe its untangling, we are able to "re-write our understandings of instruction as an actual task and practical enactment" (Macbeth, 2011, p. 445). To illustrate this point, she reports on a Japanese university student and his Brazilian teacher working together through a gap in understanding. Through the lens of interactional sociolinguistics, Leal notes that the implications for language teachers include providing meaningful opportunities for students to practice strategies of "doing" (mis)understanding.

In Chapter 7, Murray describes a study based on a course in which one of the goals was to provide foreign-born English language learners (ELLs) with an increased knowledge of their college community and an opportunity to work together to improve their English language skills. The participants were from various cultural backgrounds and were familiar with the English language but had spent only a few years in the United States. The college ESL (English as a second language) program determined that these students needed further exposure to English in order to be successful with the college program. After conducting an initial survey, it became apparent that the ELLs were expressing a sense of isolation and a need to learn more about the college environment and the American society that surrounded them. Course goals were to immerse the student participants into college life and to assist them in their adjustment to the American college system.

Jeannot and Eliason address the question of cross-cultural and cross-linguistic "incomprehensibility" in the context of higher education in the 21st century in Chapter 8. They begin by tracing through the literature to explore how incomprehensibility has been represented for L1 and L2 writers. Then Jeannot and Eliason turn toward possible responses to this question by investigating collaborative structures that bring together US domestic and international students in ways that promote reciprocity in learning and encourage cross cultural dialogue and understanding. The chapter concludes by refiguring incomprehensibility as a generative force in learning environments that are monolingual and multilingual. The authors also consider possible consequences for higher education if it ignores the question of incomprehensibility and incoherence brought on by cross-linguistic ambiguity and confusion. At the heart of the chapter lies a question about sustainability: regardless of the collaborative structures that promote reciprocity in learning in a climate of higher education where resources are always uncertain, how do teachers of writing come together to address in realistic ways the myriad challenges presented by the range of incomprehensibilities?

Chapter 9 describes the settlement experience of Hispanic immigrants in a rural town and the role of language in the process of becoming established in that community. Montoya and Leung reveal the fact that being surrounded by English as a dominant language is not perceived as negative by the immigrants, so long as there is a feeling of community support. Despite having a supportive community, the lack of Spanish speech communities may present distinct kinds of challenges in rural areas. However, Montoya and Leung also found that it also allows for certain interactions within the households of immigrants that may otherwise not be present. Furthermore, the private language that is created becomes a marker of identity and survival through a supported social network particular to this small town.

Through the lens of discourse analysis, Vegel offers in Chapter 10 a study that critically analyzes how nation-building and maintenance rely on discourse that does not often reflect state reality while showing how discourse has been relevant in Slovenia (a) in its nation-building, through the creation of its first global atlas and the development of exclusive and autonomous toponymy, while spatially "repositioning" itself towards Europe and away from the Balkans, and (b) in its national maintenance, through the promotion of ethnic nationalist ideology in opposition to state reality by diverting responsibility of particular minorities and refugees that contrast with historical revisionist goals.

In Chapter 11, Hill reminds the reader that throughout the history of education in the United States one of the most underserved groups of learners is Native American students. Schools serving Native American communities are still learning how to provide an effective learning environment where assimilation was once the norm. He argues that educators have the responsibility to create a learning environment which allows all students to be successful regardless of the context. Hill suggests that an often overlooked and underutilized method that can be employed is that of play-based learning. His chapter examines the effectiveness of play-based learning using tribal stories on a reservation in the U.S. Southwest.

Previous research on the language of gang members has generally taken a glossary rather than a contextualized discourse approach, such as how cultural and linguistic practices of gangs of one location influence the language of gangs in other territories. For this reason, Figuera and Wallace present in Chapter 12 a study on the translocalization of the "gangsta" lexicon in gang-related communities in Trinidad. This investigation uses discursive, semantic, and morphological data from within gang-affiliated communities in Trinidad as evidence of lexical adoption, re-lexical appropriation, and the re-invention of gang-related lexicon. As a result, it provides an overview of some features of gang-affiliated discourse within two communities in Northern Trinidad, while accounting for translocalized cultural influences, which have shaped language use within these local communities.

Mrak, in Chapter 13, highlights the importance of the connection between heritage language education (HLE) and the community in which the heritage language (HL) is spoken. Her study focuses on one Spanish for heritage speakers' class at the intermediate level in a public university. One of the class assignments asked students to interview two Spanish speakers from the community: one who shared the same geographic language variety as the student and one who did not. The purpose behind this activity was to (a) present students with an opportunity to study the varieties spoken by community members, (b) demonstrate to students that these varieties are worthy of study, (c) validate all the varieties, both the ones in the community and those in the classroom, (d) provide opportunities for interaction with members of the Hispanic community, since students report this as the primary reason for studying the HL, and (e) give HLLs ownership of their language. A description of the entire project in which the students participated is presented, followed by an assessment of the outcomes and suggestions for continued development that can be applied to other heritage language classrooms.

To conclude this volume, in Chapter 14 García examines initial educators' beliefs and perceptions about literacy. Ten kindergarten educators from rural communities in the south of Puebla, Mexico, participated in the study. In these communities, high levels of illiteracy, as well as a significant number of speakers of indigenous languages, are still found. Through the lens of discourse analysis and by the use of Systemic Functional Linguistics, García found that teachers' idealizations are in opposition to the stigmatized identities in the conception of the literate/illiterate binary. She also addresses findings regarding the advantages of rural communities in comparison to urban communities.

Since its inception, ISLS has had as its mission the bridging of disciplines around language studies with a particular emphasis on critical theory. With few venues, the Society, with its conference, journal, and publications initiative, now stands as a major advocate for this paradigm. *Readings in Language Studies, Volume 6,* represents contemporary issues, theory, and practices in language studies around issues of language and community. Volume 7, scheduled for publication in 2018 will continue to focus on emergent international perspectives on the intersection of language and peace studies. This forthcoming volume, as well as future volumes, will further the Society's core mission and the work of its membership.

References
Botelho, M. J., & Rudman, M. K. (2009). *Critical multicultural analysis of children's literature: Mirrors, windows, and doors.* New York: Routledge.
Goffman, E. (1959). *The presentation of self in everyday life.* New York: Doubleday.
Macbeth, D. (2011). Understanding understanding as an instructional matter. *Journal of Pragmatics, 43*(2), 438-451. doi: 10.1016/j.pragma.2008.12.006

CHAPTER 1

LANGUAGE RIGHTS FOR MINORITIES AND THE RIGHT TO CODE-SWITCH IN THE UNITED STATES WORKPLACE

Eduardo D. Faingold
University of Tulsa

Code-switching, or moving between one language and another in conversation (Myers-Scotton, 1990; Poplack, 2000), is often considered an inappropriate behavior by teachers and school officials who spend a lot of energy fighting it in the classroom and in other school settings (Palmer, 2009). Similarly, some employers make rules that prohibit code-switching and speaking foreign languages in general at work. This chapter reviews relevant neurocognitive, psycholinguistic, and sociolinguistic literature dealing with code-switching in a variety of settings. It attempts to provide a better understanding of linguistic evidence that can be used to establish a legal framework for the protection of linguistic minorities (Faingold, 2004a, 2006, 2007, 2012a, 2012b, 2014, 2015, 2016). The paper focuses on the use of Spanish/English code-switching by Hispanics in the workplace and studies rules that employers make to prohibit this behavior. It argues that code-switching is often not a matter of choice, but a natural behavior, that occurs unconsciously and unintentionally among bilinguals. Also, the chapter argues that code-switching is crucially connected to the national origin of the speakers and is of social and cultural importance to Hispanics in the United States (Haugen, 1956; Lipski, 1985; Zentella, 1997). The prohibition against speaking foreign languages at work—English-only policies—has been declared illegal under the Civil Rights Act of 1964 by some U.S. courts (Del Valle, 2003; Faingold, 2006, 2012b; Krahnke, Hoffman, & Krahnke, 2003).

English-Only in the Workplace

Title VII of the Civil Rights Act of 1964 is the legal instrument used by the Equal Employment Opportunity Commission (EEOC), the administrative agency created to enforce the statute, to combat English-only rules in the workplace in the United States. Many employees possess the ability to use a foreign language and sometimes use it along with English in the workplace. In some cases, employers make rules prohibiting employees from speaking foreign languages and have enacted English-only policies in the workplace (Del Valle, 2003). *Title VII—Discrimination because of Race, Color, Religion, Sex, or National Origin* reads, in part, as follows:

> ... It shall be an unlawful employment practice for an employer—
> 1. to fail or refuse to hire or to discharge any individual, or otherwise discriminate against any individual with respect to his compensation, terms, conditions, or privileges of employment, because of such individual's race, color, religion, sex, or national origin; or
> 2. to limit, segregate, or classify his employees in any way which would deprive or tend to deprive any individual of employment opportunities or otherwise adversely affect his status as an employee, because of such individual's race, color, religion, sex, or national origin .... (Civil Rights Act of 1964)

In a number of cases, English-only policies in the workplace have been challenged by the EEOC in U.S. courts. In 1980 the EEOC created a number of guidelines to be applied in cases of discrimination in which national origin is at issue. The guidelines define national origin discrimination broadly to include linguistic characteristics of a national origin group and specifically address English-only rules, written or unwritten, that prohibit the speaking of languages other than English in the workplace. An individual's primary language is deemed to be an essential national origin characteristic. A rule requiring employees to speak only English at all times in the workplace can be considered a burdensome term and condition of employment that violates Title VII (Del Valle, 2003). Employer rules and requirements to speak only English in the workplace can create an atmosphere of inferiority, intimidation, and xenophobia. The employer needs to show a legitimate and clearly articulated "business necessity" for such rules, and that it would suffer "undue hardship" (Del Valle, 2003, p. 151) when employees speak foreign languages at work (Krahnke et al., 2003). For example, speaking a foreign language while on the radio in a police car or fire engine can cause confusion at the time of fighting a crime or a fire. Lacking such a business necessity, English-only in the workplace or otherwise seeking a linguistically-homogenized work environment may be offensive and intimidating to Hispanics and other bilinguals, *mutatis mutandis*, not unlike the practice of slave owners intentionally mixing captured slaves who spoke different African languages to discourage the use of languages other than English on the Caribbean plantations (Holm, 1988).

In past years, several cases were decided in accordance with EEOC guidelines. For example, in *Martinez v. Lenox Health Care and Vencor, Inc.* (1999), a U.S. District Court in California ruled against an employer who created English-only rules in a nursing home. The Federal Court of the Northern District of Illinois, Eastern Division, settled a suit for eight former Hispanic plaintiffs brought against Watlow Batavia, Inc., for disciplining its workers for speaking Spanish with other co-workers on an assembly line (*EEOC v. Watlow Batavia, Inc.*, 1999). The District Court for the Northern District of Texas, Dallas Division, ruled against Premier Operator Services, Inc., in a lawsuit in which Spanish-speaking employees were fired after they refused to sign English-only agreements that would have stopped them from using only Spanish in the workplace, including during breaks (*EEOC v. Premier Operator Services, Inc.*, 2000). The EEOC reached a landmark settlement against the University of Incarnate Word in San Antonio, Texas, for 18 Hispanic housekeepers who were forbidden to use their native language of Spanish (*EEOC v. University of Incarnate Word in San Antonio*, 2001; Krahnke et al., 2003). More recently, in a language discrimination case in Oklahoma (*Maldonado v. City Altus*, 2006), 11 Hispanic city street department employees of the City of Altus, a municipal corporation, alleged that the employer's English-only policy violated Title VII of the Civil Right Act of 1964 (Faingold, 2006). A previous ruling in favor of the employer who implemented the English-only policy was reversed. The Tenth Circuit Court held that a jury could reasonably find that the English-only policy had a discriminatory impact on Hispanic workers and that the trial court had erred in concluding that the employer had established a business necessity for the policy. The Tenth Circuit Court held that the policy itself, and not just the effect of the policy, in evoking hostility from the coworkers, contributed to the hostility of the work environment. By the end of 2006, the case was settled out of court in favor of the plaintiffs (City of Altus Council Meeting Minutes, October 3, 2006).

Definition and Examples of Code-Switching

Code-switching is "the alternate use of two or more languages in the same utterance or conversation" (Grosjean, 1982, p. 145). It has also been defined as "the use of two or more linguistic varieties in the same conversation (and) can be intra- or extra-sentential and also intra-word" (Myers-Scotton, 1990, p. 85). Poplack (2000) writes that "code-switching is the alternation of two languages within a single discourse, sentence, or constituent" (p. 221). Toribio (2001a) defines code-switching as "the ability on the part of bilinguals to alternate between their linguistic codes in the same conversational event" (p. 403). She writes that code-switching "may be inter-sentential or intra-sentential" (p. 404) and provides one example of each, in sentences (1a) and (1b) below, respectively (Spanish forms appear in italics. Slashes indicate language switches in the translations):

1a. *Érase una vez una linda princesita blanca como la nieve.* Her stepmother, the queen, had a magic mirror on the wall.
Once upon a time there was a beautiful princess as white as the snow. / Her stepmother, the queen, had a magic mirror on the wall.

1b. *Por la noche, los siete enanitos* found her on the ground, seemingly dead.
At night, the seven dwarfs / found her on the ground, seemingly dead.

Neurocognitive Basis for Code-Switching

Grosjean (1997, 1998, 2001) found that bilinguals activate multiple "modes" unconsciously. Different language process mechanisms, representing the level of activation of each language at a given point in time, are activated according to such factors as language proficiency, attitudes, kinship relations, the setting (e.g., location, presence of monolinguals, degree of formality), and the stimuli (e.g., book read, TV program watched). When bilinguals interact with monolinguals, they behave in a monolingual language mode in that they are interacting with monolinguals of one of the languages that they know. In contrast, when bilinguals communicate with other bilinguals, they find themselves in a bilingual mode with bilinguals who share their two languages and with whom they can code-switch. In this case, both languages are active but the one that is used as the base language, the main language of communication, is more active than the other. Grosjean's modes are supported by his own experiments and data as well as studies of code-switching among bilingual speakers of English and several immigrant languages in Australia (Clyne, 2003), English and Dutch in the Netherlands (Hermans, Ormel, van Besselar, & van Hell, 2011), and English and Spanish in the United States (Canseco-Gonzalez, Brehm, Brick, Brown-Schmidt, Fischer, & Wagner, 2010).

In bilingual mode, when bilinguals interact with others with whom they can code-switch, they use one language as the base for the production of an utterance while the other language serves as a guest language. When code-switching occurs, both topic and addressee, as well as the conceptual and pragmatic context, affect the activation of linguistic systems (Grosjean, 1997; Myers-Scotton & Jake, 2000). In such cases, when code-switching is not appropriate, bilinguals are more likely to hesitate or produce linguistic errors. For example, bilinguals who code-switch often are obliged to use only one language, while at the same time they face competing lexicalized ideas in their first and second languages (i.e., in their L1 and L2; Green, 1998).

Pioneering work by Green (1986, 1998) and his associates (Abutalebi & Green, 2007, 2008; Costa & Santesteban, 2004; Green & Abutalebi, 2013) suggests that languages can be at different levels of activation and that bilinguals can be influenced by the nature of a language that appears to be switched off. For example, in order to use one language (e.g., an L2) rather than another (e.g., an L1), the activation level of the L2 must exceed that of the L1. Speaking in one language rather than another results in the activation of that language but not in the total inhibition of the other (Green, 1998).

Neurocognitive experiments suggest that the brain exercises control on inhibitory mechanisms and relies on multiple neural regions to manage linguistic tasks such as code-switching (Abutalebi & Green, 2008). Inhibitory neurons implement controls on language selection and code-switching and manage competition between languages (Abutalebi & Green, 2007). Physiological resources are required to maintain control, and different regions of the brain are involved in output language selection (Abutalebi & Green, 2007). Code-switching involves the frontal-parietal-subcortical network. Specifically, it appears to take place in the basal ganglia. This is because of the basal ganglia's forward and backward connections to the prefrontal cortex which are involved in the types of cognitive control necessary to produce cognitive task switching such as updating, shifting, and inhibiting mental representations (Abutalebi & Green, 2008).

According to Abutalebi and Green (2008), even for fluent speakers of a second language who do not show performance errors in the production of linguistic structures, their linguistic repertoire (i.e., their L1 and L2) remains active at all times. This suggests that bilinguals must have the means to manage competition between languages in order to select the appropriate target language, for example, to use their L2 proficiently. The need to inhibit or suppress a non-selected language requires that bilingual speakers exercise cognitive control to avoid interference from the L1 and the production of errors (Green, 1986). Separation of L1 and L2 linguistic structures in the bilingual brain requires that structures in the language not in use be successfully inhibited to avoid interference (Costa & Santesteban, 2004; Green, 1986, 1998).

Further, and of particular importance for the aims of this chapter, neurocognitive evidence shows that there is a cognitive cost in making bilinguals suppress the use of their native language. Bilingual speakers must be able to put in some "cognitive effort" (Abutalebi & Green, 2007, p. 255) or carry a "cognitive load" (Green & Abutalebi, 2013, p. 524), which can lead to impaired linguistic performance due to linguistic interference, (e.g., when going from the L1 to the L2; Green & Abutalebi, 2013). The effort to avoid such interference can be extremely demanding because both the L1 and L2 are active in the brain during the production of linguistic structures in either of the languages available to the speaker. For example, in order to name an object in the less dominant L2, the more dominant L1 needs to be strongly inhibited, resulting in an increase in "persisting inhibition" (Abutalebi & Green, 2008, pp. 560-561) or control. While the nature of control can change with proficiency, functional imaging evidence obtained from lexical access tasks shows that there is still a switch cost and that persisting inhibition is important also for highly proficient bilinguals (Abutalebi & Green, 2008). There are constraints of time and energy (i.e., cost) because of competition between languages (Abutalebi & Green, 2007). Switching languages incurs a real cost, since the inhibition of the previously irrelevant language takes unnecessary processing time. For example, it takes longer to switch into a language that is more suppressed, especially for unbalanced bilinguals (Green, 1998).

Thus, in the bilingual brain, languages can be seen as resources that require energy to operate (Green, 1986). The most dominant language requires more active suppression and activation of inhibitory processes in the production of speech by bilinguals (Abutalebi & Green, 2007). As the evidence reviewed in this section suggests, requiring bilinguals to speak a non-native language at all times has a cost, literally, in neurocognitive terms.

Psycholinguistic Constraints on Code-Switching

While we remember the content of conversations, it is very difficult to remember and repeat the exact words anyone has spoken. Bilinguals who are used to code-switching are often unaware of switching between languages. Code-switching takes place unconsciously. Speakers, including those who condemn code-switching, are unaware that they are switching from one language to another (Grosjean, 1982). Thus, bilingual speakers may not be aware of what language they are using at a particular moment in a conversation (Martinez, 2014). Bilinguals who regularly use more than one language may unconsciously code-switch or use more than one language to talk about the same subject. A good example of this was observed in a conversation among several bilinguals who code-switch frequently. At one point, according to Krahnke et al. (2003), the speakers were asked what language they had just used but they were unable to say. According to Lipski (1985),

> speakers who engage in intra-sentential shifting (code-switching) are frequently unaware of having shifted well after the fact and may not be able to recall the exact moment of the shift, or to give justification for having changed languages in midstream. (p. 3)

According to some language theorists, code-switching can be considered an underlying syntactic mechanism, part and parcel of Chomsky's unconscious rule-governed linguistic competence (Chomsky, 1981, 2006; Pinker, 1994). For example, Toribio (2001b) and MacSwan and McAlister (2010) provide strong experimental evidence that code-switching can be used to support what theoretical linguistics call the "Functional Head Constraint," a formal principle of linguistic theory that permits constituent-internal code-switching in sentences such as (2a) and (3a) but prohibits such code-switching in sentences such as (2b) and (3b) (Spanish forms appear in italics; the asterisk means that a sentence is not well-formed, that is, that it is not something that bilinguals would be likely to say):

2a. All of them *hablan español.*
 They all speak Spanish (Toribio, 2001b).

*2b. *Ellos han* completed degrees while working full time.
 They have completed degrees while working full time (Toribio, 2001b).

3a. *Mi hermano* bought some ice cream.
 My brother bought some ice cream (MacSwan & McAlister, 2010).

*3b. *El* bought some ice cream.
 He bought some ice cream (MacSwan & McAlister, 2010).

In sentences (2b) and (3b) code-switching between the functional head in Spanish (auxiliary verb *han* "had" and article *el* "the") and their complement in English (verb-phrases "have completed" and "bought") produce ungrammatical structures which would be rejected as ill-formed Spanish/English code-switching by Hispanic bilinguals who code-switch. In contrast, sentences (2a) and (3a), where no code-switching occurs between functional head and complement, would be considered legitimate examples of Spanish/English code-switching.

Because Hispanic bilinguals code-switch in their attempt to fit in linguistically with their English-speaking coworkers and bosses, their code-switching becomes something that they do naturally and without awareness. Asking them not to code-switch seems to be, *mutatis mutandis*, not unlike asking black people to bleach their black skin in order to fit in with the white-skinned majority.

Sociolinguistic Constraints on Code-Switching

In a conversation, the use of one or more languages may appear to be just a matter of choice for Hispanic bilinguals. Yet, Hispanic bilinguals feel obliged to use Spanish with Spanish-speaking relatives, teachers, friends, and others. Answering in English may be construed as an unfriendly gesture, or even dislike, by the addressee. Moreover, they feel constrained to have or show a positive attitude toward their native language (Faingold, 1999, 2004b). By the same token, language choice is also constrained by the social relationships among bilingual speakers participating in a conversation, that is, by the hierarchies found among speakers in the group (Palmer, 2009). Hispanic bilinguals of lower status may be obliged to answer in Spanish when spoken to in Spanish by other bilinguals of higher status; to answer in English may be considered an expression of disrespect (Krahnke et al., 2003). Similar considerations apply in the workplace. Here as well Spanish speakers feel that they must speak Spanish to other Spanish speakers to avoid disrespecting them.

For Spanish-speaking Hispanics in the United States, as well as other ethnic groups such as blacks, Italians, and Jews, there is a vital connection between language and ethnicity (Labov, 1978). In addition, as Fishman, Gertner, Lowy, and Milán (1986) note,

> since language is the most elaborate symbol system of humankind, it is no wonder, then, that particular languages become symbolic of the particular ethnocultures in which they are embedded and which they index. (p. xii)

More than fifty years ago Haugen (1956) noted that language

> is at once a social institution, like the laws, the religion, or the economy of the community, and a social instrument which accompanies and makes possible all other institutions. As an institution it may become a symbol of the community group. (p. 87)

Similarly, as Grosjean (1982) writes,

> it is a well-accepted notion among sociolinguists that language is not just an instrument of communication. It is also a symbol of social group identity, an emblem of group membership and solidarity. (p. 117)

Code-switching is used by bilinguals to claim membership in multilingual communities (Anzaldúa, 1987). Among U.S. Hispanics, code-switching in conversation with other Hispanics is construed as a friendly act (Faingold, 2004b; Zentella, 1997).

Mexican Americans, the largest Spanish-speaking group in the United States, as well as the other U.S. Hispanic minorities,

> are extremely attached to their language and culture and have no problems in retaining them. The region they live in once belonged to them, as the Spanish

place names remind them; they often return to Mexico to visit relatives, newcomers to the States arrive almost daily, many TV and radio stations broadcast in Spanish.... (Grosjean, 1982, p. 101; see also Faingold, 2012a, 2014)

As Lipski (1985) puts it,

> this type of language shifting (code-switching), which is characterized by a smooth flow between Spanish and English, is common in most U.S. Hispanic communities, and has even become an identifying characteristic of much of Hispanic-American literature in the United States. (p. 3)

In summary, based on the neurocognitive, psycholinguistic, and sociolinguistic evidence available, one can ascertain that code-switching between Spanish and English among U.S. Hispanics has, literally, a cognitive cost and is not a matter of choice but an unconscious and unintentional linguistic behavior as well as a crucial marker of social and cultural identity for these individuals or groups.

Monolingual English speakers often overlook the difficulty that non-native speakers of English have in expressing themselves in English, a language in which they may be fluent but not native (Grosjean, 1982). Krahnke et al. (2003) note that the vocabulary of speakers of Spanish and other languages may be limited to culturally-specific topics of conversation, for example, the family, a child's behavior, or health issues, or because of the complexity of the issue, such as legal and financial matters. They may not find it possible to talk about these topics in English because they simply do not have the language proficiency to do so. Thus, non-English speakers may be confronted either with no talking about some subjects or trying to do so in English and risk a communication breakdown. Lacking a business necessity, English-only rules may be intimidating and offensive to Hispanic and other bilingual individuals or groups because such rules prevent them from doing something that is natural and culturally relevant to them.

Note
This chapter is based on an expert witness report written by the author for the plaintiffs in a language discrimination case in Oklahoma (*Maldonado v. City of Altus*, 2006). The case was settled in favor of the plaintiffs in 2006 (City of Altus Council Meeting Minutes, October 3, 2006). The judgment in this case may constitute a landmark decision establishing a precedent that could affect the outcome of future

English-only cases pursued following the EEOC Guidelines. The reason is that the decision "may create a split in the circuit courts" because "a genuine issue of material fact existed as to the presence of a hostile work environment based solely on the employer's adoption of an English-only policy in the workplace" (Thomas, 2007, p. 2).

Acknowledgements

Revisions of this chapter have benefited from comments by audiences at the Fourth Annual Symposium of the John Hope Franklin Center for Reconciliation, Tulsa, Oklahoma, May 2013, Multidisciplinary Approaches in Language Policy and Planning Conference, Calgary, Canada, September 2013, and the Conference of the International Society for Language Studies, Albuquerque, New Mexico, June 2015. This research was supported in part by three University of Tulsa Faculty Grants in 2010, 2013, and 2014.

References

Abutalebi, J., & Green, D. W. (2007). Bilingual language production: The neurocognition of language representation and control. *Journal of Neurolinguistics, 20*, 242-275. doi:10.1016/j.neuroling.2006.10.003

Abutalebi, J., & Green, D. W. (2008). Control mechanisms in bilingual language production: Neural evidence from language switching studies. *Language and Cognitive Processes, 23*, 557-582. doi:10.1080/01690960801920602

Anzaldúa, G. (1987). *Borderlands/la frontera: The new mestiza*. San Francisco: Aunt Lute Books.

Canseco-Gonzalez, E., Brehm, L., Brick, C. A., Brown-Schmidt, S., Fischer, K., & Wagner, K. (2010). Carpet or carcel: The effect of age acquisition and language mode on bilingual lexical access. *Language and Cognitive Processes, 25*, 669-705. doi:10.1080/01690960903474912

City of Altus Council Meeting Minutes. (2006, October 3). Retrieved from http://altusok.gov/sites/default/files/ccfiles/CC100306.pdf

Civil Right Act of 1964. Retrieved from http://usinfo.state.gov.usa/info/laws/majorlaw/civilr19.htm

Clyne, M. (2003). *Dynamics of language contact: English and immigrant languages*. Cambridge, UK: Cambridge University Press.

Chomsky, N. (1981). *Lectures on government and binding*. Dodrecht, Netherlands: Foris.

Chomsky, N. (2006). *Language and mind*. Cambridge, UK: Cambridge University Press.

Costa, A., & Santesteban, M. (2004). Lexical access in bilingual speech production: Evidence from language switching in highly proficient bilinguals and L2 learners. *Journal of Memory and Language, 50*, 491-511. doi:10.1016/j.jml.2004.02.002

Del Valle, S. (2003). *Language rights and the law in the United States: Finding our voices*. Clevedon, UK: Multilingual Matters.

Faingold, E. D. (1999). The re-emergence of Spanish and Hebrew in a multilingual adolescent. *International Journal of Bilingual Education and Bilingualism, 2*, 283-295. doi:10.180/13670059908667695

Faingold, E. D. (2004a). Language rights and language justice in the constitutions of the world. *Language Problems and Language Planning, 28,* 11-24. doi:10.1075/lplp.28.1.03fai

Faingold, E. D. (2004b). *Multilingualism from infancy to adolescence.* Greenwich, CT: Information Age Publishing.

Faingold, E. D. (2006). Expert witness report: Code-switching in the workplace. Maldonado v. City of Altus, 433 F. 3d 1294 (10 Cir. 2006).

Faingold, E. D. (2007). Language rights in the 2004 draft of the European Union Constitution. *Language Problems and Language Planning, 31,* 25-36. doi:10.1075/lplp.31.1.03fai

Faingold, E. D. (2012a). Language rights in the United States Constitution and the Civil Rights Act of 1964. In P. C. Miller, J. L. Watzke, & M. Montero (Eds.), *Readings in language studies, volume 3: Language and identity* (pp. 447-457). Grandville, MI: International Society for Language Studies.

Faingold, E. D. (2012b). Official English in the constitutions and statutes of the fifty states in the United States. *Language Problems and Language Planning, 36,* 136-148. doi:10.1075/lplp.36.2.03fai

Faingold, E. D. (2014). Language rights for Mexican Americans and the Treaty of Guadalupe Hidalgo. In P. C. Miller, J. L. Watzke, & M. Montero (Eds.), *Readings in language studies, volume 4: Language and social justice* (pp. 271-281). Grandville, MI: International Society for Language Studies.

Faingold, E. D. (2015). Language rights in the European Union and the Treaty of Lisbon. *Language Problems and Language Planning, 39,* 33-49. doi:10.1075/lplp.39.1.02fai

Faingold, E. D. (2016). Language rights in Catalonia and the constitutional right to secede from Spain. *Language Problems and Language Planning, 40,* 146-162. doi:10.1075/lplp.40.2.02fai

Fishman, J., Gertner, M., Lowy, E. G., & Milán, W. G. (1986). Preface: Language and culture, the ethnic revival and the sociolinguistic enterprise. In J. Fishman, M. Gertner, E. G. Lowy, & W. G. Milán (Eds.), *The rise and fall of the ethnic revival: Perspectives on language and ethnicity (Contributions to the sociology of language,* pp. xi-xiv). Berlin: Mouton de Gruyter.

Green, D. W. (1986). Control, activation, and resource: A framework and model for the control of speech in bilinguals. *Brain and Language, 27,* 210-223. Retrieved from http://www.journals.elsevier.com/brain-and-language

Green, D. W. (1998). Mental control of the bilingual lexico-semantic system. *Bilingualism: Language and Cognition, 1,* 67-81. doi:130.64.77.193

Green, D. W., & Abutalebi, J. (2013). Language control in bilinguals: The adaptive control hypothesis. *Journal of Cognitive Psychology, 25,* 515-530. doi:10.1080/20445911.2013.796377

Grosjean, F. (1982). *Life with two languages: An introduction to bilingualism.* Cambridge, MA: Harvard University Press.

Grosjean, F. (1997). Processing mixed language: Issues, findings, and models. In A. M. B. De Groot & J. F. Kroll (Eds.), *Tutorials in bilingualism: Psycholinguistic perspectives* (pp. 225-254). Mahwah, NJ: Lawrence Erlbaum.

Grosjean, F. (1998). Studying bilinguals: Methodological and conceptual issues. *Bilingualism, Language and Cognition, 1,* 131-149. doi:10.1017/S136672899800025X

Grosjean, F. (2001). The bilingual's language modes. In J. Nicol (Ed.), *One mind, two languages: Bilingual language processing* (pp. 1-22). Oxford, UK: Blackwell.

Haugen, E. (1956). *Bilingualism in the Americas: A bibliography and research guide.* Montgomery: University of Alabama Press.

Hermans, D., Ormel, E., van Besselar, R., & van Hell, T. (2011). Lexical activation in bilinguals' speech is dynamic: How language ambiguous words can affect cross language activation. *Language and Cognitive Processes, 26,* 1687-1709. doi:10.1080/01690965.2010.530411

Holm, J. (1988). *Pidgins and creoles: Volume 1, Theory and structure*. Cambridge, UK: Cambridge University Press.

Krahnke, K., Hoffman, L., & Krahnke, K. (2003). Managing language use in the workplace. *The Journal of Behavioral and Applied Management, 4,* 148-157. Retrieved from http://www.ibam.com/jbam.html

Labov, W. (1978). *Sociolinguistic patterns*. Oxford, UK: Blackwell.

Lipski, J. (1985). *Linguistic aspects of Spanish-English language switching*. Tempe: Center for Latin American Studies, Arizona State University.

MacSwan, J., & McAlister, K. T. (2010). Naturalistic and elicited data in grammatical studies of code-switching. *Studies in Hispanic and Lusophone Linguistics, 3,* 521-532. doi:10.1515/shll20101085

Martinez. R. A. (2014). "Do they even know that they do it?" Exploring awareness of Spanish-English code-switching in a six-grade English language arts classroom. *Bilingual Research Journal, 37,* 195-210. doi:10.180/15235882.2014.934972

Myers-Scotton, C. (1990). Code-switching and borrowing: Interpersonal and macrolevel meaning. In R. Jacobson (Ed.), *Codeswitching as a worldwide phenomenon* (pp. 85-110). New York: Peter Lang.

Myers-Scotton, C., & Jake, J. L. (2000). Matching lemmas in a bilingual language competence and production model: Evidence from intra-sentential code-switching. In L. Wei (Ed.), *The bilingual reader* (pp. 281-324). London: Routledge.

Palmer, D. K. (2009). Code-switching and symbolic power in a second grade two-way classroom: A teacher's motivation system gone awry. *Bilingual Research Journal, 32,* 42-59. doi:10.1080/15235880902965854

Pinker, S. (1994). *The language instinct*. New York: Harper Collins.

Poplack, S. (2000). Sometimes I'll start in Spanish y termino en español: Toward a typology of code-switching. In L. Wei (Ed.), *The bilingual reader* (pp. 221-256). London: Routledge.

Thomas, M. D. (2007, July). A shifting burden: Recent developments related to English-only policies in the workplace. *Employment Law Commentary*. Retrieved from http://media.mofo.com/docs/pdf/ELC0707.pdf

Toribio, J. (2001a). Accessing bilingual code-switching competence. *International Journal of Bilingualism, 5,* 403-436. doi:10.117/13670069010050040201

Toribio, J. (2001b). On the emergence of bilingual code-switching competence. *Bilingualism: Language and Cognition, 4,* 203-231. doi:10.1017/S1366728901000414

Zentella, A. C. (1997). *Growing up bilingual: Puerto Rican children in New York*. Malden, MA: Blackwell.

CHAPTER 2

DO EXPERIENCES OF TEACHING ABROAD IMPACT IDENTITY TRANSFORMATION IN SECOND LANGUAGE TEACHERS?

Keiko Kitade
Ritsumeikan University

Studies of second-language teacher education (L2TE) from a sociocultural perspective (Freeman & Johnson, 1998) have emphasized that teaching practice is not primarily a knowledge-transmitting act, but rather a social activity wherein teachers negotiate between their own beliefs and values around teaching and those expected in the given context. Thus, Alsup (2006) referred to teachers' identity development through negotiations with teaching environments as crucial for their development.

To address teachers' development in particular social contexts, some studies in L2TE employ Vygotsky's (1978) genetic approach, wherein observations of the human development process, or the history of behavior, are crucial, rather than outcomes themselves, or objects. According to Vygotsky, four interrelated domains should be considered regarding development: the phylogenetic, cultural-historic, ontogenetic, and microgenetic. The phylogenetic domain is beyond this analysis, as it entails the development of humankind, or the natural species, but the remainder is necessary for analyzing teachers' development. The cultural-historic domain emphasizes the transformation of teachers' sociocultural context, for example, the national/institutional educational policy and ideology, while the ontogenetic domain highlights teachers' life trajectory. Finally, the microgenetic domain entails the concrete momentary teaching practice where teachers interact with their environments. Interactions among these domains lead to the development of higher psychological functions for teachers (Cross, 2010).

Second Language Teachers' Professional Development From a Sociocultural Perspective

Recent studies have suggested how changes in the cultural-historic domain, namely national educational reforms, impact teachers' development in local contexts. Cross (2010) investigated the experience of an English-speaking Japanese language teacher (JLT) of middle-school-aged children ages 11-15 with national educational reform, which moved from more communicative-oriented language other than English (LOTE) toward "a thinking-oriented rather than subject-based" (p. 443) approach, whereby LOTE was mainly used to support English literacy and learning for life. Although the teacher was initially employed to teach the Japanese language, LOTE became progressively irrelevant in the context of the new policy. The teacher's perceptions of himself changed to someone who assists his students to develop more generic skills for learning, rather than to enhance their communicative competence in Japanese. Cross's (2010) study illustrated how the teacher saw and reshaped his role in response to broader cultural-historic domains, using the example of national reform.

Similarly, Ahn (2011) examined South Korean English-language teachers' transformations under curricular reform based on communicative language teaching by the South Korean Ministry of Education. A novice teacher who trained at a prestigious national university to employ task-based and learner-centered instruction in imparting English had to deal with conflicting ideas when exposed to quite a different locally expected pedagogy, which considered the reality of the pupils' low English competence. Despite the teacher's initial policy of teaching in English to facilitate the development of communicative competence, she later decided to allow some Korean to be spoken, since her overuse of English limited pupils' participation.

The studies described above suggest how teachers overcome discrepancies between their beliefs and experiences developed in the ontogenetic domain, for example in training programs or previous teaching jobs, and the local expectations and policies at the microgenetic level. Furthermore, teachers may find that locally constituted teaching norms oppose national educational policy. Thus, teachers must become aware of such dissonance and seek to resolve it in each teaching context.

L2 Teachers' Identity Formation in Teaching Abroad

When teaching abroad, the locally constituted normative teaching methods or national education policy may differ from those teachers experience during training. L2 teachers may face challenges in negotiating the "past self" and different expectations in the current teaching context. Regarding teachers' study-abroad experiences, some studies have suggested that the experience increases teachers' intercultural awareness (Marx & Moss, 2011; Smolcic, 2011) via a "border-crossing" (Block, 2007) experience. But do teaching-abroad experiences guarantee teachers' development?

According to Wenger (1998), identities emerge in and through negotiation of membership in social communities. Identity is constructed neither through the individual nor the community, but via negotiation between agent and social context. Norton's (2000) investigation of immigrants in Canada suggested a two-way formation of identity between the agents, or learners, and the community, implying that L2 learners' high motivation does not always lead to investment in the language practice. Even highly motivated learners may be excluded from or resist the language practice due to nationality, race, gender, social class, and other power-related identity attributes.

Within the framework of community of practice (Lave & Wenger, 1991), which perceives learning as deepening and increasing participation in the community, rather than the acquisition of a certain type of knowledge, Wenger (1998) suggested that newcomers' participation in a community, whether "peripheral" or "marginal," is crucial for emergence of their identity. Peripheral status could involve mainly nonparticipation or partial participation, but with full participation expected in the future. Conversely, marginality prevents full participation. Newcomers in the former case are permitted community access, while those in the latter case are not. It is crucial for communities to facilitate newcomers' mutual engagement with members and allow for negotiations of activities and use of the communities' shared repertoire of resources; that is, the community's accumulated knowledge such as information, documents, experience, tools, and routines.

However, some studies have pointed out that the authority of newcomers may have an impact on their participation status. A study on a study abroad program for American college students suggested that American students or native English speakers may be prohibited from identity development through study-abroad experiences due to the world-wide *linguistic capital* (Bourdieu, 1991) of English. Block (2007) stated that American students in particular have less experience overcoming differences with host cultures. In addition to the limited length of stays, American students' sense of superiority regarding their national identity over the host community decreases their opportunities to negotiate differences. Kinginger (2010) and Kubota (2009) stated that being a speaker of English in light of its linguistic capital inhibits the development of translingual or transcultural competency.

Similarly, native-speaking teachers (NSTs) teaching abroad may face similar obstacles as when studying abroad, in terms of obtaining membership to the host community and facilitating identity development. NSTs' native authority of the language, which is caused by the linguistic ideology in the local community, may restrict the teachers' identity transformations. In addition to national or ethnic attributions, studies of L2 teachers' identity have suggested that non-native-English speakers feel inferior to native-speaking teachers and struggle to obtain legitimate status in the field (Miller, 2007; Tsui, 2007; Varghese, Morgan, Johnston, & Johnson, 2005). However, fewer studies have addressed NSTs' identity development from a critical perspective. Furthermore, NSTs' identity formation in the context of teaching abroad, and how the experience impacts their long-term professional trajectory, have received little attention. Thus, this study addresses two native-speaking JLTs who experienced teaching in South Korea at the start of their career. The research questions are: 1) What challenges are faced by novice JLTs, and what are their responses to these challenges during and after experiences of teaching abroad? and 2) How do these challenges relate to longitudinal development of the teachers' professional identity?

Method
Trajectory Equifinality Approach
To understand teachers' development in relation to their experience of teaching abroad and subsequent teaching practice in Japan, this study employs the Trajectory Equifinality Approach (TEA) (Sato, Hidaka, & Fukuda, 2009), which developed from cultural psychology considering the Vygotskian approach to human development (Vygotsky, 1978). One representative feature

of TEA is the Trajectory Equifinality Model (TEM) (Valsiner & Sato, 2006; Yasuda & Sato, 2012), which visualizes the human trajectory from narrative data and finds critical events along with social constraints/affordances at points that potentially assist in cognitive development, referred to as "bifurcation points" (BFPs) (Yasuda & Sato, 2012) in one's trajectory. Unlike other qualitative research methods, TEM positions human development as embedded in socio-historical contexts, rather than plainly categorizing or structuring notions extracted from data (Sato, 2013).

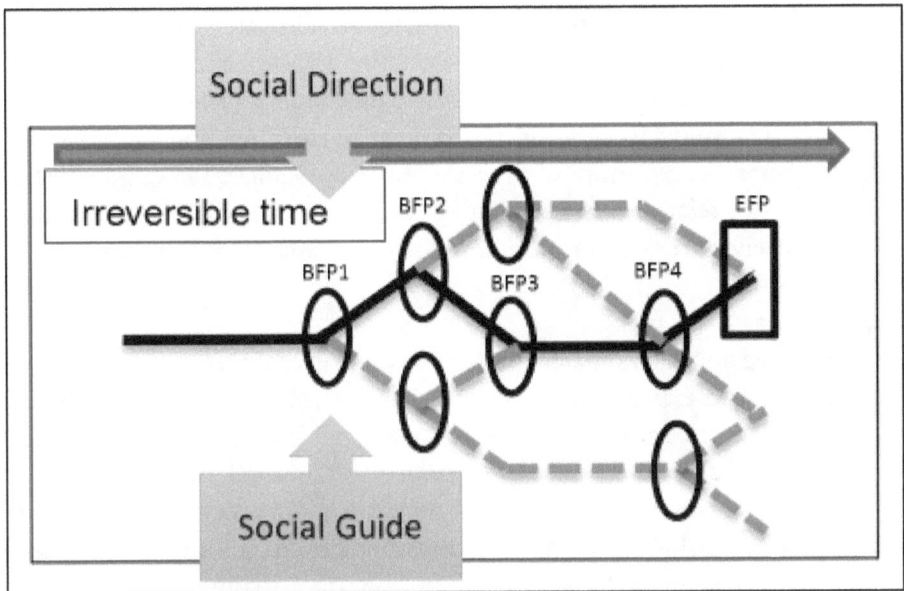

Figure 2.1. Basic concepts of TEM (adapted by author from Sato et al., 2009)

Figure 2.1 illustrates the basic concepts of TEM. With the emphasis on life as it unfolds over time (Zittoun et al., 2013), the horizontal arrow represents the irreversible flow of time, where each event and realization is placed in time order to constitute one's life trajectory overall. The rectangle represents the Equifinality Point (EFP), which is the goal of the trajectory and represents the focus, that is, the ongoing career of JLT, of the present study. As both solid and dotted lines reach the EFP, there are multiple paths to it. The ovals are crucial points, or BFPs, where one may decide to move in one direction, depicted by solid lines, rather than another, shown as dotted lines.

In addition to the concepts in Figure 2.1, social constraints, referred to as Social Direction (SD), such as social norms, traditions, and pressures, inhibit the path to EFP. Conversely, social affordances, or the Social Guide (SG), operate as a defensive force against SG and assist in achieving EFP. The SD and SG are shown with arrows from the top for the former, and from the bottom for the latter. By identifying SD and SG in relation to one's intentions or ideal self at BFP, the interrelationship between individual and social contexts may become salient in TEM.

TEA is capable of tracing the longitudinal transformation of teachers considering how their previous experience impacts later experiences and realizations. However, the dynamic negotiation process between individual and environment at the micro level is beyond the scope of TEA. To compensate therefore, this study focuses on the critical perspective and employs the aforementioned community of practice (Lave & Wenger, 1991) framework to consider the relationship between L2 teachers' identity development and the local teachers' (LTs') communities they newly enter from abroad.

Participants

As mentioned above, two participants who are currently teaching at colleges in Japan and had experience teaching at Korean colleges were invited to be interviewed. It is common for novice Japanese NSTs to start their career in other Asian countries, especially South Korea, China, and Thailand, or other developing countries because the domestic job market rarely welcomes inexperienced teachers (Okamoto, 2005). Most positions for novice teachers abroad are restricted to "NSTs of Japanese," but they do not necessarily need any prior teaching experience. The two participants in this study, referred to using the pseudonyms Ami and Saki, are no exception to this.

Ami and Saki are female Japanese teachers in their late 20s, and taught at two different Korean colleges for three years before returning to teach at a college in Japan for one year. Both found the teaching positions at the Korean colleges through Internet job announcements and had the requisite qualifications due to having graduated from Master's programs. The colleges at which they taught in Korea are both in rural districts and are distinctive from the prestigious colleges in Seoul in terms of size, students' motivation, and level of internationalization. No particular mentoring system was provided by the colleges at the start of the teachers' employment.

Ami studied in China for one year as an undergraduate, and Saki completed a three-week teaching practicum in a South Korean college during her graduate program. Both completed a Master's program in Japanese Language Teacher Education, wherein the researcher was their supervisor. Ami and Saki may have held back when recounting their negative feelings and/or experiences regarding their former supervisors; on the other hand, they may have felt relatively comfortable talking about their teaching experience with a mentor who had known them for more than five years.

Data Collection
Narrative inquiry data for two novice, native-speaking JLTs who taught in South Korea for three years before returning to teach in Japan were collected and analyzed using TEA. In addition to TEM as an analytic tool, TEA entails two significant approaches with regard to data collection and analysis. One is "Historically Structured Inviting/Invitation" (Valsiner & Sato, 2006); within this process, the researcher intentionally selects participants with identical EFPs, in this case "the ongoing career in JLT after teaching in Korea," or polarized EFPs, which is "abandoning the JLT career after teaching in Korea." The other is the "Three Layers Model of Genesis" (TLMG) (Sato, Yasuda, Kanazaki, & Valsiner, 2014), which captures how one's immediate activities at the microgenetic level relate to one's ontogenetic transformation. Details on TLMG will be discussed in the Findings and Discussion section.

Narrative data were collected through face-to-face interviews followed by several e-mail exchanges. Prior to data collection, the researcher explained the research purpose and Ami and Saki signed informed consent forms, which follow guidelines of the research ethics committee at the researcher's college.

All data were originally in Japanese and were translated into English by the researcher. First, the teachers participated in a face-to-face interview in which they answered open-ended questions regarding their teaching career, as shown in Appendix 2. To obtain detailed information on the points gathered face-to-face and to further develop the discussion, they were asked additional questions via e-mail that were developed based on their individual responses in the interviews. Finally, after completing the first draft of the TEM figures, further e-mail exchanges were conducted to validate the TEM figures and modify them according to the participants' perspectives. The e-mail exchanges following the face-to-face interviews provided the participants time for deep reflection (Feryok, 2008).

TEM emphasizes the *trans-view* (Sato, 2013) in interview data, as the data should reflect the perspectives of both interviewer and interviewee. To build intersubjectivity between interviewer and interviewee, a draft TEM figure was presented to each teacher for modification before finalization. As Yasuda and Sato (2012) suggested, the interviews incorporated the "Life-Line Interview Method" (Schroots & Ten Kate, 1989), which asks interviewees to draw a curving line to express changes in their degree of involvement in the target phenomenon, for instance, their continuing career in teaching Japanese, and to clarify what happened at curve points, whether alternative choice(s) existed besides that chosen, and whether any detrimental or advantageous circumstances arose.

Data Analysis

To describe the teachers' trajectories with TEA, interview data were analyzed following TEM to visualize the individuals' life trajectories along a timeline to identify critical points based on social affordances and constraints. First, the data that had been segmented into minimum event/meaning elements were re-placed along the time axis. Segments that related more to maintaining JLT careers, in other words, directed towards the EFP, were placed on the upper part of the figure, while segments that showed a recession away from the EFP and a move towards the P-EFP were placed on the lower part.

Then, segments explaining the same events/meanings were grouped and labeled. Next, social constraints, referred to as SDs, which included social customs, norms, and regulations, and social affordances, referred to as SGs, were identified and described using arrows from the top for SDs, and from the bottom for SGs, as shown in Figure 2.1. Finally, the labeled events were connected using a timeline and some of the events were marked as BFPs, which had a significant impact on the direction of each teacher's trajectory.

Findings and Discussion

The present section illustrates Ami and Saki's three-year teaching-abroad experiences individually by addressing their experiences in Korea, and how these experiences impacted later approaches to their careers.

Ami's Trajectory

Figure 2.2 shows the TEM figure for Ami's trajectory. As mentioned above, the connected rectangles in the middle are the events on the timeline; the arrows from the top are SDs, and those from the bottom are SGs. As shown in Figure 2.2, the bold line for Ami's trajectory fluctuates, but rises toward the EFP of the present, at the time of interview. Figure 2.3 provides a simplified version of Ami's trajectory, with Ami's transformations outlined as "guest native-speaking teacher," "teacher with the ability to teach in the 'Korean way,'" and "teacher swayed by the students' opinions."

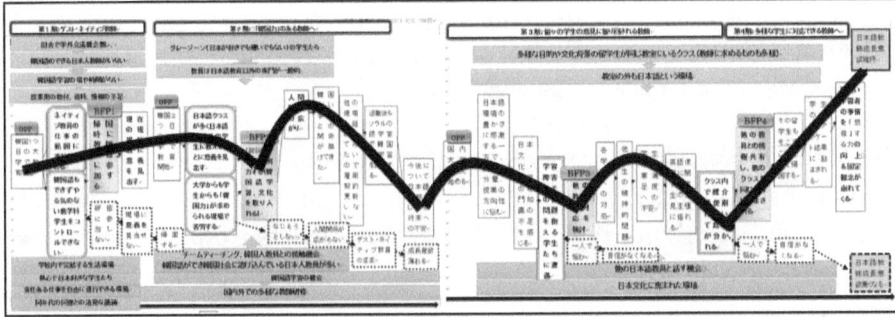

Figure 2.2. TEM figure for Ami's trajectory

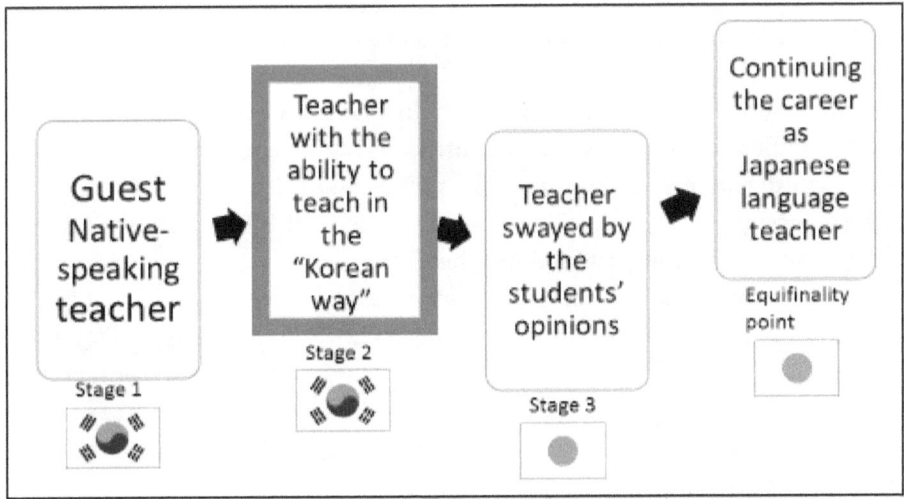

Figure 2.3. The stages of Ami's trajectory

While in South Korea, Ami's experience of teaching at the second college (C2) was quite different compared to the first (C1). Ami's first BFP occurred at C1, mainly due to her low competence in the Korean language. She had little experience of Korean prior to starting the job; however, as shown by the SGs, several of C1's staff were proficient in Japanese, and much of her life on campus was spent without speaking Korean. Ami enjoyed teaching Japanese there because the students majoring in Japanese were highly motivated to learn. However, she faced difficulties in controlling students not majoring in Japanese, but taking her classes simply for foreign language requirements.

> I initially thought that I could do without speaking the Korean language, but I could not manage the class without it. Some students' classroom behaviors were out of control. They often cheated on the exams and did nonrelated work during my class. It was terrible. (First interview)

The SG to move Ami's career on at that point was an in-service teachers' workshop she attended at the end of her first year teaching. Ami was able to share her experience with other Japanese teachers from various global teaching contexts.

> [At] the workshops, there were teachers there teaching in various countries. I realized that each teacher's experience was different and had its own meaning. This helped me to re-evaluate my teaching experience in Korea and to obtain some self-confidence in what I was doing as a teacher. (E-mail interview)

With this support, Ami decided to stay in Korea and continue teaching at another college after her two-year contract at the first. C2 transformed Ami from "guest native-speaking teacher" to "teacher with the ability to teach in the 'Korean way.'" Figure 2.4 shows Ami's second BFP and how SGs, the arrow from the bottom, assisted her therein.

C2 had some native-speaking JLTs who had married locals, lived in the area for a long time, and become fluent in Korean. The college administrators, teachers, and students at C2 did not position Ami as a native-speaking guest and expected her to teach in the "Korean way." The staff at C2's office did not speak Japanese and the students had become used to NSTs who were fluent at explaining Japanese grammar in Korean. Additionally, many Japanese classes were taught as a team, and Ami had to communicate regularly with other local Korean teachers to decide on the content, method, and exams, and to address students' problems. Above all, C2 offered no special treatment to NSTs of foreign languages, except native-speaking English teachers. Ami felt ashamed that she was unable to speak Korean and started to take Korean language classes.

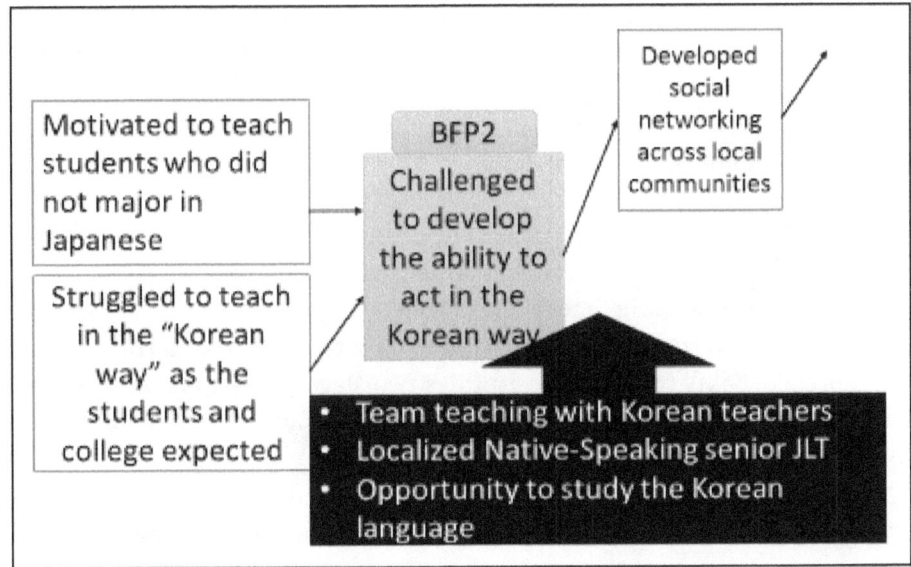

Figure 2.4. Ami's second BFP and SGs at the second stage

Additionally, she mentioned two aspects of C2 that she found crucial in her localization. One was the relationship between teachers and students. Ami felt that Korean teachers and students have closer personal relationships than Japanese. For example, teachers go out for dinner with students and have no hesitation asking students for rides. Ami stated that the native-speaking foreign teachers at C1 declined such invitations/offers by students, drawing a line in the relationship, but Ami subsequently felt that this prevented her from becoming localized, part of what she calls the "Korean way," while the Korean students were not happy with this formality.

The second aspect was the relationship with Korean teachers. Ami thought she should not visit senior teachers' offices at C1, but she was told by colleagues at the second to visit the senior teachers' offices regularly to offer assistance, even when Ami had no reason to do so. By visiting the senior teachers' office, Ami was able to communicate with other Korean teachers and had the chance to observe the local teachers' routines and locally nuanced ways of acting. Ami also often gave small gifts to the senior teachers, consistent with the local gift-giving culture. She said, "I came to feel comfortable living in Korea as I got used to acting in the Korean way at [C2]."

Overall, Ami's expected role at C2 contrasted that of the first. Ami initially struggled to meet expectations as a localized teacher at C2, but her positive attitude towards the local culture and language enabled her to improve her relationship with the students and colleagues and resulted in establishing her membership in the local community.

Saki's Trajectory
Saki's overall trajectory fluctuates like Ami's, but unlike Ami's, Saki's trajectory declines to the time of the interview, as seen in Figure 2.5. In fact, at the time the interview was conducted, Saki wanted to quit her career as a JLT. As seen in Figure 2.6, Saki's trajectory constitutes two stages, "guest native-speaking teacher" during her three years in Korea (C1), and "failed coordinator" in her teaching at a college in Japan (C2).

Unlike Ami, Saki maintained her guest status during her time at both colleges in Korea. The first BFP was at C1. After finishing the first semester, she tried to reflect on her teaching for the next semester. However, she realized that she was not expected to improve her teaching there. For example,

> I tried to grade objectively, but a lot of students complained about their grades. I asked a senior Korean teacher for advice but she said, "Well, you don't need to be so serious; just give them easy A grades because you are a Japanese native-speaking teacher. You don't need to be so strict about it. The conversation class is just for an opportunity for a cultural exchange." (First interview)

Saki came to hate the job because she felt that C1 did not want her, but just needed a Japanese person to increase the college's global image. The classes to which she was assigned were conversation classes that were not required, but an "adjunct," in Saki's words, class. Saki observed that the hierarchy of the classes' contents reflected the institutional status of the teachers assigned to the classes: Korean senior teachers taught the most important core grammar classes, local full-time teachers taught the next important classes,

Identity Transformation in Second Language Teachers 27

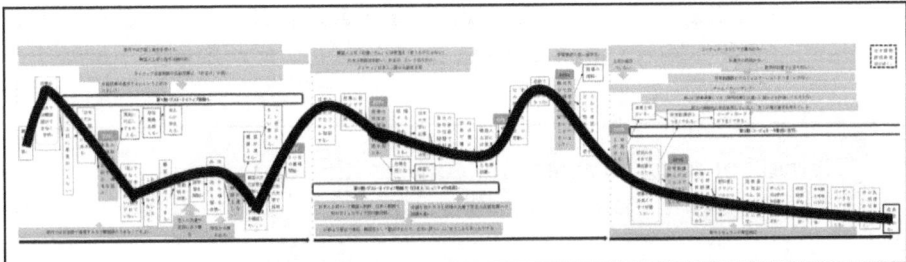

Figure 2.5. TEM figure for Saki's trajectory

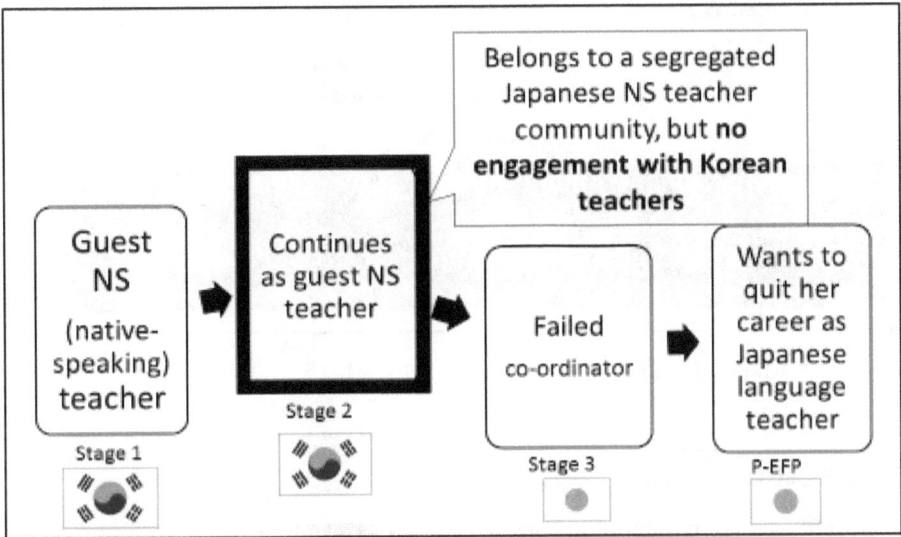

Figure 2.6. The stages of Saki's trajectory

such as reading and writing, and native-speaking adjunct teachers taught the conversation classes, which are less emphasized in the curriculum. Saki stated that the conversation classes were "perfect for a young native-speaking teacher who knows little about the local language and culture," implying that the teacher is treated as a "cultural showpiece" (Thomas, 1993) or someone whose role is primarily symbolic of the language and represents stereotypes.

However, Saki renewed her employment contract for a year because she enjoyed seeing the students who took her class progress in Japanese. After the additional year at C1, she started to wonder whether the attitudes of her Korean colleagues represented the norm across Korea. To answer this question, she decided to apply for a position at another college in Korea.

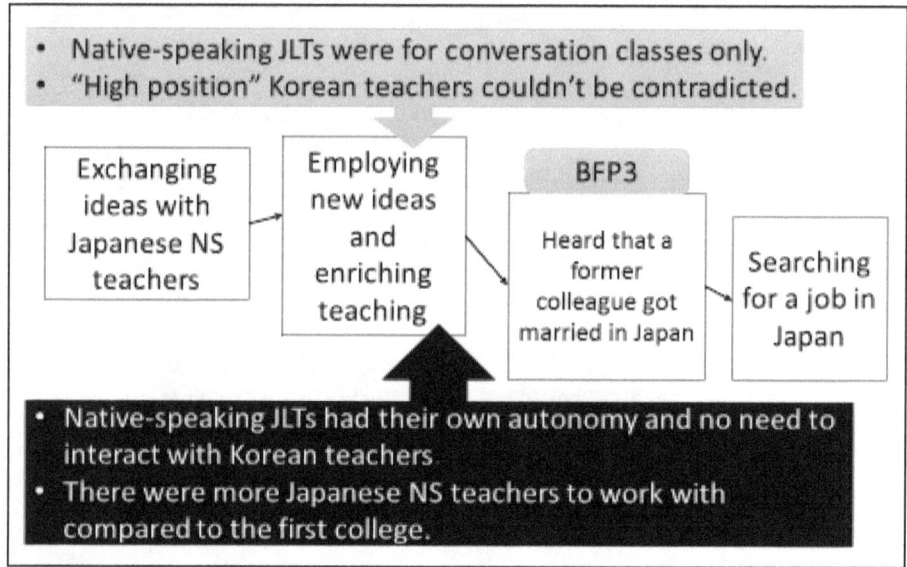

Figure 2.7. Saki's third BFP, SG, and SD

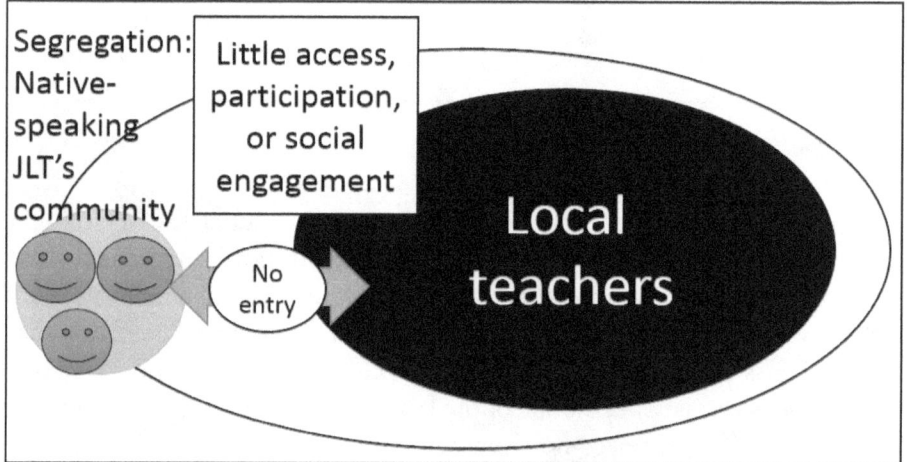

Figure 2.8. Saki's marginalized position at the second college

Saki found C2 similar; however, one difference was that there were enough native-speaking JLTs to give them autonomy and less need to interact with Korean teachers as seen in Figure 2.7. Although Saki's attitudes toward Korean senior teachers did not change at C2, she was more motivated there because she could actively exchange ideas with other NSTs to enrich her teaching.

Contrasting Ami's case, Saki had little access to, participation in, or engagement with local Korean teachers, but enjoyed teaching within the segregated native-speaking JLT community as seen in Figure 2.8.

The Impact of Teaching Abroad Experiences at the Ontogenetic Level
Although Ami's and Saki's careers started similarly, with both teaching at colleges in South Korea and returning to Japan to teach there, their identities formed during their time teaching abroad are distinguishable. Interestingly, what they felt they learned from their teaching experiences in South Korea also varied. Ami, who participated in the LTs' community and learned the local way of establishing relationships with students and colleagues, stated:

> I try to understand each student's sociocultural background and consider what each student in my class expects me to do now because of my experience in Korea. What the students expected the teachers to do was different in Korea [compared to Japan]. (E-mail interview)

By contrast, Saki, who experienced an identity of marginality in the host teachers' community, stated:

> The experience of being a minority in the society was valuable. When I run into a tourist in Kyoto, I want to help them with directions to the sightseeing spots. My experience in South Korea made me sensitive to people who are not able to ask questions easily due to the language. (First interview)

To address the critical question of how immediate momentary experience embedded in the particular social context impacts the individual's ontogenetic transformation, TEA proposes the Three Layers Model of Genesis (TLMG) (Sato, Yasuda, Kanazaki, & Valsiner, 2014). TLMG developed from Valsiner's (2007) concepts to describe the process of internalization. Vygotsky (1978) explained internalization as a process wherein all human development initially emerged socially and then moved up to the individual level, but not vice versa. TLMG conceptualizes a "mesogenetic level," located between microgenetic and ontogenetic domains, where new concepts emerge at BFPs to become contextually framed signals, which are generally derived from social habits, tendencies, and norms, and which move further up to a more stable, higher mental structure for internalization.

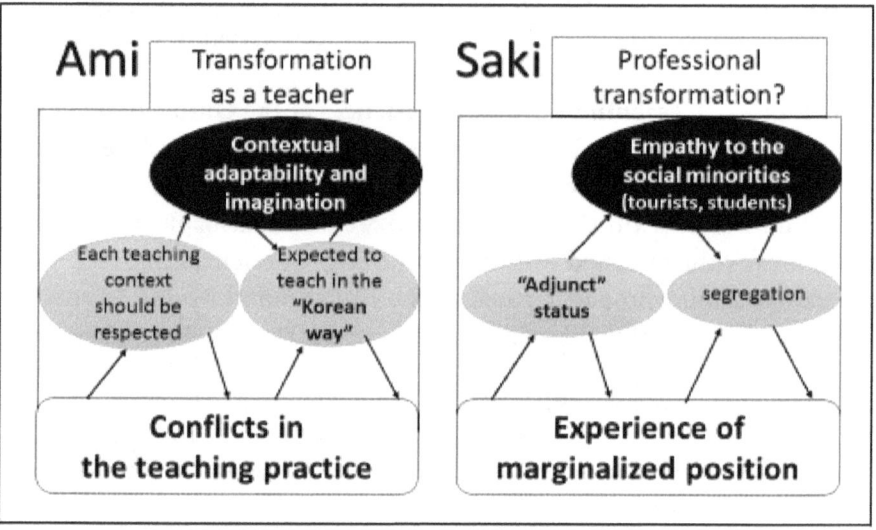

Figure 2.9. Ami and Saki's cognitive development with TLMG

Figure 2.9 illustrates how the BFPs from Ami and Saki's teaching experiences in South Korea at the micro level promoted their realization of new concepts at the mesogenetic level to impact their cognitive transformation at the ontogenetic level. As the figure shows, Ami and Saki's cognitive transformations through teaching-abroad experiences differed. Ami, realizing the significance of the contextual aspects of teaching, stated,

> What I experienced was just the Korean way. But once a teacher seriously experiences the cultural differences of teaching contexts, I think the teacher can develop a competence of "imagination," which enables him/her to expect and actively understand the differences of others. (E-mail exchange)

The role of "imagination" has been reconsidered as "expansion of experience" (Zittoun & Cerchia, 2013) in cultural psychology. Crucial experiences do not remain in the past but may play a vital role in perceiving things differently in the future as "imagination," in other words, creating the individual's Zone of Proximal Development (Vygotsky, 1978). Thus, Ami's revised image of the ideal teacher was one "who can transform themselves freely according to the environment, just like an amoeba." This contrasts Ami's previous teaching belief, that "there are some principles, such as manuals, that all teachers should follow in any context."

Conversely, Saki, who was positioned as an adjunct native-speaking foreign teacher, marginalized at C1, and who belonged to the segregated NSTs' community at C2, developed sensitivity towards social minorities.

Ami and Saki's identity development and the experiences of their positions in the local contexts while teaching abroad significantly impacted their later careers. Saki took a five-year full-time contract at a Japanese college. However, she struggled with the position, which required her to coordinate the college's Japanese language program. Besides the overwhelming workload, she faced difficulties in communicating and collaborating with part-time teachers; she had previously never been in a position to negotiate the curriculum or address students' problems with teachers who have different opinions or perspectives.

Ami became employed as a part-time lecturer of exchange students at a college in Japan. Ami faced some difficulties in dealing with a student who asked her to use English to explain Japanese grammar, and consulted with other teachers to overcome the matter. Ami spent a lot of time in the JLTs' staff room at the college in order to have opportunities to communicate with other teachers. The strategy that Ami had attained at C2 in Korea enabled her to access the shared norms in this particular teaching context.

Discussion
Linguistic Capital in Local Systems?
The data illustrate the contrasting transformation of the two teachers due to their differing participation status in the host-teacher communities during their sojourns. The two research questions can be answered as follows. The challenges faced during the teachers' stay in Korea related to their low competency in the local language and culture, which prevented them from

managing the classes effectively and developing relationships with the other LTs and students. Ami was able to overcome the obstacles to become a legitimate member of the local community at C2 by accommodating local norms, while Saki remained marginalized during her whole sojourn. Their experiences in Korea further impacted their teaching beliefs and reactions to problems faced in their later careers.

What appears to be salient in their narratives is "nativeness" as JLTs at the Korean colleges. Unlike the common job requirements for JLTs in English-speaking countries, the native authority of JLTs enables novice teachers to find jobs in Asian areas where Japanese, as well as English, is perceived to have linguistic capital, regardless of teachers' experience, academic degrees, or ability to speak the local language (Hirahata, 2009). However, positions for "NSTs" are mostly for "adjunct" teachers, who only teach conversation and sometimes writing classes. Teachers applying for these positions are rarely fluent enough in the local language to conduct administrative work besides teaching or have little interest in the local culture/language. Hirahata (2008), investigating native-speaking JLTs' roles in Asia, revealed that local non-NSTs feel inferior toward "native-ness/Japanese-ness," but are discouraged by attitudes of native Japanese teachers, who just want to teach Japanese but are rarely willing to understand the local culture or educational policy.

Unlike the privileged image of native-speaking over non-native-speaking teachers, particularly regarding English teachers in previous studies (Duff & Uchida, 1997; Pennycook, 2001), native-speaking adjunct teachers in foreign-language environments in some rural communities commonly experience marginality. These teachers may encounter a disparity in the perception towards NSTs at national and local levels. The linguistic capital of English worldwide, and of Japanese in some Asian countries, is highly valued in the national ideology as the government encourages colleges to employ native-speaking or foreign teachers to achieve "global standards." However, teachers with different cultural/linguistic backgrounds are not always welcomed or respected in local systems, where the locally constituted normative customs are dominant.

At C2, Saki was happy with the autonomy of her teaching; however, with minimal contact with Korean teachers, she remained marginal and ultimately joined the segregated Japanese community, rather than achieving legitimacy in the local community. Neither realization of the contextual nature of the teaching practices nor negotiation of the differences was observed in Saki's data. The sojourners' statuses within the community were constituted through the interplay between the teachers and their environment, not solely the attitudes of the host community, but Saki's lack of intercultural experience prior to teaching abroad compared to Ami may have had an impact on her stances and perceptions.

Implications for L2TE
To assist in the professional development of novice native-speaking language teachers, approaches across domains related to human development should be considered. In the local context, as illustrated by Ami's case at C2, the role of senior NSTs may be crucial in shaping the participation status of new NSTs. Locally accustomed senior NSTs assist new teachers in obtaining access to the shared resources of the LT community. Following advice from the senior NST, Ami frequently visited the senior Korean teacher's office, where she could observe and learn the local norms followed by the teachers. Such assistance is necessary for new teachers to obtain legitimate access to community practice where norms, curricula, and policies are usually taken for granted and not explained to newcomers.

At the ontogenetic level, both pre- and in-service L2TEs should develop ways to promote teachers to be contextually responsible for the teaching environment (Cross, 2010). Ami obtained legitimacy at C2 not simply because of the assistance of senior NSTs, but because she actively participated in workshops for in-service teachers, where she reflected on and realized the meaning of her teaching practices at C1. By realizing the significance of contextual aspects, Ami tried to establish not only interpersonal relations, but also mutual engagement in practice with other members of the local community, as well as gaining access and contributing to the joint enterprise and resources in use (Tsui, Edwards, & Lopez-Real, 2009).

Due to the emphasis that L2TEs place on grammar and theoretical aspects of pedagogy, teachers are in danger of perceiving colleges/schools as neutral spaces (Morgan, 2004). Thus, teachers must understand the complexity and significance of context (Miller, 2009). For in-service teachers, reflective practices (Burton, 2009; Freeman, 1996) have been suggested to increase contextual awareness and understanding. For instance, Miller (2009) suggested undertaking critical sociocultural reflection on teachers' identities and related issues in particular environments, and the functions of discourse in (re-)forming experience. Considering the cultural-historic domain in relation to other domains, Hawkins and Norton (2009) emphasized critical ideological realization as essential for L2TEs by reflecting on the teachers' own positioning in the local community, power differences among cultural groups, and linguistic capital of NSTs during teaching experiences abroad, by which teachers may realize their self-perceptions and thus their ability to act within the community.

Limitations of the Study
This study is limited in terms of its narrative inquiry and focus on the subjects' perspectives. The data on these two teachers, and the implications of this data, are unique to these specific contexts and cannot be generalized. The teachers' competency in the local language, along with their age, gender, academic qualifications, as well as previous teaching experience, may have impacted on their positions as NSTs. Moreover, the employment systems and policies of the institutions, and the local teachers' attitudes toward foreign language teachers, may vary by college in Korea. Thus, further ethnographic investigation including the voices of host communities and observations may highlight the other side of adjunct native-speaking JLTs' teaching-abroad experiences.

Conclusion
This study suggests that the impact of teaching abroad on teachers' professional development may vary depending on the constructed positions of novice NSTs in local teaching contexts. As teachers' identities form through the interplay between teacher and teaching contexts, the LTs' community, as well as the NSTs/L2TE, need to re-evaluate the current system. The analysis also highlights a possible gap regarding NSTs across domains in Asian colleges. The ideology shared at national and institutional levels encourages hiring of foreign teachers with linguistic capital, while local communities are unlikely to admit such teachers as peripheral members. Thus, to promote teachers' life-long development, L2TEs should offer reflective opportunities for teachers not only to improve classroom pedagogical practices, but also to foster their awareness of the power relations reflecting such ideological disparities. Additionally, the study highlights variations in the status of NSTs

compared to those found in previous studies, and suggests that teachers' positions regarding their social attributions are contextually driven. Further study on L2 teachers from critical ideological perspectives will benefit future L2TEs.

References

Ahn, K. (2011). Learning to teach under curricular reform: The practicum experience in South Korea. In K. E. Johnson & P. R. Golombek (Eds.), *Research on second language teacher education: A sociocultural perspective on professional development* (pp. 239–253). New York: Routledge.

Alsup, J. (2006). *Teacher identity discourses: Negotiating personal and professional spaces*. Mahwah, NJ: Lawrence Erlbaum Associates.

Block, D. (2007). *Second language identities*. London: Continuum.

Bourdieu, P. (1991). *Language and symbolic power*. Cambridge, MA: Harvard University Press.

Burton, J. (2009). Reflective practice. In A. Burns & J. C. Richards (Eds.), *The Cambridge guide to second language teacher education* (pp. 298–307). Cambridge: Cambridge University Press.

Cross, R. (2010). Language teaching as sociocultural activity: Rethinking language teacher practice. *The Modern Language Journal, 94*, 434–452. doi:10.1111/j.1540-4781.2010.01058.x

Duff, P., & Uchida, Y. (1997). The negotiation of teachers' sociocultural identities and practices in postsecondary EFL classrooms. *TESOL Quarterly, 31*(3), 451–461. doi:10.2307/3587650

Feryok, A. (2008). An Armenian English language teacher's practical theory of communicative language teaching. *System, 36*, 227–240. doi:10.1016/j.system.2007.09.004

Freeman, D. (1996). The "unstudied problem": Research on teacher learning in language teaching. In D. Freeman & J. Richards (Eds.), *Teacher learning in language teaching* (pp. 351–378). Cambridge: Cambridge University Press.

Freeman, D., & Johnson, K. E. (1998). Reconceptualizing the knowledge-base of language teacher education. *TESOL Quarterly, 32*, 397–417. doi:10.2307/3588114

Hawkins, M., & Norton, B. (2009). Critical language teacher education. In A. Burns & J. C. Richards (Eds.), *The Cambridge guide to second language teacher education* (pp. 30–39). Cambridge: Cambridge University Press.

Hirahata, N. (2008). Asia ni okeru bogowasha Nihongo-kyoshi no aratana yakuwari: bogowasha-sei to nihonjin-sei no shiten kara [The new roles of native-speaking Japanese language teachers in Asia: Nativeness and Japaneseness]. *Sekai no nihongo kyoiku [Japanese language education for the world], 18*, 1–19.

Hirahata, N. (2009). Tayoka e no taio ni muketa Nihongo-kyoshi yosei no kadai [The tasks for JLT education in facing diversification]. *Canadian Journal of Japanese Language Education, 10*, 107-125.

Kinginger, C. (2010). American students abroad: Negotiation of difference? *Language Teaching, 43*, 216-227. doi:10.1017/S0261444808005703

Kubota, R. (2009). Internationalization of universities: Paradoxes and responsibilities. *The Modern Language Journal, 93*, 612-616. doi:10.1111/j.1540-4781.2009.00934.x

Lave, J., & Wenger, E. (1991). *Situated learning: Legitimate peripheral participation.* Cambridge: Cambridge University Press.

Marx, H., & Moss, D. M. (2011). Please mind the culture gap: Intercultural development during a teacher education study abroad program. *Journal of Teacher Education, 62*(1) 35-47. doi:10.1177/0022487110381998

Miller, J. (2007). Identity in the ESL classroom. In Z. Hua, P. Seedhouse, L. Wei & Cook (Eds.), *Language learning and teaching as social interaction* (pp. 148-162). Hampshire: Palgrave Macmillan.

Miller, J. M. (2009). Teacher identity. In A. Burns & J. C. Richards (Eds.), *The Cambridge guide to second language teacher education* (pp. 172-181). Cambridge: Cambridge University Press.

Morgan, B. (2004). Teacher identity as pedagogy: Towards a field-internal conceptualization in bilingual and second language education. *Bilingual Education and Bilingualism, 7*(2&3), 172-188.

Norton, B. (2000). *Identity and language learning: Gender, ethnicity and educational change.* London: Longman.

Okamoto, S. (2005). Nihongo kyoshi yousei no genjo to kadai [The current issues and tasks of Japanese teachers training program]. *Hokkaido Bunkyo daigaku ronshu [Collection of essays for Hokkaido Bunkyo University], 6*, 121-133.

Pennycook, A. (2001). *Critical applied linguistics: A critical introduction.* Mahwah, NJ: Lawrence Erlbaum Associates.

Sato, T. (2013). Shitsu-teki kenkyu to human computer interaction no yutaka na setten to mirai e mukete [Towards the enriched point of contact and future between the qualitative research and human computer interaction]. *The Human Interface, 15*, 303-308.

Sato, T., Hidaka, T., & Fukuda, M. (2009). Depicting the dynamics of living the life: The trajectory equifinality model. In J. Valsiner, P. Molenaar, M. Lyra, & N. Chaudhary (Eds.), *Dynamic process methodology in the social and developmental sciences* (pp. 217-240). New York: Springer.

Sato, T., Yasuda, Y., Kanazaki, M., & Valsiner, J. (2014). From describing to reconstructing life trajectories: How the TEA (Trajectory Equifinality Approach) explicates content-dependent human phenomena. In B. Wagoner, N. Chaudhary, & P. Hviid (Eds.), *Cultural psychology and its future: Complementarity in a new key* (pp. 93-106). Charlotte, NC: Information Age.

Schroots, J. J. F., & Ten Kate, C. A. (1989). Metaphors, aging and the life-line interview method. In D. Unruh & G. Livings (Eds.), *Current perspectives on aging and the life cycle: Vol. 3 personal history through the life course* (pp. 281–298). London: JAI Press.

Smolcic, E. (2011). Becoming a culturally responsible teacher: Personal transformation and shifting identities during an immersion experience abroad. In K. E. Johnson & P. R. Golombek (Eds.). *Research on second language teacher education: A sociocultural perspective on professional development* (pp. 15–30). New York: Routledge.

Thomas, S. (1993). Proposition: Resolved, debating toward the future. *JET Journal, 88,* 86-91.

Tsui, A. B. M. (2007). Complexities of identity formation: A narrative inquiry of an EFL teacher. *TESOL Quarterly, 41,* 657–680. doi:10.1002/j.1545-7249.2007.tb00098.x

Tsui, A. B. M., Edwards, G., & Lopez-Real, F. (2009). *Learning in school–university partnership: Sociocultural perspectives.* New York: Routledge.

Valsiner, J. (2007). *Culture in minds and societies.* New Delhi: Sage.

Valsiner, J., & Sato, T. (2006). Historically Structured Sampling (HSS): How can psychology's methodology became tuned in to the reality of the historical nature of cultural psychology? In J. Straub, D. Weidemann, C. Kolbl, & B. Zielke (Eds.), *Pursuit of meaning. Advances in cultural and cross-cultural psychology* (pp. 215–251). Bielefeld: Transkript.

Varghese, M., Morgan, B., Johnston, B., & Johnson, K. A. (2005). Theorizing language teacher identity: Three perspectives and beyond. *Journal of Language, Identity, & Education, 4,* 21–44. doi:10.1207/s15327701jlie0401_2

Vygotsky, L. S. (1978). *Mind in society.* Cambridge, MA: Harvard University Press.

Wenger, E. (1998). *Communities of practice: Learning, meaning, and identities.* Cambridge: Cambridge University Press.

Yasuda, Y., & Sato, T. (2012). *TEM de wakaru jinsei no keiro: Shitsu-teki kenkyu no shin tenkai* [Understanding life trajectory with the Trajectory Equifinality Model: A new perspective in qualitative research]. Tokyo: Seisho Shobo.

Zittoun, T., & Cerchia, F. (2013). Imagination as expansion of experience. *Integrative Psychological and Behavioral Science, 47,* 305-324.

Zittoun, T., Valsiner, J., Vedeler, D., Salgado, J., Gonçalves, M. M., & Ferring, D. (2013). *Human development in the life course: Melodies of living.* Cambridge: Cambridge University Press.

Appendix 2
Questions Prepared for the First Interview for Ami and Saki

1. During your time teaching in South Korea, did you find anything interesting or different compared to your previous experience? If yes, please explain.

2. Do you think your experience of teaching abroad and/or studying abroad has impacted on your current teaching beliefs? If yes, how?

3. Please draw a curved line on the paper to express changes in your degree of involvement in your teaching career. Then, please clarify what happened at the curved point and tell me if alternative choice(s) existed besides the one chosen. (Following the "Life-Line Interview Method", Schroots & Ten Kate, 1989).

4. Have you ever experienced points in your teaching career when you needed to choose one option over another, or when you had to do something against your will? Was any social assistance provided to help you move in these new directions, or did any social obstacles prevent you from doing so?

5. Do you think your beliefs regarding teaching and learning Japanese language have changed at all since you were a graduate student? If yes, please tell me how your beliefs changed, and what made them change. If no, please tell me how they stayed the same.

6. Please describe, in your own words, each of the teaching contexts you have experienced so far. Also, Please also tell me why you see them this way.

CHAPTER 3

LANGUAGE ENGINEERING IN TOTALITARIAN RÉGIMES:
Controlling Belief and Behavior Through Language

Timothy G. Reagan
University of Maine

In her book *The Language Imperative*, Elgin (2008) cogently observed that:

> It is all too easy to underestimate the power of language... because almost every human being knows and uses one or more languages, we have let that miracle be trivialized.... We forget, or are unaware of, the power that language has over our minds and our lives; we use that power ourselves as casually as we use the electric power in our homes, with scarcely a thought given to its potential to help or harm. We make major decisions about language on the most flimsy and trivial—and often entirely mistaken—grounds. (p. 239)

Although its ubiquity may go largely unnoticed much of the time, language is nevertheless profoundly important, both in terms of how we construct our daily activities and in developing and articulating our broader understandings of society, politics, ideology, and culture. This, of course, was precisely the point that George Orwell made in his masterpiece *1984*, in which the goal of Newspeak, the created language of the State, was ultimately to prevent creative or innovative thought, that is, precisely the kind of thought that might endanger the State by resulting in (or even making possible) "thoughtcrime." As Winston's friend Syme explained in the novel,

> Don't you see that the whole aim of Newspeak is to narrow the range of thought? ... Has it ever occurred to your, Winston, that by the year 2050, at the very

latest, not a single human being will be alive who could understand such a conversation as we are having now? ... The whole climate of thought will be different. In fact, there will be no thought, as we understand it now. Orthodoxy means not thinking—not needing to think. Orthodoxy is unconsciousness. (Orwell, 1989, pp. 60-61)

The desire to control language and language use is especially powerful, as Syme noted, precisely because it controls thought (Young, 1991). In its extreme form, this view is essentially a rearticulation of the Sapir-Whorf hypothesis (or, more accurately, of the doctrine of linguistic relativism) in its strongest form,[1] and while most linguists do not accept it in such a form, it is nevertheless widely recognized as quite important in its weaker forms.[2] If one is unable to discuss or articulate a topic, then it is also extremely difficult (if not impossible) to think about that topic. As Whorf (1956) explained,

We dissect nature along lines laid down by our native language. The categories and types that we isolate from the world of phenomena we do not find there because they stare every observer in the face; on the contrary, the world is presented in a kaleidoscope flux of impressions which has to be organized by our minds—and this means largely by the linguistic systems of our minds. We cut nature up, organize it into concepts, and ascribe significances as we do, largely because we are parties to any agreement to organize it in this way—an agreement that holds throughout our speech community and is codified in the patterns of our language ... all observers are not led by the same physical evidence to the same picture of the universe, unless their linguistic backgrounds are similar, or can in some way be calibrated. (pp. 212-214)

In this chapter, I will explore historical efforts to engineer and control language use in two totalitarian societies: in the USSR in the years immediately following the 1917 Revolution and in Nazi Germany. I will then discuss the implications of these cases for understanding an important aspect of totalitarian régimes, as well as the implications of the issues raised for citizens of modern democratic societies.

Language in the USSR

The Bolshevik Revolution, which ended more than three centuries of rule under the Romanov dynasty, resulted in the creation of a radically new society in Russia with impacts on virtually all aspects of everyday life, not the least of which was language (Blank, 1988; Gorham, 2003; Hirsch, 2005; Kreidler, 1982). However, as Ryazanova-Clarke and Wade (1999) note,

> although 1917 has traditionally been regarded as a major watershed in the development of the Russian vocabulary, the language had in fact been evolving continuously since the end of the nineteenth century and into the early years of the twentieth, but had not undergone a thorough-going revolution. (p. 3)

It was the Bolshevik Revolution that provided the context for this thorough-going revolution in language and language use in Russia. For the new Soviet state, nationalism presented a number of challenges (Haarmann, 1995; Hirsch, 2005). The Soviet Union was a multinational, multiethnic, and multilingual state, much as the Russian Empire that preceded it had been. The challenge facing the newly established USSR was to balance the need to seem to protect and promote local nationalisms, but to do so within the framework of a common, unified socialist State. Although into the 1930s the USSR did in fact promote what was called коренизацииа (indigenization), under Stalin this approach steadily declined, and, as Fierman (2006) has noted,

> From the decline of коренизацииа in the 1930s until the late 1980s, the Communist party (CPSU) actively promoted the Russian language as a common bond uniting the multiethnic "Soviet people" . . . In [this] capacity, Russian was assigned a central role in fostering rapprochement (сближение) of the many nationalities inhabiting the USSR. According to official Soviet ideology, linguistic and other differences would progressively weaken and eventually lead to their merger (слияние). (p. 98)

Following the Revolution, Soviet leaders sought to address two specific language issues. As Smith (1998) explains,

> Soon after creating their new federal state, Soviet leaders marshaled the forces of linguistic agents and diverse citizens to conquer two specific national frontiers. One was between the standard, urban Moscow literary language and the provincial and rural Russian dialects. Linguists and policy makers now began to reshape the historical, literary Russian into a living, popular Russian; what once had been appropriate for an elite now had to serve the masses of workers and peasants as well. They dreamed of an epic linguistic "union" (смычка) between city and village. Another frontier was between the Russian language center and the non-Russian national peripheries. (p. 3)

Language presented the Soviet leadership with an opportunity to promote a common ideology, while at the same time promoting a "safe" kind of nationalism that was compatible with the common ideology of Marxism-Leninism. As Smith (1998) notes,

> Of all the "foundations" of nationhood, then, language was the least offensive to the Marxist mindset. It was one of the most fundamental signs of difference, by which the common people identified their friends and strangers, or by which a government might measure loyalty to itself. But the Bolsheviks also appreciated its plasticity, how language was a register of what we now call the "imagined community" of the nation, which people created on the basis of common native tongues, and all the legends, folklore, and literatures spoken or written in them . . . Working within the tension between these principles, the Soviet government sanctioned a broad initiative in language reform, what it eventually called, with characteristic certainty, "language construction" (языкогое строительство). The term betrays an image of the government excavating the USSR's national sites, linguists drawing up architectural plans, and the nationalities themselves placing the bricks. (p. 4)

Beyond these concerns, though, the Russian language itself underwent profound changes. Perhaps most visibly in the short term were changes to the orthography of the language in the 1918 reform. Russian (at least in its historical versions) has arguably been a written language for nearly a millennium, during which time it has consistently been written in the Cyrillic script. With the Revolution, a successful effort was made to modernize the alphabet by eliminating nine letters (all of which were remnants of Old Church Slavonic and hence were no longer relevant for modern Russian) and to significantly reduce the use of the твёрдый знак (the "hard sign," ъ). The specific letters which were eliminated were Ѳ ѳ, I i, V v, Ѱ ѱ, Ѡ w, Ѣ ѣ, Ѫ ѫ, Ѧ ѧ, and Ѭ ѭ. In addition, although not concerned with the Russian language itself, as a parallel linguistic reform, there was also a mass shift in orthography for the Central Asian languages from the use of the Arabic script to the use of the Latin script, which was later followed by a shift to the Cyrillic script (see Sebba, 2006, and Shorish, 1984, for excellent discussions of this topic)—the final change, from the collapse of the USSR and independence in the Central Asian countries, being in turn reversed with the Latin script again being implemented.[3]

The vocabulary of Russian also changed with the coming of the Revolution. Extensive borrowings from European languages had already been occurring prior to the Revolution, but 1917 marked the start of massive lexical borrowing into Russian. Examples, many of which are political changes (or reflect political changes) that occurred in the society, are presented in Appendix 3A. Some new lexical items were not merely compatible with the new ideology, but were explicitly Marxist-Leninist in their flavor, including such words as коммуна (commune), чистка (purge), and подытоживать (to sum up). As Smith (1998) noted, "Language, especially the nomenclature of Marxism-Leninism, was their fundamental tool of political power, economic production, and social management" (p. 7).

It was not simply in the lexicon that the Russian language exhibited changes. One fascinating development was the widespread use and adoption in popular speech of various abbreviations. In essence, as Ryazanova-Clarke and Wade (1999) have suggested, abbreviations in the Russian language following the Revolution fall into three primary groups: abbreviations created from initials, abbreviations consisting of "stumps" (i.e., from pieces or stems drawn from other words), and abbreviations that are a mix of these other two types of abbreviations. Characteristic of all three kinds of abbreviations is that they are lexicalized and are thus used as lexical items themselves. Examples of each are provided in Appendix 3B.

Changes in style to the written Russian language also quickly emerged after the Revolution, with the powerful rhetoric of individuals like Lenin and Trotsky often cited as models. And yet, if Lenin and Trotsky were models of the ideal Soviet use of language, such an ideal was all too rarely achieved. As Lenin himself commented about the language commonly used in Soviet Russian-language newspapers in the early 1920s, "What language is this written in? Some kind of gibberish? This is Volapük,[4] and not the language of Tolstoy and Turgenev" (quoted in Smith, 1998, p. 36).

There were also a number of euphemisms that were used in the Soviet era. "Rootless cosmopolitan" (безродный космополит), a phrase used commonly during the Stalinist era, was used to describe Zionists (and, actually, all Jews). "Sluggishly progressing schizophrenia" (вялотекущая шизофрения) was a serious psychological disorder, characterized by public criticism of the State, Party and party leadership, and treated by internment in psychological facilities. "Parasites" (паразиты) were individuals who were unemployed and who sought to live off of the labor of others. This included workers who were fired (often for politically unacceptable behavior) and were then unable to find new work. "Bourgeois/reactionary pseudoscience" (буржуазная/реакционная псевдонаука) was the term used to dismiss western scientific discoveries that contradicted politically acceptable Soviet scientific theories (such as Lamarkian evolutionary theory, Trofim Lysenko's work in agricultural genetics, and Nikolai Marr's Japhetic theory in linguistics). Euphemisms were especially popular in such areas as politics, world events, and the like.

In short, as Smith (1998) has noted, "We should not underestimate the dynamism and treacherousness of language. It was conductive... in values which Soviet leaders were able to control, and in ways they never could [control]" (p. 7). In their efforts to control language, and to use language to control society, Smith goes on to say that "linguists became the government's primary agents in language reform, applying their rudimentary structural principles to codify new national literary standards: alphabets, spelling systems, grammars, as well as scientific-technical and literary languages" (p. 10).

Language in Nazi Germany

The second case to be examined here is that of Nazi Germany. As was the case with the USSR, the Nazis sought to radically recreate their society, and language played a key role in their efforts (Hutton, 1999). The use of German that emerged during the Nazi era was a distinctive variety of the language that Doerr (2002) has called "an ideological language of exclusion, domination, and annihilation" (pp. 27-46). In his book *The Language of the Third Reich*, Klemperer (2000) posits a central question about the Nazi era and offers an extremely compelling response:

> What was the most powerful Hitlerian propaganda tool? Was it the individual speeches of Hitler and Goebbels, their pronouncements on this or that theme, their rabble-rousing against the Jews, against Bolshevism? .... Certainly not, because a lot of this was not even understood by the masses, or it bored them in its endless repetition .... No, the most powerful influence was exerted neither by individual speeches nor by articles or flyers, posters or flags; it was not achieved by things which one had to absorb by conscious thought or conscious emotions .... Instead Nazism permeated the flesh and blood of the people through single words, idioms and sentence structures which were imposed

on them in a million repetitions and taken on board mechanically and unconsciously. (p. 15)

It is important to note that "all studies of Nazi German are in agreement that its specificity cannot be found in German linguistic structures, but in a particular use of the German language, in its application to certain situations and thus in conveying certain ideas" (Pajević, 2014, p. 13). In other words, the changes to German that took place during the Nazi régime were largely lexical and semantic in nature, although there was an orthographic reform—the planned "German Spelling Reform," initiated by Reich Education Minister Bernard Rust, that was to be introduced in 1944, but which was never implemented because of the war (Birken-Bertsch & Markner, 2000). The Nazi period also saw the widespread replacement, beginning in 1940, of the traditional *Fraktur* script.[5]

A number of lexical items were introduced into German during the Nazi era, most of which can be classified as political, ideological, or military-related, and many of which clearly indicated the influence of militarism in Nazi German (Michael & Doerr, 2002). Examples of such terms are presented in Appendix 3C. Much of the explicitly Nazi terminology has become taboo in modern German, except when specifically discussing the Nazi era. Especially sensitive terms include *Endlösung* ("final solution," i.e., the Shoah), *Entartet* ("degenerate"), and *Selektion* ("selection," at the concentration camps, the decision of whether inmates would be killed immediately or pressed into service as slave labor). Even the name of the German military is a sensitive issue; the *Wehrmacht* has been replaced with the *Bundeswehr*, and the two are anything but synonymous (see Kucharz, 2008). Some of the words, though, have continued to be part of the daily German lexicon, generally unrecognized or acknowledged as a remnant of the Nazi past: *Autobahnen* ("highways"), *Fernsprecher* ("telephone," a Nazi-created alternative for the more international *Telefon*), and *Volkswagon* are all examples of this phenomenon.

Virtually all of the abbreviations used by the Nazis were created directly from initials, examples of which can be seen in Appendix 3D. Although few in number, there are abbreviations that consist of either "stumps" or of a mix of initials, including *Gestapo* (for *Geheime Staatspolizei*), *Kripo* (*Kriminalpolizei*), *Orpo* (*Ordnungspolizei*), *SiPo* (*Sicherheitspolizei*), and *Nazi* (for *Nationalsozialistische*). As was the case with abbreviations in the USSR, in Nazi Germany many became lexical items themselves and were used as such.

Euphemisms were especially important for the state in Nazi Germany, since they were used to hide or disguise activities that it is believed might generate public concern (Mitchell, 2000). The extent to which many of the euphemisms that were employed were really effective in hiding what was taking place under the régime is somewhat debatable, but their use is incontrovertible. Some of the euphemisms employed by the Nazis are listed in Appendix 3E.

During the Nazi era, one of the more striking characteristics of the German language, both in terms of its popular and literary forms, was its dramatic deterioration from its earlier heights. The language of Goethe, Heine, Mann, and so many other great writers descended into a sterile and bleak kind of jargon. Writers in exile (both domestic self-imposed exile and external exile) such as Brecht, Mann, Remarque, and Zweig continued to use the language brilliantly, but the public use of German in Germany throughout the era was deeply impoverished. As Klemperer (2000) noted, the language of the Third Reich was "destitute. Its poverty is a fundamental one; it is as if it had sworn a vow of poverty" (p. 19).

Common Characteristics of Totalitarian Language Engineering

In our examination of the cases of the USSR and Nazi Germany, a number of common features of language engineering have emerged. Although these features are not necessarily to be found in all instances of totalitarian régimes, their presence, especially when taken together, does indicate a strong concern with and commitment to the utilization of language to enforce social control. The features that we have identified are script reform, lexical reform, the extensive use of both euphemisms and abbreviations, and the overall poverty of language in such settings. Further, it is clear that language tends to be used to obfuscate and to sanitize reality, and it is often tied to the dehumanization of "Others." All of this is reminiscent of Arendt's (1968) description of "the banality of evil."

Concluding Reflections

The focus of this chapter has been on language engineering in two specific historical totalitarian states. Similar kinds of language manipulation might be identified in other similar states, for instance, Mussolini's Italy, Perónist Argentina, and in apartheid South Africa. At the same time, it is important to note that even the most dedicated of such efforts to control human thought and behavior can only be so successful. As Smith (1998), referring to the earlier work of Pocock (1984), has observed, "even the language of authority is more a discourse open to play and interpretation rather than an unambiguous signal of control and obedience" (p. 7).

Perhaps more interesting might be the implications of the arguments offered here for non-totalitarian societies. In recent years, the United States has been involved in numerous "actions" (wars) in the Middle East, has been involved in the occasional "abuse of prisoners" (torture), has had "assets" (weapons) on the ground, has been concerned with ensuring that it has the required "coercive potential" (military power) in certain settings, has employed "discriminant deterrence" (pinpoint bombing), as well as "enhanced interrogation methods" (that is, torture again), not to mention using "extraordinary rendition" (sending prisoners to countries where they can be more easily tortured), "neutralizing" (killing) individuals, and placing individuals in "protective custody" (imprisonment without a charge or trial) when it is deemed necessary. Unfortunately, such actions have also all too often resulted in "collateral damage" (generally, civilian casualties). I do not mean to make the case here that the United States has necessarily become a totalitarian society, nor that its use of euphemisms is any more cynical than that of other nations. Similar linguistic phenomena are ubiquitous in the language of states; they are not intrinsically bad, they are just dangerously misleading. At the very least, citizens of democracies should be exceptionally sensitive to the language and misuses of the language of their governments and politicians. The late Christopher Hitchens once warned of "the moral offense of euphemism," and his warning needs to be taken more seriously today than ever.

Notes

1. The Sapir-Whorf hypothesis, which is also called "linguistic relativism," in its stronger version, argues that language determines thought, that is, that the language we speak limits how we can make sense of and understand that world.
2. The weaker version of linguistic relativism argues that language can influence thought and behavior. In essence, the idea here is that particular languages determine what must be communicated, and what may be communicated,

differently. Thus, if Kim is my friend, in English there are no clues about whether Kim is male or female, while Spanish requires me to provide his or her gender (by choosing between *amigo* and *amiga*).
3. This process has already been completed in most of Central Asia. Kazakhstan currently continues to use the Cyrillic alphabet but is planning to shift to the Latin alphabet in the next few years.
4. Volapük was the first reasonably successful international auxiliary language. Lenin was being sarcastic, and was in fact disparaging Volapük, although the USSR would later (in some periods at least) be quite supportive of Esperanto, Volapük's successor.
5. *Fraktur* script had been used from the 16th century onward, not just for German, but also for a number of other European languages, including Danish, Swedish and Norwegian.
6. *Asoziale* people and groups were the socially marginalized and were thus basically unwanted in Nazi society. They were also called *Ballastexistenzen* ("ballast-existences," dead weight, waste-lives). The term was used to refer to the homeless, migrant workers, beggars, vagrants, the "work shy," alcoholics, prostitutes, and so on. The Roma were considered to be "foreign race *asoziale*," although their status was somewhat ambiguous, as there was a belief that they were originally "Aryan."

References

Arendt, H. (1968). *Eichmann in Jerulsalem: A report on the banality of evil* (rev. ed.). New York: Viking. (Originally published 1963)

Birken-Bertsch, H., & Markner, R. (2000). *Rechtschreibreform und nationalsozialismus: Ein kapitel aus der politischen geschichte der deutschen sprach* [Spelling reform and National Socialism: A chapter from the political history of the German language]. Göttingen: Wallstein.

Blank, S. (1988). The origins of Soviet language policy, 1917-21. *Russian History*, *15*(1), 71-92. doi:10.1163/187633188X00050

Doerr, K. (2002). Nazi-Deutsch: An ideological language of exclusion, domination and annihilation. In R. Michael & K. Doerr, *Nazi-Deutsch/Nazi German: An English lexicon of the language of the Third Reich* (pp. 27-46). Westport, CT: Greenwood.

Elgin, S. (2008). *The language imperative*. New York: Basic Books.

Fierman, W. (2006). Language and education in post-Soviet Kazakhstan: Kazakh-medium instruction in urban schools. *The Russian Review, 65*, 98-116. doi:10.1111/j.1467-9434.2005.00388.x

Gorham, M. S. (2003). *Speaking in Soviet tongues: Language culture and the politics of voice in revolutionary Russia*. DeKalb, IL: Northern Illinois University Press.

Haarmann, H. (1995). Multilingualism and ideology: The historical experiment of Soviet language politics. *European Journal of Intercultural Studies, 5*(3), 6-17. doi:10.1080/0952391950050302

Hirsch, F. (2005). *Empire of nations: Ethnographic knowledge and the making of the Soviet Union*. Ithaca, NY: Cornell University Press.

Hutton, C. (1999). *Linguistics and the Third Reich: Mother tongue fascism, race and the science of language*. London: Routledge.

Klemperer, V. (2000). *The language of the Third Reich: LTI–Lingua Tertii Imperii: A philologist's notebook*. London: Continuum. (Original publication in German, 1957)

Kreidler, I. (1982). Lenin, Russian, and Soviet language policy. *International Journal of the Sociology of Language, 33*, 129-135.

Kucharz, C. (2008, February 1). Beware of Nazi words. *ABC News On-Line*. Retrieved from http://abcnews.go.com/International/story?id=4227660

Michael, R., & Doerr, K. (2002). *Nazi-Deutsch/Nazi German: An English lexicon of the language of the Third Reich*. Westport, CT: Greenwood.

Mitchell, C. (2000). Of euphemisms and euthanasia: The language games of the Nazi doctors and some implications for the modern euthanasia movement. *OMEGA-Journal of Death and Dying, 40*(1), 255-265. doi:10.2190/K68E-762E-3U3E-QRKX

Orwell, G. (1989). *1984*. London: Penguin Books. (Original publication 1949)

Pajević, M. (2014). German language and national socialism today: Still a German "*Sonderweg*"? In P. Davies & A. Hammel (Eds.), *Edinburgh German yearbook 8: New literary and linguistic perspectives on the German language, national socialism, and the Shoah* (pp. 7-24). Woodbridge, UK: Boydell & Brewer.

Pocock, J. G. A. (1984). Verbalizing a political act: Toward a politics of speech. In M. Sharpiro (Ed.), *Language and politics* (pp. 25-43). New York: New York University Press.

Ryazanova-Clark, L., & Wade, T. (1999). *The Russian language today*. London: Routledge.

Sebba, M. (2006). Ideology and alphabets in the former USSR. *Language Problems and Language Planning, 30*, 99-125. doi: 10.1075/lplp.30.2.02seb

Shorish, M. (1984). Planning by decree: The Soviet language policy in Central Asia. *Language Problems and Language Planning, 8*, 35-49. doi:10.1075/lplp.8.1.03sho

Smith, M. (1998). *Language and power in the creation of the USSR, 1917-1953*. Berlin: Walter de Gruyter.

Whorf, B. (1956). *Language, thought and reality*. Cambridge, MA: MIT Press.

Young, J. (1991). *Totalitarian language: Orwell's Newspeak and its Nazi and communist antecedents*. Charlottesville, VA: University Press of Virginia.

Appendix 3A
Examples of Soviet Russian Neologisms
(Ryazanova-Clarke & Wade, 1999, pp. 3-4)

Russian Neologisms	English Meaning
автономия	autonomy
агитация	agitation
аграрный	agrarian
активный	active
анархизм	anarchism
аннексия	annexation
бойкот	boycott
буржуазия	bourgeoisie
декрет	decree
дезертир	deserter
делегат	delegate
демонстрация	demonstration
депутат	deputy
дирекивы	directives
комиссар	commissar
контрреволюционер	counter-revolutionary
лозунг	slogan
мандат	mandate
манифестация	demonstration
митинг	mass meeting
ордер	warrant
пролетаиат	proletariat
трибунал	tribunal

Appendix 3B
Examples of Lexicalized Abbreviations in Soviet Russian

Abbreviation	Source	English Meaning
Type 1 Abbreviations		
ВСНХ	Высший совет народного хяйства	Supreme Council of the National Economy
СССР	Союз Советских Социалистических республик	Union of Soviet Socialist Republics
Type 2 Abbreviations*		
Агитпроп	агитация пропаганда	political propaganda and agitation
Военкор	военный корреспондент	war correspondent
Исполком	исполнительный комитет	executive committee
Совдеп	Совет депутатов	Council of Deputies
Type 3 Abbreviations		
Губоно	губернский отдел народного образования	local education authority
Роста	Российское телеграфное агентство	Russian Telegraph Agency
* Some stems used in particular abbreviations became thematic and widely used, such as *Сов-* (Soviet), *Парт-* (Party), and *Полит-* (Political).		

Appendix 3C
Examples of Nazi German Lexical Items

Nazi Terminology	Meaning
Anschluss (*Anschluß*)	"annexation" (in particular the annexation of Austria)
Ariernachweis	"Certificate of Descent" (to show "Aryan" heritage)
Asoziale	"asocial" people[6]
Ausrichtung	"alignment" (referred to the external uniformity of dress corresponding to an inner ideological alignment with respect to Nazi goals)
Autobahnen	"national freeway system"
Blitzkrieg	"lightning war"
Daseinkampf	"struggle for existence" (used to describe the perceived struggle against perceived enemies – Jews, Slavs, Communists, Roma, etc.)
Deutscher Gruß	"German greeting" (also known as the "Hitler salute," Hitlergruß)
Deutschkunde	"study of German culture"
Endlösung	"Final Solution" (referred to the Shoah)
Ersatz	"substitute product"
Feindhörer	"person who listens to enemy broadcasts"
Gleichschaltung	"restructuring" (refers to the restructuring of German society into streamlined, centralized hierarchies of power, with the intention of gaining total control and coordination of all aspects of society)
Judenfrei	"free of Jews" (areas "ethnically cleansed" from any Jewish presence)
Judenknecht	"servant of the Jews" (Gentile individuals, groups, or states opposing Nazi Germany)
Judenrampe	"Jews ramp" (at death camps and concentration camps, the rail platform for unloading newly arrived, often Jewish, internees)
Judenrat	"Jewish Council" (the Gestapo established Judenräte in ghettoes to have them carry out administrative duties)

Judenrein	"cleansed of Jews" (areas from which any trace of Jews had been completely eradicated)
Kriminalpolizei	"Criminal Police" (the national Criminal Police Department for the entire Reich from July 1936)
Kristallnacht	"Crystal Night" (refers to the "Night of Broken Glass," November 9-10, 1938) (also known as Reichskristallnacht)
Lebensraum	"living space" (specifically living space for ethnic Germans and generally referring to territories to be seized in Eastern Europe)
Männerbund	"bond of men" (a distinctly masculine mystique which was an essential part of Nazi, and especially SA, ideology)
Mischling	person of "mixed race" (in Nazi German, this term was used in reference to an individual with alleged partial Jewish ancestry)
Neuordnung	"The New Order" (the formation of a hegemonic empire in Europe in order to ensure the supremacy of Nazi Germany and the Nordic-Aryan master race)
Rassenhygiene	"racial hygiene" (the Nazi eugenics program)
Selektion	"selection" (refers to the selection of inmates for execution or slave labor at a concentration camp)
Siberiakentum	"Siberiadom" (used euphemistically to refer to the planned annihilation of the Poles as a result of their forced assimilation into the native populations of Siberia after the intended wholesale expulsion to Siberia)
Volk	people, folk-community, nation, or ethnic group

Appendix 3D
Examples of Nazi German Abbreviations

Abbreviation	German	English
BDM	*Bund Deutscher Mädel*	League of German Girls (the female branch of the Hitler Youth)
DAF	*Deutsche Arbeitsfront*	German Labor Front
DAP	*Deutsche Arbeiterpartei*	German Workers' Party (original name of the NSDAP)
DFO	*Deutscher Frauenorden*	German Women's Order
DJ	*Deutsches Jungvolk*	Middle school-aged boys' Hitler Youth organization
DNSAP	*Deutsche Nationalsozialistische Arbeiterpartei*	Austrian German National Socialist Workers' Party
FHA	*Führungshauptamt*	Leadership Head Office (administrative headquarters of the Waffen-SS)
HJ	*Hitlerjugend*	Hitler Youth organization
KdF	*Kraft durch Freude*	"Strength through Joy" (Nazi slogan)
KZ	*Konzentrationslager*	Concentration camp
NPEA	*Nationalpolitsche Erziehungsanstalten*	National Political Educational Establishment
NSDAP	*Nationalsozialistische Deutsche Arbeiterpartei*	National Socialist German Workers' Party (Nazi Party)
NSDDB	*Nationalsozialistischer Deutscher Dozentenbund*	National Socialist German University Lecturers League
NSF	*Nationalsozialistische Frauenschaft*	National Socialist Women's League
NSLB	*Nationalsozialistische Lehrerbund*	National Socialist Teachers League
OKW	*Oberkommando der Wehrmacht*	High Command of the Armed Forces

PzKpfw, PzKw	*Panzerkampfwagen*	armored fighting vehicle (tank)
RAD	*Reichsarbeitsdienst*	State Labor Service
RFV	*Reichskommissariat für die Festigung des deutschen Volkes*	Reich Commissariat for the Strengthening of the German People
RKPA	*Reichskriminalpolizeiamt*	Reich Criminal Police Department (more often called the *Kriminalpolizei*)
RSHA	*Reichssicherheitshauptamt*	Reich Main Security Office
SA	*Sturmabteilung*	Storm (or Assault) Detachment (refers to the Stormtroopers or the Brownshirts)
SD	*Sicherheitsdienst*	Security Service of the SS
SS	*Schutzstaffel*	Protection Squadron
SS-TV	*SS-Totenkopfverbände*	Death's Head Units

Appendix 3E
Examples of Euphemisms Employed in Nazi German

Euphemism	Meaning
Aktion T4	The code name for the forced extermination of mentally ill and handicapped individuals. The abbreviation refers to "Tiergartenstraße 4," the address of the Chanellery department set up in 1940 in Berlin which recruited and paid personnel associated with the Aktion T4 project.
Endlösung	The "Final Solution," the term used by the Nazis to refer to their efforts to eliminate the Jewish people.
Erbgesundheitsgerichte	The "Hereditary Health Courts" that determined whether or not to sterilize individuals
HIB-Aktion	The "Into-the-Factories Campaign"; an effort to recruit factory workers.
Selektion	The selection of inmates for execution or slave labor at a concentration camp.

CHAPTER 4

DRAMATURGICAL CRITICAL ANALYSIS:
A Case for Performance Plays to Stage Critical Multicultural Analysis of Literature

Paulo Andreas Oemig
New Mexico State University

Introduction

The act of reading can assume different layers of engagement. There is no reason to consider one as superior to another (e.g., reading for pleasure or reading for research); it remains a case of intentionality and purpose. However, through schooling children are socialized not only into academic language or the school language (Gee, 2001), but they are also routinized into a particular, and often times narrow, reading of the world (Freire, 1983; Freire & Macedo, 1987). This alone merits inquiry; the irony is that academic language and the processes aimed at arriving at its proficiency should enable deeper level of engagement with any literary text. My focus in this chapter is to explore the utility of critical multicultural analysis as constructed by Botelho and Rudman (2009) in the field of performance plays. It is common to emphasize the performative nature of plays, as opposed to their literary elements (Hubberman, Ludwig, & Pope, 1997). Despite this preference, and for the purpose of this chapter, a play is both a literary work intended to be read, performed and fully engaged in by the characters.

Botelho and Rudman (2009) examine children's literature to unearth deeper layers of readings by applying critical multicultural analysis (CMA). CMA deconstructs essentialized stories, stereotypical portrayals of disenfranchised people, questions power relations and covert and overt ideological propositions, as well as problematizes representations of class, gender, and race. Detecting whose voices are heard, or not, through texts, illustrations, and performances invite a reading that is inclusive and inquisitive. CMA demands a deeper level of engagement to question not only the authors within a sociopolitical and historical context but also to question ourselves, our ingrained assumptions, prejudices, and ideologies.

Statement of the Problem

Overall, children's literature portrays stereotypical representations about race, gender, and class. Students arriving to theatre classes in high school have little or no exposure to critical literacy. Botelho and Rudman (2009) undertake a traditional understanding of literacy in general as a singular event, that is to say a reader's interaction with texts. Literacy, however, is not limited to language alone, as there are "multiple literacies" (New London Group, 1996). In this broader sense, CMA can inform all spheres of life. Multiple literacies include visual, audible, gestural, spatial, and multimodal meanings. Ultimately, Spencer (1986) argues that literacy has to be reflected upon and considered in relation to what counts as knowing in one's society. This recognizes the sociopolitical significance of knowledge, skills, life realities, and demands.

Whereas Botelho and Rudman (2009) examine book sets arranged by themes and genres, I present here recommendations for classroom application through the enactment of stories, by staging, deconstructing and reconstructing plots, and through performance plays to reach deeper levels of critical engagement. In combining Botelho and Rudman's critical multicultural analysis and Goffman's (1959) dramaturgical analysis, I envision a critical engagement of all dimensions of text and language in a new framework: dramaturgical critical analysis (DCA).

Literature Review

All literature is a human product created in the midst of cultural understandings. When we attend a play, a recital, or a musical, we are insightfully entertained. The experience also changes us, or at least prompts feelings and thoughts within. It creates a space for reflection that must be filled in order to become a complete act. "The reader is best equipped when multiple reading strategies are available…readers are often constructed intertextually" (Botelho & Rudman, 2009, p. 112). The experience of reading a text also demands reflection, equipped with multiple sets of questions; the richness of the message emerges with multiple meanings and possibilities. It is "critical" intertextually only if we are able to bring various strategies into play, which allows for a more inclusive understanding. This is especially demanding because "ideology is most effective when its workings are least visible" (Stephens, 1992, p. 69).

"Our goal as readers," maintains Botelho and Rudman (2009), should not be "to freeze or isolate these positions [domination, collusion, resistance, and agency], but to demonstrate their fluidity by examining the social processes of power in texts and demonstrate how these positions are constructed" (p. 118). The examination of power relations is complex, and requires the organization of distinct positions. The interrelation among these positions can be elusive. The ultimate goal should be one that reaches or facilitates agency, to move us to act not so much with self-determination, but with collective-determination. In the collectivity of our encounters, domination can be disputed and "social processes" of life understood. A sense of selfhood as a critical reader/actor cannot be isolated from a sense of collective-hood in community; one strengthens the other. The performance of a play on stage commands a collective endeavor of solidarity through a community of practice (Lave & Wenger, 1991).

Stage plays present a unique opportunity to "help students examine the ways in which some people are more powerful than others, ask questions about what is fair, and name what is not fair" (Bomer & Bomer, 2001, p. 18). Consider how plays such as *Le Misérables, West Side Story, Annie, Into the Woods,* and *Little Shop of Horrors* have the potential to raise students' sociopolitical awareness and reach deeper levels of engagement. This does not happen naturally, thus, students must be shown how to use tools to unearth prejudices, power differentials, and isms. As they have experienced a transmission model of education, most students entering secondary school are ill-prepared to identify social justice issues (Moje, 2008), let alone in disrupting unjust conditions that many of them may experience. Since theatre has always been a medium through which people define and understand their world (Brockett, 1995), dramaturgical critical analysis in conjunction with stage performance can achieve a deeper understanding and mobilize action. Theatre, according to Paley (2004), is an arena for examining the social and emotional worlds that are the foundations of literacy learning as well as a window into the meaning-making of social issues. In academics it is common to point to inequalities, racism, or corporate greed, while in the public schools historical accounts are sanitized lest the mainstream complain about ideologies that do not match their own (Loewen, 1995). Reading, therefore, has to be accompanied with the reenactment of situations being read. What I propose is a theatre of possibilities, where scripts are analyzed, acted out in front of an audience, and a transactional engagement is sought out. Within these possibilities, not only through reading, but also through the emotions of re-enacting, we can explore the meaning of social class, gender, and power. In other words, the realm of power relations surfaces to create transformative possibilities with language.

Goffman (1959) proposed a dramaturgical analysis of the world. Social life, through this lens, is like a drama or the stage where socialization takes place. The stage is where we make our thoughts public, the use of language takes center stage whereas backstage is where future plans develop and careful reflection can take place. Through the medium of language, which I consider not only written and oral but also all visual symbolism, we can manage the impressions that others receive of us. Three factors determine impression management: social setting (where the action unfolds), the appearance (the props we use), and language (the manner in which language is communicated). Within the script, texts can hide dissonance of roles and actions that through dramaturgical critical analysis can be made evident.

In connecting Goffman's (1959) *Presentation of self in everyday life* with literacy analysis, I am proposing a dramaturgical critical analysis. Providing this opportunity to students to dramatize the message of the story, "rehearse, modify, and integrate their interpretations of the author's presentation into their reality...they [students] have the chance to enhance the construction of meaning" (Goodman, Watson, & Burke, 2005, p. 55). Dramaturgical analysis examines social life as if it were a drama taking place on stage. Socialization consists of playing assigned roles. Social roles are "enactments of rights and duties attached to a given status" (Goffman, 1959, p. 16). Roles are taken for granted, or as given according to the social class one is born into. Goffman, however, does not examine how language is used to negotiate power. It does provide the reason why a social role exists, but not how it came to be socio-politically and historically constructed. The theatre classroom fosters a particular community of practice (Gee, 2000; Lave & Wenger, 1991) in which a literate identity is performed through word, action, and body.

Knowledge and understanding is collaboratively produced while leading to the performance of a play or musical. The proposed approach requires more than just viewing "culture as text" (Geertz, 1973, pp. 452-453) and being open to interpretation; it requires critical scaffolding for students to be able to crystallize the sociopolitical dimensions of human activities.

Research Question

Given the performance nature of plays these can lead to internalizing emotions, attitudes, and life's experiences. Thus, the overall guiding question in this study is how readings of plays and their performances can unveil ideological positions, prejudices, and injustices? I contend that performance plays can be utilized by high school students to practice dramaturgical critical analysis. In particular, in working with students' rehearsing for two plays, *The Least Offensive Play in the Whole Darn World* and *Hard Candy*, both written by Jonathan Rand, I seek to evaluate students' understandings of corporations prior and after to being exposed to DCA.

Theoretical Framework

The theoretical framework through which this chapter is built is based on social practice. Literacy understood as social practice is best exemplified through the work of Brian Street (1984). The distinction Street makes between *autonomous* vs. *ideological* notions of literacy assists in understanding language teaching practices. The autonomous notion reflects a transmission model of literacy education whereas the ideological model considers literacy as a set of practices confined to cultural and power structures. Emphasizing practices brings about the notion of cultural production; the construct of how cultural meanings are produced, accepted, or challenged in relation to social structures (Eisenhart & Finkel, 1998; Holland & Lave, 2009; Wortham, 2006). In complementing this framework, Bourdieu (1991) offers insight into critical theories. In relating language use, power, and politics, Bourdieu builds on his concepts of *habitus*, or dispositions that favor a particular way of thinking and acting, and *cultural capital*, which signifies status level and degree of authority according to how language is enacted. How language is practiced or performed, thus, represents how all "linguistic exchanges [including written texts and scripts] are also relations of symbolic power in which the power relations between speakers or their respective groups are actualized" (p. 37). The way language is used can symbolically reproduce social differences. Teachers engage in acts of symbolic violence when they deny their students the opportunity to question and disrupt inequities, marginalization, and the status quo.

Literacy, language, and communication in all their manifestations comprise a vast array of meaningful semiotic human interactions seen in connection to social, cultural, and historical patterns of use. Literacy cannot be isolated from the richness of human activities; it cannot be understood as simply reading, writing, and speaking. Literacy must be enacted in order to be purposeful; to merely think about a text without having to express the thoughts generated is an incomplete act. "School literacies tend to privilege reading and writing over other modalities" (Botelho & Rudman, 2009, p. 44). All "modalities" must be considered to fully attend to what here is called the inescapability of ideology.

Schools favor a narrow theoretical framework supporting students' analyses of literacy. It often takes the form of a literary approach (Botelho & Rudman, 2009, pp. 25-27), which focuses on the aesthetic elements of the text. This tends to essentialize a particular meaning over time despite the context. The treatment in general has been to celebrate the positive aspects of diversity or to stereotype the behaviors of gender or of racial groups (Lubienski, 2003). It is important, then, to contextualize human activities and its by-products. Literacy, as such product, transforms our environment into an ideologically meaningful one and vice versa.

Methodology

Case study (Zainal, 2007) was the method used in this study. As a window into understanding whether students can assume a social justice stance through reading and performing plays, this method provides the most appropriate way to examine the data within the context of a theatre class. This case study was the result of collaborating with a high school theatre teacher, Mrs. Bartolome.[1] There were freshmen and sophomore students ($N = 24$) engaged in this project, 13 of which were female, 17 of which received free/reduced lunch, and 16 of which were Hispanic, with the remaining eight participants all Anglo students. Students were recruited from Mrs. Bartolome's theatre class; all assented to participate.[2] Classroom activities such as improvisation exercises and plays were selected from Mrs. Bartolome's lessons. I approached

Mrs. Bartolome with the idea to carry out this study in early May 2014. As a volunteer at Mountain High in their science and theatre departments, I have come to know the teachers and many of the students. In the theatre program every year I often help with set production and construction with other community members. Many of the students already knew me in that capacity, and when I formally met them all on September 6, 2014, I explained the purpose of the study, answered questions, and handed out assent forms.

The plays to be read and performed were selected from a list given to me by the teacher. Two plays were performed: *The Least Offensive Play in the Whole Darn World* and *Hard Candy*. The former play was the focus of the study. All the students in the class participated in either one or both plays. In *The Least Offensive Play*, the ScriptCleaner5000 is a product sold by Cynocorp to high schools to edit (censure) scripts from plays considered too offensive by the establishment. In *Hard Candy*, job applicants at Banff Enterprises try anything to succeed in the corporate world. Through a series of interviews aspirants showcase their duplicity as the play provides cues into the nature of capitalism. Plays are usually read by students who will perform them with the intention of memorizing the lines, and students limit their assessment of scripts to a plot analysis, that is, to identify the structure of the play. In this study, through dramaturgical critical analysis, students were given opportunities to reflect and make connections between their worlds and that of the plays, while elaborating on social justice issues.

The questions for the study of the plays combined Ada's (2003) creative dialogue model and Bomer and Bomer's (2001) concepts for critical reading. A questionnaire instrument was given to students prior to engaging in the dramaturgical critical analysis and performance of the plays. Multiple focus group conversations were guided by the creative dialogue model during the project. A post-questionnaire was given to assess the quality of critical analysis. The questions and prompts on the pre- and post-questionnaires were the same,[3] but the order of the questions was changed for the latter. A sociology class, the control group, took part in completing the same post-questionnaire (see Appendix 4A for questionnaire sample). This class watched the performance of both plays.

Ada's (2003) creative dialogue stimulates readers to move from a literal comprehension of texts to achieving deeper understanding while questioning the nature of the message in the text. As such this model develops through phases from a descriptive phase, with a focus on addressing the who, what, how, and why questions to literally understand the text; to a personal interpretative phase, with a focus on making personal connections; to a critical multicultural phase, with a focus on analyzing the issues raised in the text; to a creative phase, with its focus on discovering what actions can be taken to resolve the issues. The conversational nature of the creative focus group dialogues led me to view myself as a "discussion leader to facilitator to observer/participant" (Bomer & Bomer, 2001, p. 47).

The sociology class was chosen for two reasons: first, none of these students had taken theatre or were, at the time of the study, enrolled in the theatre class. Second, Mrs. Johnson had a reputation for challenging students to think critically, as she had stated that the goal for her class was to "have them [her students] make connections between history and peoples' biographies and question their own assumptions" (T. Johnson, personal communication, October 22, 2014). The performance of both plays took place on November 18 during school hours in Mrs. Bartolome's theatre classroom, which has an elevated open stage and ample space for an audience of about 70 people. The performance is considered a big component of the final exam in the theatre class. Earlier that month Mrs. Bartolome had emailed all English classes as well as the sociology class, asking them to attend and to RSVP. There were two shows, with one in the morning and one in the afternoon. The pre-questionnaire was administered on October 14, 2014, and the post-questionnaire on November 20. Focus groups and observations of classroom activities took place throughout the months of October and November.

Data Analysis

I focused this study on an inquiry of literature use, specifically plays, in the classroom. I chose a theatre class at Mountain High School in a city in the Southwestern United States. This is an elective class that the vast majority of the students have chosen to take. The reputation of Mrs. Bartolome as an engaging theatre teacher and her interest in students has made this a popular program in the school. In classes that all students are required to take for graduation credit purposes, not all students engage willingly with the content. Yet, this theatre class has facilitated the participation of all its students.

The elements of Botelho and Rudman's (2009) CMA, as I have used them, are:

1. Characters and social processes among them. This represents the focalization and social dynamics of the story.
2. Genre as social construction. Genres prescribe certain anticipations by the reader.
3. Sociopolitical and historical elements. What are the cultural themes that the text is responding to? What are some historical developments of the cultural theme?

Social interactions are determined by the triangulation of race, gender, and class (and I should add age) within a recursive power continuum of domination, collusion, resistance, and agency (Botelho & Rudman, 2009).

The classroom discussion transcripts were analyzed using Flick's (1999) thematic coding method in which recurring themes are identified from the data. Thematic domains are linked to the developed categories (e.g., domination, collusion, resistance, and agency), and cross-checked to students' responses to questionnaires and Ada's (2003) conversation model.

Findings

In order to address the research question of how readings of plays and their performances can unveil ideological positions, prejudices and injustices, Botelho and Rudman's (2009) critical multicultural analysis and Goffman's (1959) dramaturgical analysis were incorporated to render a dramaturgical critical analysis (DCA) interpretation of plays as sites of sociopolitical contestations.

Play

The Least Offensive Play in the Whole Darn World
Want to perform a classic play too offensive for your high school? Then the ScriptCleaner5000 is the product for you! Sit back and relax as Cynocorp representatives Shelly and Tom present sample scenes from plays that have been treated with this exciting new technology. Wipe away that dirty David Mamet profanity! Violence in Shakespeare? Gone. And what about those pesky sex scenes? The ScriptCleaner5000 has got you covered! (http://www.playscripts.com/play/388)

Genre

Plays, in general, are a genre unto themselves. Unlike the neat categorizations found in Botelho and Rudman (2009), attempting to circumscribe a play to a particular category takes away from the experience of the play in performance. Moreover, categories such as melodrama, tragicomedy, neoclassical drama, and farce (Worthen, 2002) speak to the extraordinary complexity of plays. This is not surprising as they depict life itself. As Wilson (1994) asserts, "the attempt to separate and organize plays according to categories can be a hindrance in developing free and open understanding of theater" (p. 167). Thus, for the purpose of this study, I will be classifying *The Least Offensive Play in the Whole Darn World* as a comedy. The plays written by Jonathan Rand are aimed at a high school audience; the comic element is present and offers unique possibilities to examine social issues.

Focalization and Social Processes Among the Characters
The main characters are Tom and Shelly, spokespeople and Big Corporation Incorporated representatives. They are "presentational and phony" (Rand, 2010, p. 9); their job is to sell the ScriptCleaner5000, a product designed to clean scripts of offensive language and graphic scenes, to high school drama programs across the nation. Throughout the play Tom and Shelly demonstrate how the product works with different scripts, such as Mamet's *Glengarry Glen Ross*. This play is full of curse words as it follows four real estate agents as they participate in illegal acts, such as bribery and burglary, to sell unwanted properties to unsuspecting buyers.

Tom and Shelly demonstrate how ScriptCleaner5000 functions by showing the audience. Characters appear on stage to demonstrate a scene from Glengarry, but in this rendition all offensive words are replaced. For instance, the lines for the character Roma in Glengarry are transformed by ScriptCleaner5000 into

> Eight thousand dollars. And one flipping Chrysler. What do you have to say to that? What do you have to say to that, jerky, jerk jerk jerk? You gosh darn piece of *horse manure*. How did this happen, huh? You son of a gun. You son of a gun...[emphasis in original]. (Rand, 2010, p. 11)

The ScriptCleaner5000 can even get rid of all "those things" that "are bad" in the musical *Rent*. It is a "rock opera that deals with a number of issues, including sex, drug use, mugging, strippers, violence, rioting, gays, lesbians, homelessness, drag queens, suicide, and AIDS" (Rand, 2010, p. 18). During the whole play Tom and Shelly have complete agency, equally complement each other, and collude to prove how successful the product is with various scripts. There is no resistance; Tom and Shelly have complete control on stage as they advertise and demonstrate the corporation's product.

Sociopolitical and Historical Context
In order to describe corporations with the power to affect public opinion (such as our imaginary "Cynocorp" represented in our play, or real world media conglomerates) and set economic trends, Kumashiro's (2008) *Seduction of Common Sense* and *The Powell Manifesto* (reclaimdemocracy. org/powell_memo_lewis/) provide the framework for this section.

In the class it was common for students to engage in structured improvisation. In these exercises the teacher provided groups of students with a card stating a situation, setting suggestions, and objectives. In one of my observations, students participated in structured improvisation exercises with socio-political messages. One of the groups was given the setting suggestion of a cage (see Appendix 4B for this card's prompts) in which "a person has been imprisoned by a political leader and placed in a cage. His freedom of movement is also limited by various obstacles." Objectives: "To demonstrate the physical and mental effects of limited freedom." The four students in the group created their own script and movement around the stage and classroom. The police (two students) at one point tell the protester, "This is American't for you," replying to a student in handcuffs who stated, "This is America; I have the right to protest." These proved to be rich activities to enact injustices and social justice issues.

Today, more than ever before, the master narrative crafted by CEOs, lobbyists working for big corporations, and the super wealthy has percolated the minds "of the people." This successful implant of a deceiving message in the minds of most Americans is undeniable. As Kumashiro (2008, p. 97) states, "the Right has been successful at addressing multiple issues and framing its initiative in ways that mask its intentions, divide and conquer the Left, and bring many from the middle on board." The United States portrays an illusion of democracy. Special interest groups drive government policies; the concerns of the general citizenry are used to gain votes and thereafter ignored.

The Powell Memo (1971) is an important catalyst precipitating the watershed consequences of the Right. Before his nomination to the Supreme Court, Lewis Powell wrote this memo to the U.S. Chamber of Commerce; in it is a framework for countering what he viewed as an "attack of American free market enterprise system" from the Left. He identified college campuses as breeding grounds of socialist ideas and people like Ralph Nader as enemies of corporate power. What followed from this manifesto is an organized and steady build-up of corporate greed. Citing Demarrais, Kumashiro (2008, p. 11) explains its effects in four programs: fostering a cadre of students supporting Rightist ideologies in universities, securing a generation of scholars whose research supports free enterprise, creating conservative policy think tanks, and the restructuring of media networks to advocate for the Right agenda. With these four programs concretized today, we can see how corporations thrive at the expense of the people and influence people's thinking and values.

The insensitive nature of a vast number of large corporations in search of profit maximization and mind control is suggested in Rand's statement:

> during a brainstorming session I thought about all the absurd censorship I'd faced with many of the productions of my plays over the years, and decided to channel that absurdity into a new script called *The Least Offensive Play in the Whole Darn World*. (J. Rand, personal communication, November 5, 2014)

Social Reproduction

In interviewing students arranged in creative dialogue groups (Ada, 2003), the theme of performance as a purpose for reading emerged. A student named Brian expressed this cogently: "We read with the purpose of performing and not messing up the lines" (Brian, personal communication, November 5, 2014).

Conversing about the play, John, another student, stated that "In the play itself they say 'this is America, where we do everything to make sure no one is offended about anything.'" Another student, Emily, interjected: "Well, it's also about making sure everybody buys their product, for them [the corporation] it is more important they sell the product than what the product is about." The social reproduction effect that schooling (Bourdieu & Passeron, 1990; Bowles & Gintis, 1976; Willis, 1981) has on students can also be disrupted. The readings and performances of plays become mediational means by which students can take on multiple histories and position themselves through different identities and social groups. The theatre class as a community of practice (Lave & Wenger, 1991) offered the space in which students could analyze and contest social reproduction via dramaturgical critical analysis.

Interviewer (PAO): Do you think that this happens in real life?
Group: Yeah.
Eddie: Just look at iPhones.
Claudia: I couldn't live without mine.
Andrea: I wouldn't trade mine for any other.
Interviewer: How many of you own an iPhone? (Four out of nine students in this group raised their hands; the rest in the group had Android phones).
Interviewer: How are things sold, or who makes you want a particular thing or brand of something?
Emily: Just as in the play if you are good at selling something they are going to sell you more of that product (personal communication, October 28, 2014).

Another student, David, talked about his part in stealing money from his dad to buy drugs, and Carl stated, "How do I put this, oh this is a big thing in America but they are trying to cover up something sweet and innocent where drugs are very badly."

Interviewer: Why do we have drug use in the United States?
David: Because we have a lot of people who use drugs.
Interviewer: But that doesn't answer the question.
Carl: Like, basically in the play when they brought up sex, drugs and violence are very big in America where people go and abuse that fact, people are killing other people, and where there is abuse of drugs.
Interviewer: Do you think we need more legislation or laws?
Jennifer: It probably wouldn't go very well, especially with younger people.
Gabby: There are laws, the problem is that they are not enforced, which is what they should do.
Interviewer: Very good…Who benefits from the use of drugs? Who is benefiting from all that?
Carl: The people who make them.
Gabby: The drug dealers.
John: The media.
Interviewer: The media?
John: Yeah, the media from covering all those stories, the publicity as when they follow a drug bust, or cover a drug raid.
Interviewer: That's interesting. The media covers things that will sell…What else doesn't the media cover?
Carl: Discrimination of women, discrimination in general.
Gabby: Discrimination is bad. I shouldn't be treated differently because I'm a woman.
Interviewer: Why does discrimination exist?
Carl: People don't like other people, and make shit up; oh, excuse my language.

> *Jorge* [up to this point did not say anything]: Yeah, like when Mexicans are called beaners or wetbacks. That's discrimination.
> *Interviewer:* Good example, Jorge. Now, who is discriminating?
> *John:* White people.
> *Interviewer:* Why is that?
> *John:* They are afraid.
> *Interviewer:* They are afraid of what?
> *John:* They are afraid we are invading and taking over the country…

In another group dialogue, the following exchange took place.

> *Carl:* There are real things in life that are going on with drugs, sex, violence, whereas people, like in our play, how do I describe it, they are trying to cover it up, but these are actual things that are going on in the world and they say, well let's shun away from that, let's focus on that…pretend that that doesn't exist, whereas in real life it does.
> *Gabby:* Just like pretending that discrimination doesn't exist.
> *Interviewer:* Beautiful, thank you Gabby… (personal communication, November 12, 2014).

In our conversations, as manifested above, the play became a reference point to make connections that the students use to illustrate their thoughts and opinions. The meanings the students elicited from their own lives unearthed different layers of reality through which inadvertently, but forcefully, the hidden curriculum of knowledge production was contested. Dramaturgical critical analysis is a methodical process; facilitating conversations anchored in the reading and performance of plays, students' awareness surfaces to identify social justice issues. This was the fourth conversation I had with these students as a group. By now, students' awareness is heightened by prompts such as: Who is benefiting from it? Is discrimination a good thing? Who controls information? Think of your character and how it relates to real life. Why does it exist? This creative dialogue occurred in every one of my visits, seven in total, except for the one in which students performed their two plays on November 18, 2014, to other classes at Mountain High. Students are used to analyzing plays from a literary standpoint (see Appendices 4C and 4D for guidelines students use to read and write a play summary). However, they are not accustomed to critically contesting the portrayal of power relations.

Results: Pre- and Post-Questionnaires
One male student in the pre-questionnaire responded to the question "Do you think social programs such as food stamps, Medicaid (health care for the poor), or Social Security are necessary? Explain" as follows: "Yes, to a certain extent because most people take advantage of that free hand out and they don't work for it." In the post-questionnaire, the same student answered: "This is because people need the money to survive and feed their families." Another student, female, responded to the same question in the post-questionnaire: "Because some people are trapped in poverty, so it is needed for them to get basic human needs."

Another male student responded to the question: "Who usually has power in stories that you read in novels, or in your English classes? Think of gender (male/female) and race (African American, White, Hispanic, Native American" with "Can't say I can…" And in the post-questionnaire: "Male and White."

A female student replied to "A corporation is a way to formally organize a big business. Its goal is to create profit. What do you think are the effects of corporations on people living in poverty?" with the following: "They take potential money from the poor and distribute it to the wealthy."

A male student added, when prompted to add anything or about the questions: "A question I would add is: Are there at least 3 plays/movies you can name that have strong female protagonists?" This a thoughtful and valid commentary prompted perhaps by one of the questions in which I asked, "Can you provide the title of a story/book you have read to support your answer?" Another male student in the post-questionnaire added to the last question of would you like to add anything?: "The randomness of these questions make it very difficult.".

Overall, the project can be summarized by a response to the last question in the post-questionnaire: "Do you have any comments regarding any of the questions or would you like to add anything?" A female student in the theatre class wrote: "I think these questions help young people think more about reality" (November 20, 2014). Other important information came from the quantification of questions using the Likert scale. It provided a discreet comparative measurement between pre-intervention (pre-DCA) and post-DCA. Also, the post-questionnaire was given to a control group, a sociology class that attended the performance of the play.

Table 4.1

Quantification of Questions Using the Likert Scale

	SA Pre	SA Post	A Pre	A Post	D Pre	D Post	SD Pre	SD Post
Success (or lack of) is individually achieved	3	5	13	11	6	8	1	0
Plays can portray SI	10	13	10	10	2	1	1	0
Do you think you could a write play on SI and propose a solution?	6	13	15	11	2	0	0	0
No matter the race to which one belongs, all people have the same opportunities to succeed in life	14	10	6	5	8	5	1	1

The statement in the pre-questionnaire: People are treated differently according to their gender, race, or social class was not included in the pre/post comparison as it has a confounding effect. It was, however, disaggregated for the post/control questionnaires.

The four statements were:

1. The success (or lack of) we achieve in life is determined by individual efforts alone.
2. Plays and musicals can portray social issues (examples: global warming, poverty, racism) on stage.
3. Do you think you (as part of a small group) could write a play about a social issue (SI) and propose a solution?
4. No matter the gender, social class and race to which one belongs, all people have the same opportunities to succeed in life. (This statement cofounds three variables, but left as is to have students consider the interplay of them in prospects to be successful in life.)

Each of the four statements had the following scale and students had to circle one choice: *strongly agree* (SA), *agree* (A), *disagree* (D), *strongly disagree* (SD).

Overall, there was an increased awareness in, for instance, identifying that success in one's life is not only due to individual efforts. In the pre-questionnaire, there were 13 Agrees versus 11 Agrees in the post; 6 Disagrees versus 8 Disagrees in post. This issue, however, was not directly addressed during the creative dialogue discussions. The other three were and it is here that we see the largest gain toward critical awareness.

Table 4.2
Comparison Responses in Relation to Control Class

	SA Post	SA Cont	A Post	A Cont	D Post	D Cont	SD Post	SD Cont
Success (or lack of) is individually achieved	5	5	11	9	8	5	0	0
Plays can portray SI	13	6	10	9	1	4	0	0
Do you think you could write a play on SI and propose a solution?	13	3	11	11	0	5	0	0
No matter the race to which one belongs, all people have the same opportunities to succeed in life	10	6	5	8	5	4	2	1
People are treated differently according to race	8	4	13	9	3	5	0	1
People are treated differently according to gender	7	3	13	11	4	4	0	1
People are treated differently according to social class	10	4	11	10	3	5	0	0

Considering that the control (Cont) class was a sociology class with 11th and 12th grade students, we can see in the last three statements that the intervention theatre class demonstrated a heightened awareness of race, class, and gender than did the control class. The results for Strongly Agree, for the last three statements, are almost double that of those for the control class. When students were asked to consider whether they could write a play regarding a social issue while proposing a solution and perform it, theatre students, not surprisingly, concurred. Worth noticing is the fact that the statement includes "propose a solution," which is an act to do something.

Conclusions

I began this project with the question of: "How can readings of plays and their performances unveil ideological positions, prejudices, and injustices?" This was for the purpose of examining the role of multiple literacies (plays and performances in this case) and how different readings are possible. Schools favor a narrow theoretical framework that sustains an unproblematized view of the world. Students' examination of literary elements and script analysis offer a limited comprehension of text, and because author's motives go unquestioned, they are often taken as truths."

A dramaturgical critical analysis approach empowers the student to realize the meanings beyond words, which are associated with a sociopolitical world. The student assumes responsibility for learning through the engagement of guided critical inquiry. Students will be able to remove the multiple layers of meanings that maintain inequalities, and by acting out publicly be able to reposition themselves and imagine new possibilities. A repositioning of a student's mind is a latent transformative act.

Results from instruments and dialogues show a more complex understanding of power relations, stereotypical portrayals, and essentialized stories. There was an overall increase of critical awareness. This is demonstrated through pre/post comparison and post/control class comparison. Creative dialogue facilitated critical awareness and the richness of the data. Despite having to disregard the confounding statement in the pre-questionnaire, the disaggregated version in the post-questionnaire is a valid source of data as it compares another class' responses. Compared to the sociology class, the theatre class' responses suggest the positive effect of dramaturgical critical analysis. This project makes an inroad in the literature of critical literacy and enriches it by providing a sample study as performed in a non-mainstream classroom. When literature is performed and critically analyzed students experience multiple perspectives (more reflective of multiple literacies and real life) from where to contest implicit ideologies. The results of this study support the use of performance plays by high school students to practice dramaturgical critical analysis in the theatre class, and it heightens awareness of social justice and injustices in a community of practice.

Dramaturgical critical analysis takes advantage of performances and encourages students to examine the text through students' lived experiences. Pineau (2002) maintains that "any performative exercise is the refinement of one's kinesthetic senses." Moreover, "performance enables an imaginative leap into other kinds of bodies, other ways of being in the world, and in so doing, it opens up concrete and embodied possibilities for resistance, reform and renewal" (p. 51). As learning becomes enfleshed in this unique literate space, those possibilities take on a new meaning. The improvisation exercises and performances alone could not have manifested the level of critical creativity without group dialogues. Creativity and a critical reading of the world can be nourished and performed on and off stage.

The multimodal encounter found in this theatre class affords knowledge construction and representation embodied in performative experiences that are lived, enacted, and felt. Active engagement with the social realities of life transforms passivity into dynamic interactions with the world. In approaching this study the intent was to look beyond the appropriation of literacy by reframing literacy research around a dramaturgical critical analysis that defies generalizations and includes the performing arts as spaces where students' diverse backgrounds are acknowledged. Future studies should address these spaces as well as how to increase academic engagement in core subjects through performativity. This, I believe, has far reaching consequences, especially when students are given opportunities to problematize the text, perform the word, and create new possibilities in their world.

Notes
1. All names and locations mentioned throughout are pseudonyms.
2. Institutional Review Board was approved from the school district and New Mexico State University prior to study.

3. The pre- and post-questionnaires had the same questions. The post-questionnaire, however, had more questions as I disaggregated the following confounding statement from the pre-questionnaire: "People are treated differently according to their gender, race or social class." The questions were shuffled in the post-questionnaire as well; the first five became the last five for a set of five questionnaires, rotating them in such fashion within five groups.

References

Ada, A. F. (2003). *A magical encounter: Latino children's literature* (2nd ed.). Boston, MA: Allyn & Bacon.

Bomer, R., & Bomer, K. (2001). *For a better world: Reading and writing for social action.* Portsmouth, NH: Heinemann.

Botelho, M. J., & Rudman, M. K. (2009). *Critical multicultural analysis of children's literature: Mirrors, windows, and doors.* New York: Routledge.

Bourdieu, P. (1991). *Language and symbolic power.* (G. Raymond & M. Adamson, Trans.). Cambridge, MA: Harvard University Press.

Bourdieu, P., & Passeron, J. C. (1990). *Reproduction in education, society and culture* (2nd ed., R. Nice, Trans.). London: Sage Publications.

Bowles, S., & Gintis, H. (1976). *Schooling in capitalist America: Educational reform and the contradictions of economic life.* New York: Basic Books.

Brockett, O. G. (1995). *History of the theatre* (7th ed.). Boston: Allyn & Bacon.

Eisenhart, M., & Finkel, E. (1988). *Women's science: Learning and succeeding from the margins.* Chicago, IL: University of Chicago Press.

Flick, U. (1999). *An introduction to qualitative research.* London: Sage Publications.

Freire, P. (1983). The importance of the act of reading. *Journal of Education, 165*(11), 5-11. Retrieved from http://serendip.brynmawr.edu/exchange/files/freire.pdf

Freire, P., & Macedo, D. P. (1987). *Literacy: Reading the word and the world.* South Hadley, MA: Bergin & Garvey.

Gee, J. P. (2000). The new literacy studies: From socially situated to the work of the social. In D. Barton, M. Hamilton, & R. Ivanic (Eds.), *Situated literacies: Reading and writing in context* (pp. 180-196). New York: Routledge.

Gee, J. (2001). What is literacy? In E. Cushman, E. R. Kintgen, B. M. Kroll, & M. Ross (Eds.), *Literacy: A critical sourcebook* (pp. 537-544). Boston: Bedgord/St. Martin's.

Geertz, C. (1973). *The interpretation of cultures.* New York: Basic Books.

Goffman, E. (1959). *The presentation of self in everyday life.* New York: Doubleday.

Goodman, Y., Watson, D. J., & Burke, C. L. (2005). *Reading miscue inventory: From evaluation to instruction* (2nd ed.). Katonah, NY: Richard C. Owen.

Holland, D., & Lave, J. (2009). Social practice theory and the historical production of persons. *Actio: An International Journal of Human Activity Theory, 2,* 1-15.

Hubberman, J. H., Ludwig, J., & Pope, B. L. (1997). *The theatrical imagination* (2nd ed.). Fort Worth, TX: Holt, Rinehart & Winston.

Kumashiro, K. (2008). *The seduction of common sense: How the Right has framed the debate on America's schools*. New York: Teachers College Press.

Lave, J., & Wenger, E. (1991). *Situated learning: Legitimate peripheral participation*. Cambridge, UK: Cambridge University Press.

Loewen, J. W. (1995). *Lies my teacher told me: Everything your American history textbook got wrong*. New York: New Press.

Lubienski, S. T. (2003). Celebrating diversity and denying disparities: A critical assessment. *Educational Researcher, 32*(8), 30-38.

Moje, E. B. (2008). Foregrounding the disciplines in secondary literacy teaching and learning: A call for change. *Journal of Adolescent & Adult Literacy, 52*(2), 96-107.

New London Group. (1996). A pedagogy of multiliteracies: Designing social futures. *Harvard Educational Review, 66*(1), 60-92.

Paley, V. (2004). *A child's work: The importance of fantasy play*. Chicago, IL: University of Chicago Press.

Pineau, E. L. (2002). Performative pedagogy. In N. Stucky & C. Wimmer (Eds.), *Teaching performance studies* (pp. 41-54). Carbondale, IL: Southern Illinois University Press.

Powell, L. (1971). *The Powell memo (also known as the Powell manifesto)*. Retrieved from http://reclaimdemocracy.org/powell_memo_lewis/

Rand, J. (1997). *Hard candy*. New York: Playscripts.

Rand, J. (2010). *The least offensive play in the whole darn world* (2nd ed.). New York: Playscripts.

Spencer, M. (1986). Emergent literacies: A site of analysis. *Language Arts, 63,* 442-453.

Stephens, J. (1992). *Language and ideology in children's fiction*. London: Longman.

Street, B. (1984). *Literacy in theory and practice*. London: Routledge.

Willis, P. E. (1981). *Learning to labor: How working class kids get working class jobs*. New York: Columbia University Press.

Wilson, E. (1994). *The theater experience* (6th ed.). New York: McGraw-Hill.

Wortham, S. (2006). *Learning identity: The joint emergence of social identification and academic learning*. New York: Cambridge University Press.

Worthen, W. B. (2002). *The Harcourt anthology of drama*. Boston, MA: Tomson & Heinle.

Zainal, Z. (2007). Case study as a research method. *Jurnal Kemanusiaan, 9*(1), 1-6.

Appendix 4A

1. What image does the Barbie doll represent for 5-7 year old girls, for 5-7 year old boys and for adults who are parents?

2. Why are there social programs such as food stamps, Medicaid and Social Security?

3. A corporation is a way to formally organize a big business. Its goal is to create profit, to make money for its executives and shareholders. What do you think are the effects of corporations on people living in poverty?

4. People are treated differently according to their gender.
   Circle one:
   Strongly agree   *Agree*   *Disagree*   *Strongly disagree*

5. The success (or lack of) we achieve in life is determined by individual efforts alone.
   Circle one:
   Strongly agree   *Agree*   *Disagree*   *Strongly disagree*

6. Plays and musicals can portray social issues (examples: global warming, poverty, racism) on stage.
   Circle one:
   Strongly agree   *Agree*   *Disagree*   *Strongly disagree*

7. Do you think you (as a part of a small group) could write a play about a social issue and propose a solution?
   Circle one:
   Strongly agree   *Agree*   *Disagree*   *Strongly disagree*

8. No matter the race to which one belongs, all people have the same opportunities to succeed in life.
   Circle one:
   Strongly agree   *Agree*   *Disagree*   *Strongly disagree*

9. Who usually has power in stories that you read in novels or in your English classes? [Think of gender (male/female) and race (African American, White, Hispanic, Native American)] Can you provide the title of a story/book you have read to support your answer?

10. If the character in your script has problems, can you see how those problems are about having or not having money, struggling with others for power, or being cheated or helped by society's rules?

11. People are treated differently according to their social class.
Circle one:
Strongly agree　　　*Agree*　　　*Disagree*　　　*Strongly disagree*

12. People are treated differently according to their race.
Circle one:
Strongly agree　　　*Agree*　　　*Disagree*　　　*Strongly disagree*

DO YOU HAVE ANY COMMENTS REGARDING ANY OF THE QUESTIONS OR WOULD LIKE TO ADD ANYTHING?

Appendix 4B
Sample of a Structured Improvisation Card

Setting Suggestion:
A cage

Situation:
A person has been imprisoned by a political leader and placed in a cage. His freedom of movement is also limited by various obstacles.

Optional factors you can add to change the scene:
a. Keep adding obstacles and limitations
b. Repeat with several different students, discussing the feelings of each

Objectives:
To demonstrate the physical and mental effects of limited freedom

Appendix 4C
How to Read a Play

To read drama well requires a theatrical imagination attuned to the possible realizations of the dramatic script onstage.

1. Imagine the physical environment (setting)
   a. When is the play set?
   b. Where is the play set?
   c. What are the main markers in that location (i.e., a door, a throne, a dining room)

2. Imagine the scenic environment
   a. What are the specific physical layouts of the particular scenes?
   b. Which characters are present in the particular scenes?

3. Imagine each character's appearance
   a. What do they look like?
   b. What do they wear?
   c. How do they move?

4. Imagine the language of the play
   a. The spoken text (i.e., dialogue; literally what the characters say to each other)
   b. The action text (i.e., the physical language of the play, the gestures and movements)
   c. The subtext (i.e., the unspoken thoughts, feelings, and intentions of the characters)

5. Imagine the production elements of the play
   a. How would you light the play?
   b. How would you costume the play?
   c. How would you design the set?
   d. How would you stage the play?

Appendix 4D
How to Write a Play Summary

1. **Title:** Plays use quotation marks unless they are considered classics, in which case you underline.

2. **Author:** Use full name please

3. **Publishing Information:** Be sure to include the year!

4. **Character Descriptions:** A sentence to cover age, personality, etc. of each character.

5. **Setting:** A few sentences that give information on time, place, period of time, etc.

6. **Plot Summary:** Include in a few paragraphs the basic plot of the play. Indicate how many Acts and scenes. You can discuss each in a separate paragraph. Be careful not to "rewrite" the play. This should be on page unless the play is very complicated.

7. **Production Elements:** One paragraph on what you think production of this play would require in the way of sets, costumes, make-up, and lighting.

8. **Your Opinion:** Did you like the play? Why or why not? Is it something you would enjoy seeing? What type of audience would enjoy this play? Is it something we should consider doing at Mountain High HS? Is it something you would like to go see if it is available in production in the area? Be honest. If you did not like the play be sure to explain why.

CHAPTER 5

CRITICAL SOCIOLINGUISTICS AND COMMODIFICATION:
Studying English as a Foreign Language in Mexico

Gerrard Mugford
University

Introduction

In Mexico, learning English as a Foreign Language (EFL) is often seen as a gateway to educational advancement, opportunities to travel abroad, and job progression (British Council, 2015). As a result, adult students will invest significant amounts of time and money in learning English. Whilst acquiring an additional language undoubtedly brings social, cultural, and educational benefits, foreign language proficiency may not automatically lead to the economic and financial prosperity that is often touted. I argue that learner aspirations are often encouraged through EFL *commodification* (Fairclough, 1992, p. 2010) as courses are often neatly packaged into a convenient number of levels to be studied intensively over a short period of time and that on their completion learners are purportedly able to pass international examinations with ease and apply for enviable jobs. In this paper, I critically examine learners' goals and objectives in studying English as a foreign language and attempt to match their aspirations with more down-to-earth realities in the Mexican context, specifically in the Guadalajara metropolitan area, Mexico's second largest conurbation.

To undertake this research, I adopt a critical sociolinguistics perspective and, following Mey (1985), attempt to identify the social and economic misrepresentations that language learners are faced with. Whilst critical research strongly focuses on linguistic imperialism (Phillipson, 1992, 2009), resistance perspectives (Canagarajah, 1999), and politics of pedagogy (Pennycook, 2001), I follow an emic approach by interacting with the learners themselves. To investigate their aspirations, I administered a written questionnaire to 70 beginner adult students regarding what they hoped to achieve, the best way to do this, and what economic, social, and cultural advantages they sought through studying English. The results indicate that learners may have their hopes dashed when confronted with educational and work realities but, at the same time, are also aware of what they want to achieve personally and interactionally through the study of English as a foreign language.

Commodification of ELT
Commodification, or the marketisation, of education has been especially highlighted by Fairclough, who examined how university prospectuses have been converted into an example of a promotional genre (1992), and characterised by "personalisation of the reader (*you*) and the institution (*we*)" (2010, p. 102). For instance, educational institutions in Mexico use slogans such as ¡*Tenemos un lugar para ti!* (We have a place for you!) and *Estamos cerca de ti* (We are near you). Furthermore, commodification in education, whether it be aimed at prospective university students or foreign-language learners, has the potential to confuse or disorient since it combines "[t]exts of the information-and-publicity or telling-and-selling sort" (Fairclough, 1992, p. 117). Therefore, language school advertising may be informative about the course being offered and/or persuasive regarding how English can give people the power to change their lives. This can lead to the confusing use of terminology. For instance, Fairclough argues that "[i]t is no longer surprising, for example, for sectors of the arts and education such as theatre and English language teaching to be referred to as 'industries' concerned with producing, marketing and selling cultural or educational commodities to their 'clients' or 'consumers'" (1992, p. 207).

This phenomenon can be seen for instance, in Guadalajara, where English-language school publicity addresses potential students as *clientes* (clients) where they can enrol for a course by making an online *compra* (purchase). One of Spanish's leading linguistic authorities, *La Real Académica de Español,* defines *cliente* as *Persona que utiliza con asiduidad los servicios de un profesional o empresa* (Person who regularly uses the services of a professional or company). The idea of a language learner using the services of a company radically changes the student-teacher relationship. Indeed, Fairclough argues that there is "a widespread ambiguity about who educational commodities or 'packages' are being sold to. Is it the learner, or the firms that currently employ or are likely to employ learners?" (1992, p. 208).

In Mexico, commodification is especially evident in how language schools offer prospective students a successful outcome as well as offering them marketable skills. The focus on skills is taken up by Fairclough who examines how prospective students are viewed:

> On the one hand, they are constructed in the active role of discerning customers or consumers aware of their "needs" and able to select courses which meet their needs. On the other hand, they are constructed in the passive role of elements or instruments in production processes ... targeted for training in required skills or "competences," with courses designed around precise "attainment targets" and culminating in "profiles" of learners, both of which are specified in terms of quite precise skills. (Fairclough, 1992, p. 208)

English-language courses in Guadalajara are packaged in terms of learning the four skills with the result that students will be able to 'dominate' the target language.

In this chapter, I take up two questions raised by commodification: What are language courses in private language institutions trying to achieve? Secondly, what is the effect of commodification on language learners themselves as they consider what English-language courses promise to offer them and in what time period?

Critical Sociolinguistics

Whilst commodification examines language use, critical sociolinguistics differs from traditional sociolinguistics in that it attempts to understand how people may be manipulated and misled by language. Traditional sociolinguistics describes language and society in terms of stability and orderliness which can be conveniently placed into such categories as geographical location, social class, gender, etc. In contrast, critical sociolinguistics "seeks to recognise the political and economic distortions that our society imposes upon us" (Mey, 1985, p. 342). In the case of learning a foreign-language, students often invest considerable amounts of income in learning the target language in the hope of increased employment prospects when the realities may be quite different. Too often ELT pedagogy promotes a "banking" approach to education (Freire, 1993) where students are all crammed with the same information often described in terms of grammar structures and communicative functions. They may be led to believe that this can be achieved over a relatively short period of time through purely constructing and practising an inventory of language patterns and skills (speaking, listening, reading, and writing) which is easy to "deliver" pedagogically. However, in reality, such teaching practices may have questionable results.

Furthermore, critical sociolinguists are interested in seeing people not as categories or numbers but as thinking and reflective individuals who have their own goals and aspirations. Within the ELT industry, language learners are rarely seen as individuals who may want to exploit, appropriate, or even resist English for their own purposes (Benesch, 2012; Canagarajah, 1999). Furthermore, learners' existing attitudes, beliefs, histories, and values, or what Bourdieu (1972) terms *habitus*, are seldom taken into consideration in contemporary teaching practice. For example, Kecskes (2013) argues that every foreign-language learner interacts in the target language (TL) using prior first language (L1) background, building on second-language situational experiences, and co-constructing interactions with other TL users (pp. 148-149). Consequently, language learners may not uncritically or wholeheartedly embrace concepts such as English as a global language but rather see the learning of English as a foreign language as a way for personal betterment and increased job prospects.

In this chapter I examine how the participants were willing to accept packaged language courses that can be delivered in a neatly packed time frame but at the same time establish their own aims and objectives. Critical sociolinguists are interested in understanding contradictions as students may be willing to accept imported methodologies but reject the goals behind those methodologies.

In examining why beginner students in Guadalajara, Mexico, embark on learning English as a foreign language, I wanted to understand their attitudes and motives. In order to identify the participants' priorities and how they use English for their own purposes, I have identified the benefits that foreign-language users perceive by learning the target language.

Consequently, I have adopted an emic approach rather than imposing the "conceptual framework of the researcher" (Cohen, Manion, & Morrison, 2000, p. 313). An emic research stance examines language learning from the students' point of view rather that employing a previously established framework as a point of departure. Whilst an etic viewpoint which reflects the researcher's perspective, an emic approach reflects "the concern … to catch the subjective meanings placed on situations by participants" (Cohen et al., 2000, p. 139). If the researcher is to understand the participants' view of English language learning, foreign-language students need to be able to describe their objectives and goals. Given the emic focus of the study, I have used everyday categories such as work and educational prospects that learners can identify with rather than more obscure academic terms such as instrumental and integrative motivation.

Therefore to understand the participants' point of view, my overarching research question is: What benefits do students see themselves as attaining by studying English? I need to understand the goals, aims, and motivations of the students themselves in studying English. To answer this key question, I have developed three specific research questions:

1. Do students learn English as a foreign language for materialistic, personal, or interactional reasons?
2. Do students believe that learning English results in more than just knowing and using an additional language and whether it opens up new worlds?
3. Do students approach foreign-language learning in terms of amassing information by constructing and practising an inventory of language structures and skills?

To examine the possible benefits of studying English, my first specific research question asks whether students learn English as a foreign language for materialistic, personal, or interactional reasons. Materialistic reasons provide language learners with a perceived tangible benefit such as finding a better job or achieving a salary increase. Personal motives may be to travel abroad or the strengthening of the curriculum vitae. Interactional reasons involve constructing, developing, and maintaining social relationships. From a critical sociolinguistics perspective, the commodification (or the marketisation) of education may mislead students into believing that learning English can readily satisfy learners' materialistic, personal, or interactional goals and ambitions.

My second specific research question asks whether students believe that learning English results in something more than just knowing and using an additional language and whether it opens up new worlds and unlimited opportunities as often touted through the commodification of foreign language learning.

My third specific research question examines whether students approach foreign-language learning in terms of Freire's banking approach (i.e., the amassing of information by constructing and practising an inventory of language structures and skills). Such approach is often promoted through the commodification of language as students are led to believe that a compendium of verb tenses, topic vocabulary, along with an understanding of the four skills (speaking, listening, reading, and writing), are all that is necessary to become proficient in the target language. I asked respondents whether learning is best achieved through studying grammar and vocabulary or whether there are other ways of achieving foreign-language proficiency and, also, how long this process should take.

Method

In this section, I detail how the data was collected, describe the participants, and review the advantages and disadvantages of using questionnaires. Furthermore, I illustrate that besides reflecting an emic approach, the methodology is quantitative in that it seeks to measure participants' motives and attitudes.

Participants

The 70 Mexican participants in this study were all working adults, aged between 20 and 40 years old. There were 46 women and 24 men, which reflects the usual predominance of women in studying English as a foreign language in Guadalajara. The students were studying on an extremely low-cost English-language course at the university's teaching training centre. Guadalajara hosts numerous international companies that actively seek English-speaking employees. These transnational firms include call centers, information technology companies, and manufacturing units, and many students are looking for work opportunities in these companies.

The researcher asked the programme coordinator for permission to approach the students and, on receiving her agreement, subsequently asked the students if they were willing to fill out a questionnaire and, if so, to give their assent in writing. The students were told that participation was voluntary. However, all of them agreed to participate. This may be because they were appreciative of the low price of the course.

Through the administration of a diagnostic examination the students had been placed at an elementary level. They studied on three-hour intensive courses in the mornings from Monday to Thursday. This was their first course studying English.

Research Instrument
The study was carried out through the use of a written questionnaire that contained four open-ended questions with no fixed response options and two closed-ended questions with response options. See Appendix 5. The two closed-ended questions allowed respondents to offer alternative answers. The questionnaire was written in Spanish and it was expected that students would respond in Spanish. However, one respondent answered in English. The questionnaire as a research instrument was adopted because it provided fast information from respondents who led busy lives and did not have time to be interviewed or answer long questionnaires.

Procedures
To answer the research question, I asked the 70 students studying in the intensive four-week course to respond to the written questionnaire in Spanish. This was completed in the classroom at the end of class during their first week of study. No time limit was given. Learners were asked about their motives for learning English and whether they thought that a new language would change their way of thinking and especially attitudes to their own country. In the questionnaire, I also asked participants to describe their goals in terms of how learning may affect their values and attitudes rather than using such theoretical constructs as Bourdieu's (1972) *habitus* and social capital. By asking about values and attitudes, learners were given the opportunity to reflect on any socio-cultural changes that may occur through learning a foreign language.

Although the data analysis was quantitative in terms of adding up the number of answers, I was more interested in a qualitative analysis of the reasons behind their answers.

Results

In this section, I present the respondents' motives for learning English and report on whether foreign language learning changes the participants' ways of thinking and perceptions about themselves and their society and country. Focusing on English-language learning and teaching, I also asked them what they considered to be the most desirable method to learn English as a foreign language and how long they thought it should take.

In Question 1, I asked participants about their motivation for learning English, especially given that there is significant local demand from transnational corporations for English-speaking employees. To guide them, they were given a list of possible reasons. However, they were also given the option of adding their own reason. The results can be seen in Table 5.1:

Table 5.1
Participants' Motives for Learning English as a Foreign Language

Reported Motive for Studying English	n	Percentage
Work & employment	30	42.9
Travel abroad	12	17.1
Increase their CV	7	10
Talk with friends & family	3	4.3
Postgraduate studies	3	4.3
Other (Culture; education, hobby, individual interest)	4	5.7
No reason	1	1.4
Invalid (more than one answer)	10	14.3
Total	70	100

The results indicate that an overwhelming number of respondents (42.9%) believe that English-language proficiency leads to greater job opportunities. Whilst travelling abroad was a comparatively strong category (17.1%), miscellaneous reasons for learning English indicate that language students' motivations do not always respond to commodification (or the marketisation) of education. Furthermore, four respondents added their own motives for learning English: increasing cultural knowledge, creating educational opportunities (e.g., pursuing postgraduate studies), enjoying English as a leisure time activity, and developing individual interests and personal knowledge.

Question 2 examines whether the respondents' main reason for learning English is purely economic or materialistic. The question asks whether learning English is designed to increase one's income or reflects more scholarly or cultural aspirations. Respondents were encouraged to give a reason for their answer and the results are seen in Table 5.2:

Table 5.2

Respondents' Degree of Economic Motivation for Learning English

Economic motive for learning English?	n	Reasons	n	% of total
Yes	42			60
		Higher salary	26	
		Career development	24	
		Capitalism / globalisation	2	
No	20			29
		Personal	11	
		Cultural	5	
		Basic necessity	2	
		Obligatory	1	
		No reason	1	
No answer	3			4
Invalid answer	5			7
Total	70			100

The results indicate that economic and materialistic reasons (60%) were predominantly the main motivations for learning English especially since the respondents thought that they could command higher salaries and/or forward their careers. However, it should be noted that nearly 30% of respondents rejected economic and materialistic considerations and believed that personal and cultural objectives were more important.

Question 3 asks respondents whether they believed they would change their values, attitudes, opinions, and beliefs as a result of learning English as a foreign language. The question explores the idea that language learning not only entails developing new ways of communicating but also alters the way people think and reflect about themselves and their surroundings. Respondents were encouraged to give a reason for their answer and the results are seen in Table 5.3:

Table 5.3
Learning English Develops New Values, Attitudes, Opinions, Beliefs, etc.

Language learning affecting values, attitudes etc.	*n*	Reasons	*n*	% of total
Yes	58			82.9
		Personal way of being	28	
		Understanding other cultures	29	
		No reason	1	
No	12			17.1
		Only a language	9	
		No reason	3	
Total	70			100

The results indicate that 82.9% of language learners believe that learning a new language results in a change in behaviour and culturally understanding other people in new ways. The respondents were more or less evenly divided as to whether they thought they would change their behaviour as individuals or how they would view other cultures. Approximately half the participants felt they would interact differently whilst the other half thought they would understand others differently.

Question 4 examines whether respondents expected to view their own culture and society differently as a result of learning English. Language learning may not only change people as individuals but also the way that they participate in their own society. Respondents were encouraged to give a reason for their answer and the results can be seen in Table 5.4:

Table 5.4
Changes in Perception of One's Own Culture/Country/Society

Does learning another language affect view of own country?	n	Reasons	n	% of total
Yes	34			48.6
		Comparative	25	
		Development	2	
		No reason	2	
No	34			48.6
		Only a language	17	
		Already formed views on society	6	
		No reason	10	
Yes & No	2			2.8
Total	70			100

The results indicate that respondents were evenly divided (48.6%) as to whether they expected to view their own country differently after having learned the target language. It is impossible to predict whether such a development would be positive or detrimental. Respondents largely believed that learning a new language would result in making comparisons between their own country and the target-language country rather than in developing new ways of examining their own beliefs and attitudes. Of those who did not envisage a change in how they would view their culture/country/society, most respondents (17) felt that they were only learning a language and not constructing a different perception of society. A further six respondents said that their view of society was already formed and was unalterable.

Question 5 focused on what respondents thought was the most effective way to learn a language. Participants were given options so as to give them the opportunity to perhaps contemplate other ways of learning the target language. The results can be seen in Table 5.5:

Table 5.5
Preferred Approach in Learning English

Approach	Methodology	n	% of total
Structures	Grammar & skills based	54	77
Interaction	Socialisation	6	9
Task focus	Problem-solving	4	6
Communicative	Functional language	3	4
Classical	Studying culture and literature	3	4
	Total	70	100

The results indicated overwhelmingly that the respondents opted for grammar and skills-based approaches. That they had put their faith in such approaches may be surprising given that they had previously attempted to learn English at school. They apparently had not been successful since they had now been placed at the elementary level. On the other hand, respondents may not have been aware of alternative approaches to teaching a foreign language.

In Question 6, respondents were asked how long they thought it would take to learn English really well. The question aimed to find out whether student expectations correlated with those language institutions that claim that English can be learned within a relatively short period of time (see Table 5.6).

Table 5.6
Estimated Time to Learn English

Duration	n	% of total
Less than one year	3	4.3
1 - 1.9 years	14	20.0
2 - 2.9 years	25	35.7
3 - 3.9 years	15	21.4
More than 4 years	11	15.7
No answer	2	2.9
Total	70	100

The results indicate that 24.3% of respondents believe that English can be learned well in less than two years. This goal may be unrealistic for working adults, and less than three years may be a more realistic target depending on time and effort dedicated to studying the target language. The 21.4% who estimated 3 - 4 years may have established a much more attainable target given their work and perhaps family commitments.

In conclusion, the respondents articulated clear motives for wanting to learn English and what they expected to achieve in terms of better job opportunities, individual advancement, development of their own values, attitudes, opinions, beliefs, and interaction with other cultures. Many respondents felt that language learning was best achieved by focusing on grammar and learning the four skills (speaking, listening, reading, and writing). However, few felt that English as a foreign language could be learned sufficiently well in less than two years, and the majority opted for between two and four years.

Discussion

Students of English as a foreign language in Mexico all too often believe learning the target language will improve their economic status. Little research has been carried out on this perception but, as Alsagoff, McKay, Hu and Renandya (2012) argue, it is unlikely that English alone will improve one's career prospects: "A very prevalent belief is that being proficient in English allows one better and more job opportunities. Whereas English proficiency alone is not sufficient for a good job, for a growing number of professional jobs, English does appear to be great asset" (2012, p. 32). Answers to Question 1 indicate that respondents were studying English principally to increase their job prospects and for career development. However, at least in the Mexican context, there may not be a simple correlation between foreign language education and increased job prospects as argued by Hausmann (2015):

> In Mexico, the average income of men aged 25 - 30 with a full primary education differs by more than a factor of three between poorer municipalities and richer ones. The difference cannot possibly be related to educational quality, because those who moved from poor municipalities to richer ones also earned more.

Therefore, the implications of this finding is that English-language students in poorer areas may not necessarily enhance their employment prospects through the study of English if they are unwilling to relocate. Therefore the promises forwarded through the marketisation and commodification of English language learning need to be critically examined as to whether knowing English can really give people the ability and the power to change their lives.

In Question 2, the finding that 60% of respondents studied English for economic and materialistic reasons would appear to support the argument that the teaching and learning of English should focus on communication for business purposes rather than for interactional or social reasons. (As I argue later, respondents' answers to Question 3 challenge this argument.) English-language students may not be particularly interested in concepts such as English as a global language or becoming part of an international community of language users. Rather, they are more concerned with trying to better their immediate economic situation. From a critical sociolinguistic perspective, learners may be investing a sizable proportion of their wages and salaries to pursue an economic ambition that may never be accomplished.

In Question 3, 82.9% of respondents believe that language learning changes behaviour and understanding. Therefore, teaching cannot be reduced to purely focusing on transactional language use, as suggested in the answers to Question 2. The apparent conflict between the two sets of answers suggests that over the short-term, respondents may look for economic gain but that over the long term they have more individualistic and interpersonal goals. If language learning is indeed about changing attitudes and beliefs, pedagogy also needs to focus on interactional language use and how to express ideas and opinions in the target language.

The interpersonal value of foreign language learning is further underlined in the answers to Question 4 as the respondents see themselves changing how they view their own society and becoming more tolerant and understanding of other cultures. These motivations reinforce arguments that language learning is not just about travel and work but trying to understand other worldviews and diminish one's own ethnocentricity.

Answers to Question 5 suggest that learners had not adopted a critical stance towards their own learning of English and perhaps recent failure to grasp a second language. The teaching of English as a foreign language has been a school subject in primary schools since 1992 (Davies, 2009). Given that all the interactants were adults and had previous experience of (and perhaps frustration with) learning English, it might have been expected that they would be critical of grammar and skills approaches to learning English. However, they appear to be willing to accept methods and approaches forwarded through the marketisation and commodification of English language learning that neatly package English-language instruction into conveniently "learnable" units.

In the answers to Question 6, respondents seem to be skeptical of being able to learn English in less than two years. The results indicate that less than 25% of respondents believe that this is possible. This raises the question as to why language institutions continue to sell courses that promise results in less than a year. Perhaps marketisation is so strong that potential customers are convinced by arguments of immediate success or, perhaps, there are no viable alternatives coming from the foreign-language industry. The 35.7% of respondents who believe that English can be learnt well in less than three years may reflect a more considered and feasible approach to learning English.

Limitations
This study has limitations regarding the choice of research instrument, the investigative procedure, and the selection of participants. First of all, I discuss the advantages and disadvantages of using a questionnaire. I then examine whether the research should have been undertaken over a longer time period, and finally I reflect on the choice of participants.

The questionnaire offers a structured way to collect data that can be later analysed in a systematic manner. Questionnaires can measure factual, behavioural, and attitudinal questions (Dörnyei, 2007). In this study I examine the students' beliefs and expectations regarding the learning of English as a foreign language. Whilst questionnaires have the advantages of being economical to administer, easy to arrange, and accurately record respondents' answers (Denscombe, 2010), they can be seen as limiting participants' choices or unduly encouraging them to think in a certain way. To overcome this, I allowed respondents to offer alternative answers in the closed-ended questions.

However, I justify the use of the questionnaire because it raises awareness about beliefs and attitudes in language learning and teaching that the respondents may not have expressed in an interview or which might not have surfaced through ethnographic research.

With regard to the investigative procedure, it is important to take into consideration that students' objectives for learning a foreign language may change during a course of study and therefore, the motives for learning English may change. Future research needs to take into consideration, perhaps through a diachronic study, how foreign-language students change and/or develop their learning objectives.

Finally, the number of participants was relatively small. Future research should increase the sample size as well as examine possible differences in participant gender, social class, and educational background.

Conclusion
In this Mexican context, learners share common interests and motivations in learning English, and the English Language Teaching (ELT) industry builds on their aspiration that a knowledge of English will open up economic opportunities and provide golden job opportunities. However, in reality language learners are individuals who exploit, appropriate, or even resist

English for their own purposes (Benesch, 2012; Canagarajah, 1999). Students are not only interested in English for economic gain but also for personal and societal reasons. Therefore, the identification of learner needs should mean that teaching objectives, teaching content, material design, classroom instruction, language curricula, and assessment practices should consider the needs and aspirations of the individual learner. The ELT industry needs to stop treating learners as a homogenous group and resist the mass-marketing and packaging of foreign-language courses to be delivered in less than two years.

In this chapter, I have answered the overarching research question as to whether students want to learn English as a foreign language for purely instrumental reasons. Whilst initial answers indicated that students were interested in the economic and work benefits from learning English, they also expect to experience personal change and development. In answer to my first specific research question which asks whether students are persuaded through the commodification of language that English will open up new worlds and unlimited opportunities, students believe that learning English can readily satisfy materialistic goals and ambitions. But, at the same time in response to my second specific research question, students do have their own personal or interactional goals and ambitions and see the study of English as more than just learning a language. In answer to my third specific research question, respondents appear to accept the tenet that learning is most effectively achieved studying grammar, vocabulary, and the four skills of speaking, listening, reading, and writing (i.e., Freire's banking approach).

The research reflects an initial attempt to understand how Mexican students view the language learning process. A larger-scale investigation needs to collect more data on the students themselves (e.g., previous experience of learning English, their current and desired professions) and see how, from a critical sociolinguistic perspective, foreign-language teaching can effectively empower students to pursue their own language learning goals and not be manipulated by the commodification processes that lie behind the marketing of English as a foreign language and, following Fairclough (1992), resist being constructed as passive recipients of language learning courses.

References

Alsagoff, L., McKay, S. L., Hu, G., & Renandya, W. A. (2012). *Principles and practices for teaching English as an international language*. London: Routledge.

Benesch, S. (2012). *Considering emotions in critical English language teaching*. New York: Routledge.

Block, D., & Cameron, D. (2002). Introduction. In D. Block & D. Cameron (Eds.), *Globalization and language teaching* (pp. 1-10). London: Routledge.

Bourdieu, P. (1972). *Outline of a theory of practice*. Cambridge: Cambridge University Press.

British Council. (2015). *English in Mexico: An examination of policy, perceptions and influencing factors*. Mexico: British Council. Retrieved from https://ei.britishcouncil.org/sites/default/files/latin-americaresearch/English%20in%20Mexico.pdf

Canagarajah, S. (1999). *Resisting linguistic imperialism in English teaching*. Oxford, UK: Oxford University Press.

Cohen, L., Manion. L., & Morrison, K. (2000). *Research methods in education* (5th ed.). London: Routledge Falmer.

Davies, P. (2009). Strategic management of ELT in public educational systems: Trying to reduce failure, increase success. *The Electronic Journal for English as a Second Language, 13*(3), 1-22. Retrieved from http://www.tesl-ej.org/wordpress/issues/volume13/ej51/ej51a2/

Denscombe, M. (2010). *The good research guide for small-scale social research projects*. Maidenhead, UK: Open University Press/McGraw Hill.

Dörnyei, Z. (2007). *Research methods in applied linguistics: Quantitative, qualitative and mixed methodologies*. Oxford: Oxford University Press.

Fairclough, N. (1992). *Discourse and social change*. Cambridge, UK: Polity Press.

Fairclough, N. (2010). *Critical discourse analysis*. Harlow, UK: Pearson.

Freire, P. (1993). *Pedagogy of the oppressed*. New York, Continuum.

Hausmann, R. (2015) *The education myth*. Retrieved from http://www.socialeurope.eu/2015/06/the-education-myth/

Kecskes, I. (2013). *Intercultural pragmatics*. New York: Oxford University Press.

Mey, J. (1985). *Whose language? A study in linguistic-pragmatics* (Pragmatics and beyond companion, Volume 3). Philadelphia: John Benjamins.

Pennycook, A. (2001). *Critical applied linguistics: A critical introduction*. Mahwah, New Jersey: Lawrence Erlbaum.

Phillipson, R. (1992). *Linguistic imperialism*. Oxford: Oxford University Press.

Phillipson, R. (2009). *Linguistic imperialism continued*. New York: Routledge.

Appendix 5

1. ¿Cuáles son las razones principales por las que las personas quieren aprender inglés? Marca sólo una opción.

   - Trabajo y empleo.
   - Incrementar su CV.
   - Viajar al extranjero.
   - Hablar con familiares y amigos.
   - Otras razones (Por favor específica).
   - Ninguna razón en particular.

2. ¿Cree usted que la razón principal para aprender inglés es económico y materialista? Escribe sí o no. Especifica las razones de tu respuesta.

3. Cuando aprendes ingles ¿Desarrollas nuevos valores, actitudes, opiniones, creencias, etc.? Escribe sí o no. Especifica las razones de tu respuesta.

4. Cuando aprendes inglés ¿Piensas de manera diferente acerca de tu propio país y cultura? Escribe sí o no. Especifica las razones de tu respuesta.

5. ¿Cuál es el curso ideal de lengua extranjera? Marca sólo una opción.

   a) Gramática, vocabulario, pronunciación, leer, escuchar, hablar y escribir actividades. ( )
   b) Actividades de comunicación, por ejemplo: Pedir información, agradecer, disculparse, discutir, sugerir, felicitar, etc. ( )
   c) Actividades que usen Inglés, por ejemplo: Planear unas vacaciones, encontrar un lugar para vivir, buscar trabajo, resolver problemas. ( )
   d) Socializar: Hacer amigos, platicar en conversaciones informales, conocer gente. ( )
   e) Estudiar países de habla inglesa, cultura, sociedad y literatura a través de lecturas, videos y audios. ( )

6. ¿Cuánto tiempo cree usted que se necesita para aprender otro idioma realmente bien? Calcula el número de meses/años.

Gracias por responder este cuestionario. Por favor escribe sí, si estás de acuerdo en que tus respuestas pueden ser usadas para propósitos académicos.

English translation:

1. Why do people principally want to learn English? Mark just one option.

    - Work and employment
    - Increase their CV
    - Travel abroad
    - Talk with friends and family
    - Other reasons (Please specify)
    - No particular reason

2. Do you think that the main reason for learning English is economic and materialistic? Say yes or no. Give reasons for your answer:

3. When you learn English do you develop new values, attitudes, opinions, beliefs, etc.? Say yes or no. Give reasons for your answer:

4. When you learn English, do you think differently about your own country and culture? Say yes or no. Give reasons for your answer:

5. What is the ideal foreign-language course? Mark just one option.

    a) Grammar, vocabulary, pronunciation, reading, listening, speaking and writing activities. ( )
    b) Communication activities, such as asking for information, thanking, apologising, arguing, suggesting, greeting, etc. ( )
    c) Activities that use English, such as planning a holiday, finding a place to live, looking for work, solving problems etc. ( )
    d) Socialising: to make friends, to chat in informal conversations, to get to know people. ( )
    e) Studying English-speaking countries, cultures, societies, and literature through readings, videos and audio recordings. ( )

6. How long do you think it takes to learn another language really well? Estimate the number of months/years:

Thank you for answering this questionnaire. Please write yes, if you agree that your answers can be used for academic purposes.

CHAPTER 6

(MIS)UNDERSTANDING IN THE LANGUAGE CLASSROOM:
The Case of a Japanese Student and a Brazilian English Language Teacher

Priscila Leal
University of Hawai'i at Mānoa

Introduction

(Mis)understandings are part of everyday life. Whether we are at home, work, school, church, or during customer service situations, interaction has the potential for misunderstanding. We frequently take for granted the act of comprehension and understanding and only take notice of understanding when we feel something has gone "wrong"—someone has misinterpreted something we have said or has responded differently to our expectation, or vice-versa. In a language classroom, the potential for misunderstandings to happen is surefire. This study reports on how Hoshihiko, a Japanese university student, and I, his Brazilian English language teacher, worked together through a gap in understanding between task instruction and task interpretation (Ohta, 2001).

(Mis)understanding is under-researched in the field of education and further research is necessary because when teachers examine misunderstandings in their class, they take the first step towards the discovery that instruction is an actual task in itself and that it may be adjusted on a moment-to-moment basis. Such is the case in this study. As I analyzed the (mis)understandings that took shape in the instructional interaction between Hoshihiko and me, I realized that I redesigned the instruction based on the understandings we developed in our interaction. In other words, how I went on instructing was directly related to our moment-to-moment achievement of understanding.

The task required students to create evaluative questions about a text. However, Hoshihiko and his partner did not use a modal verb (i.e., should) to signify that their question requested an opinion. Their answer was deemed incorrect due to the lack of a modal verb. Initially it seemed as though Hoshihiko was contesting or challenging me, but the interaction led to collaborative effort and the seeking of mutual understanding. Conversational inferences and each other's actions and turn-taking guided the interaction as both student and teacher attempted to make meanings understood. The lines between the teacher's and the student's institutional roles became blurred as we navigated between checking, claiming, and demonstrating understanding (or lack thereof).

This chapter is structured in the following way: first, I discuss the current literature on understanding and how one checks, claims, and demonstrates it. Second, I present the context of the study, the methods of data collection, and analysis. And finally, I analyze the data and their contextual, sequential, and socio-interactional interdependent nature. I conclude with a discussion of the implications for language teachers.

Understanding in Instructional Settings

Understanding has received renewed interest in the pragmatics and educational fields. In 2011, the *Journal of Pragmatics* dedicated an issue (43) featuring articles on understanding specifically in instructional settings. In the issue, the editor, Timothy Koschmann, stated, "The connection between instruction and understanding is not accidental. Instruction, by its nature, calls for the production of new understandings" (Koschmann, 2011, p. 436). Students are required to connect new understandings with previous knowledge and demonstrate these understandings to satisfy institutional requirements (i.e., assessment).

Although pragmatics is concerned with *how* understanding happens, my goal in this article is to analyze *whether* Hoshihiko and I understood each other; therefore, an interactional sociolinguistics framework guided the analysis of our interaction. Like other scholars before me, I conceptualize understanding as a situated, interactive process (e.g., Mondada, 2011). Nevertheless, I wondered, was Hoshihiko's and my understanding of each other also collectively achieved and publicly displayed (Mondada, 2011)?

Understanding as Collectively Achieved and Interactively Oriented

Understanding is publicly displayed as a speaker takes a turn in conversation (Koole, 2010; Macbeth, 2011). Understanding is interactively built across sequences (Mondada, 2011) as the second speaker infers on the first speaker's intentions and acts upon her inference. From this logic, one could argue that misunderstanding is then the absence of a speaker's inference on the first speaker's intentions and thus the absence of the second speaker's action or turn (i.e., silence). To follow this logic would be to deny that misunderstanding can promote interaction and mutual understanding. Linell (2009) believed misunderstandings have the potential to keep a conversation going. His hypothesis was that if speakers cared about the topic or the goal of the interaction, speakers would then work together through their misunderstanding to achieve mutual understanding. A speaker's turn would seek clarification or confirmation of the first speaker's intentions, which is evidenced throughout the interaction between Hoshihiko and me.

From my experience in intercultural communication (namely as a language learner conversing with native language speakers), conversations often continue when both parties care about the goal of the conversation. Even when there is misunderstanding, speakers can continue to take turns in order to achieve understanding collectively. Customer service is one such example. Once, when I was in Chile visiting for the holidays, I went shopping for *lembracinhas* (souvenirs). As I attempted to describe (with very basic Spanish language) the type of *lembracinha* I was looking for, the staff joined me in the process of working through this lack of understanding with the goal of arriving at a mutual understanding and therefore potentially scoring a sale. It was a joint effort towards discovery of each other's intention: mine, in trying to describe the type of *lembracinha* I was looking for, and in trying to understand the staff's suggestions or questions for clarification; the staff's, in trying to understand my description, and attempt to offer suggestions or asking questions for clarification. Misunderstanding then may promote interaction and mutual understanding, and misunderstanding does not necessarily hinder communication but it can push the interaction forward, especially when there is mutual interest.

Understanding as Publicly Displayed: Clarifying and Confirming by Claiming and Demonstrating Understanding

Hoshihiko and I guided each other's interpretations of what was being said through a range of potentially relevant factors and empirically detectable signs (Gumperz, 1992). One of those detectable signs is related to the notion of confirming understanding by claiming and demonstrating understanding. Sacks (1992) argued that both claiming and demonstrating understanding can be evident in conversations. Demonstrating is evident in explicit communicative acts (e.g., "I get it," "I know what you mean"); claiming, when a speaker draws a relevant inference. The interaction between Hoshihiko and I suggest a different aspect of Sacks' (1992) notion of claiming and demonstrating understanding; the claiming and demonstrating of a *lack of* understanding.

The distinction between claiming and demonstrating, and clarifying and checking (lack of) understanding is relevant here. It helps researchers recognize the kinds of understanding the speakers experience during the interaction. Furthermore, it helps researchers recognize how these kinds of understanding guide the embodied, sequential organization of interaction (Kääntä, 2014). A speaker's verbal and non-verbal actions serve to confirm whether the other speaker's inference is adequate. When the inference is inadequate, these actions invite clarifying and checking understanding.

In the classroom, verbal and non-verbal actions serve as observable cues for teachers to check and clarify students' understanding (Koole & Elbers, 2014). Observable cues or signs are a teacher's main source for inferring when students (mis)understand instruction or content; however, these signs are socio-culturally normative and can themselves be a source of misunderstanding. Teachers may not notice a cue or may interpret it differently than originally intended (Ishida, 2006). Such was the case in the interaction between Hoshihiko and I; Hoshihiko displayed certain signs and I misinterpreted them, and vice-versa. Ultimately, the misunderstanding was resolved as we continued to confirm, claim, demonstrate, clarify, and check each other's and our own understanding.

Methods

The data for this article are part of a larger study on critical language pedagogy. Critical language pedagogy sees teaching as a cultural, moral, social, and political practice. It is adapting traditional instructional practices to encourage student-centered teaching and to question taken-for-granted, dominant worldviews and ideologies (Crookes, 2013). In the spring of 2014, eight Japanese English language students attended my course *English Reading and Writing* as part of an intensive, four-week program at a university in Hawai'i, USA. The data for the larger study included thirty hours of audio recordings of classroom interaction, my daily reflective journal, student questionnaires, and student artifacts (e.g., journals entries and writings). The data were collected as part of my teacher development and approved by the Social and Behavioral Sciences Institutional Review Board (IRB).

The Course
I developed the curriculum and lesson plans for the course with tasks that would incrementally challenge the students to think critically about the texts and the world (cf. Leal, 2015). I have learned from experience not to assume that students come to class prepared to engage in discussion of taken-for-granted, dominant worldviews. It can be quite a leap for some students to go from a traditional teacher-centered classroom to having an active role in the classroom, let alone questioning the status quo.

The curriculum included potentially controversial topics such as Japanese immigration in Hawai'i and the attack on Pearl Harbor. Before presenting the students with these topics, I devised a unit that would serve as the foundation for preparing them to engage in discussions, and to help them become comfortable with sharing their opinions with each other. For this foundational unit, I selected a familiar text, *Little Red Riding Hood*, based on the notion that the students would already be familiar with it; therefore, they would not need to focus (so much) on its content but on the format of the task (see Leal, 2015 for a detailed description of the tasks).

The Classroom
I include the layout of the classroom and seating arrangement at the time of the interaction with Hoshihiko (cf. Figure 6.1). The seating arrangement is relevant because it represents Hoshihiko's and my places in relation to each other, in relation to other students, and in relation to the physical space of the classroom—all of which can influence the level of interaction and engagement (Simonsen, Fairbanks, Briesch, Myers, & Sugai, 2008). It is

speculated that had we been in different places (e.g., farther away from each other), this interaction might not have occurred, or it might have happened in a different way. The location of the audio recorder was in the middle of the communal table, close to myself, Hoshihiko, and another student. One of the limitations I faced with audio data was that they missed aspects of non-verbal expressions, embodied actions, and manipulation of artifacts. To remediate such limitation, I made note of these paralinguistic aspects in my field notes immediately after class.

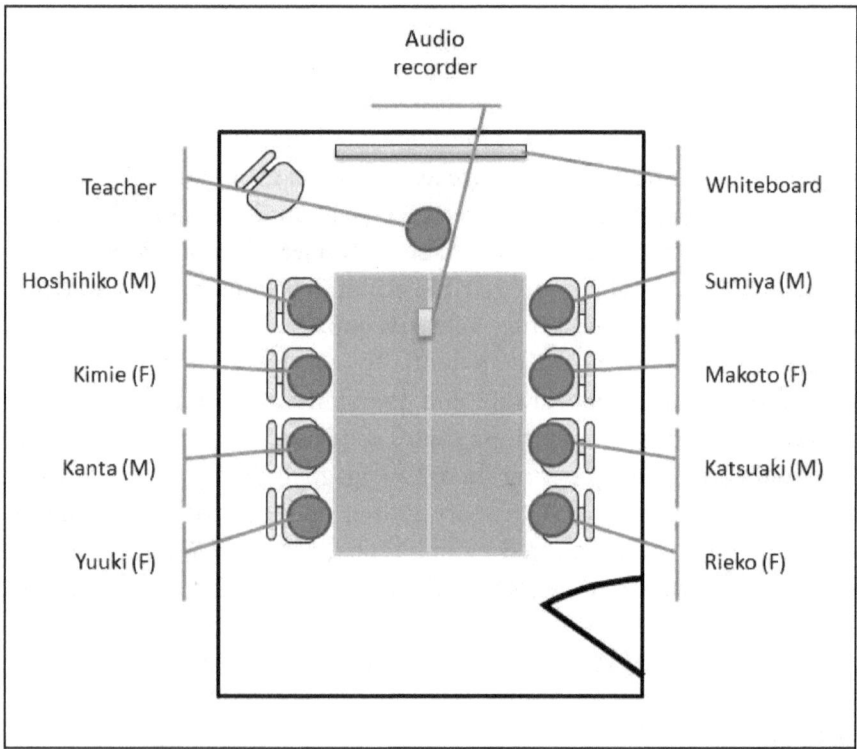

Figure 6.1. Classroom layout

The Task
The task was a "Create your own question," which was a two-part task. The first part consisted of:

a) Students reading two different versions of *Little Red Riding Hood* (one by Charles Perrault and the other by the Brothers Grimm);
b) In pairs, students creating text comprehension questions (e.g., what color was Little Red Riding Hood's hood?);
c) Students exchanging their questions with another pair; and,
d) Students discussing their answers with their partners, and then as a class.

Part two consisted of students creating questions that were evaluative in nature (e.g., why was Little Red Riding Hood's hood red?). Evaluative questions were defined as questions whose answers could not be found in the text. I explained that the answers to the evaluative questions would be "in one's minds and hearts" (Leal, 2015, p. 210), referring to opinion and emotion, respectively. Such was the context of the data presented in this article: it was lesson number six (out of 14), right after I had instructed part two. The entire interaction of (mis)understandings between Hoshihiko and I occurred over 42 minutes of audio data. In this chapter, I discuss seven selected excerpts from this interaction.

Communicative Projects

I frame our 42-minute interaction within a Communicative Projects Theory. A theory of communicative projects conceives interaction as other-oriented and jointly accomplished (Linell, 2009). A speaker's single utterance (e.g., communicative act) is not a decontextualized, autonomous speech with a unique semantic representation (Linell & Marková, 1993), but rather it is part of a communicative project (CP) (Linell, 2009). Communicative projects are tied to particular social situation types and form Communicative Activity Types (CATs) (Linell, 2009). The CATs demonstrated in this chapter involves Hoshihiko and I working together (i.e., CP) in the language classroom (i.e., social encounter type) to solve our misunderstanding (i.e., social situation type).

In the excerpts discussed in this article, CP has multiple meanings and functions. How Hoshihiko and I acted was a result of and response to the previous communicative acts and directly related to their multiplicity of meanings and functions. In addition, CP dealt with topics and actions with which Hoshihiko and I were concerned at least for that moment of the interaction (cf. Linell, 2009; Zheng, 2012 for other examples of CP in use).

Analysis and Findings

I present the analysis and findings of seven excerpts from the 42-minute interaction. Each excerpt highlights the strategies that Hoshihiko and I utilized in the moment-to-moment meaning-making process. These excerpts also include the communicative acts that preceded and followed the moment when understanding was negotiated. The first excerpt began after I had instructed the students on the second part of the task (e.g., to create two evaluative questions).

As briefly explained in the previous section, one of the goals of the task was to support students as they gradually learned to question taken-for-granted assumptions (Shor, 1993). For most of the students, this was their first time creating evaluative questions in the class (Leal, 2015). With that goal in mind, I made very little to no corrections of students' grammatical deviations. I was most interested in *what* they had to say (e.g., content) rather than *how* they said it (e.g., form). I was concerned that if I focused on the latter that students might become self-conscious and therefore less willing to participate. In the case of Hoshihiko, I believe if I had focused on form rather than content, it would have affected his openness in explaining his reasoning.

As Hoshihiko near-transferred the task of creating both knowledge-based and evaluative questions, our misunderstanding became visible. Below (Excerpt #1) is Hoshihiko's response to my suggestion to change his and his partner's question from "How did the girl answer the wolf?" (knowledge-based) to "How do you think the girl should have answered the wolf?" (evaluative). I justified my suggestion by saying, "basically now we need to think; [the answer is] not in the text".

Excerpt #1: "This is - is also we need uh we think"(28m20s)

60.	Hoshihiko	This is- is also we need uh we think
61.	Teacher	How?
62.	Hoshihiko	((smiling)) I think so
63.	Teacher	You're right. You need to think. Any questions you need to think
64.		but the answer can be in the text or it can be in here ((points to
65.		forehead)) and here ((points to heart)) so when you ask "what do
66.		you think?", "what is your opinion?", "do you agree?" Then the
67.		answer comes from here ((points to forehead and heart at the same
68.		time)) it's not in the text (.)

69.	Hoshihiko	Mmm hmm ((voicing agreement))
70.	Teacher	because that's author (.) that's somebody else's opinion (.) does it-?
71.	Hoshihiko	Mmm hmm ((voicing agreement))
72.	Teacher	so you're right you need to think to answer, but what about the::
73.		answer? Where do you find the answer? We want questions that
74.		we find the answer here ((points to forehead and heart at the same
75.		time)) yes? Hard?
76.	Hoshihiko	Okay (.)

A communicative act can suggest a range of functions and have numerous interpretations; I interpreted Hoshihiko's comment, "This is- is also we need uh we think" (line 60), to function as an indirect signal of disagreement. By using positive grammatical features, he seemed to agree (on the surface) with my explanation and evaluation ("basically now we need to think; [the answer] it's not in the text"). However, rather than explicitly denying my evaluation, his comment seemed un-imposed as he offered an alternative way of interpreting the "need to think" by saying "also" (line 60). I was especially interested in Hoshihiko's disagreement because my previous experiences with Japanese students demonstrated that they rarely directly disagree with the teacher. With that in mind, I hoped to encourage him to think further and share his reasoning. Additionally, I wanted to create a meaningful classroom environment where interactions and negotiations of meaning were authentic, natural, dynamic, and spontaneous (Willis, 1996, as cited in Guariento & Morley, 2001, p. 350). I also hoped that he would feel validated about his previous yet potentially face-threatening comment (line 60), and that he would feel valued as an individual who had a different opinion than mine. I validated his comment, and sought clarification and further information as I asked, "How?" (line 61).

I was surprised by his response. Hoshihiko did not offer an explanation, but provided a short, indirect answer "((smiling)) I think so" (line 62) that reinstated his (disagreeing) opinion. I interpreted his indirectness as a friendly avoidance because he spoke smilingly; however, his response was not enough for me to gauge whether he had comprehended the task instruction of creating evaluative questions. Again, my prior experience in teaching Japanese students was what guided my interpretations of his actions and my reaction (lines 63-68). In line 63, I oriented to common ground by agreeing with him ("You're right. You need to think."), and I added a layer of embodied actions (pointing to my forehead and heart in lines 64, 65, 67, and 74). My intention in using gestures was to support and reinforce my verbal message. They were also used in an attempt to explain the task in a way that would make sense to him. Because Hoshihiko offered acknowledgment tokens ("Mmm hmm ((voicing agreement))," lines 69 and 71), I interpreted it as us having understood each other, and as a signal that I should continue (Walsh, 2011)—which I did in line 70 and lines 72-75. I interpreted Hoshihiko's last comment ("Okay," line 76) as an agreement, claiming understanding, and closure of this CP.

Excerpt #2: "Almost understand" (29m30s)
77.	Hoshihiko	Almost understand
78.	Teacher	It's easy to say- to ask what color was her hood? Easy right?
79.	Hoshihiko	Yea
80.	Teacher	[the answer] is in the text. Right. Why did the author choose red to
81.		be the color [of her hood]? (.) Easy or hard?
82.	Hoshihiko	Hard
83.	Teacher	Is the answer in the text?
84.	Hoshihiko	No
85.	Teacher	No. It makes us think differently. It's a different (.) different exercise.
86.		Does that make sense?
87.	Hoshihiko	Makes sense

My goal as a critical language teacher is to not only have the students complete an assigned task (in this case, create two evaluative questions), but also that they understand the task instruction, experience the task-in-progress, and produce new ways of interpreting taken-for-granted assumptions. For a short moment, I felt like Hoshihiko had finally understood. However, Hoshihiko's comment ("Almost understand," line 77) brought that into question and I reopened the conversation. I shared this excerpt with a Japanese colleague and, as we listened together to the audio recording, she brought to my attention another layer of interpretation to this intercultural interaction—Hoshihiko may have transferred a common Japanese way of displaying stance and refusing (cf. Takahashi & Beebe, 1987). The signs and expressions of understanding are culture-specific and can be a source of misunderstanding. Because I could only assess Hoshihiko's understanding by relying on his observable displays of understanding (Koole & Elbers, 2014, p. 60), and because these observable displays of understanding are dictated by socio-cultural norms.

The confusion was evident as I interpreted Hoshihiko's epistemic stance literally and was not satisfied with my task instruction being partially (i.e., "almost," line 77) understood, and I pursued in making sure he understood what was expected of him and his partner. I modified my approach and altered the questions I had initially used as examples. From abstract questions such as "what do you think?," "what is your opinion?," and "do you agree?" (lines 65-66), I now offered examples of questions which I believed to be of a more obvious nature—"What color was her [Little Red Riding Hood's] hood?" (line 78) and "Why did the author choose red to be the color [of her hood]?" (line 80). These questions however were not genuine in the sense that I did not know their answers. On the contrary, I expected specific answers from Hoshihiko and I believed that the manner in which he responded would demonstrate his current (mis)understanding of the task. In lines 79 ("Yea"), 82 ("Hard"), and 84 ("No"), Hoshihiko provided the expected answers. I then performed what I attributed as a final comprehension check ("Does that make sense?," line 86) to which he confirmed ("Makes sense," line 87).

Excerpt #3: "Maybe (.) different culture" (30m00s)
88. Teacher   ((smiling)) So so?
89. Hoshihiko   Almost
90. Teacher   ((smiling)) Almost?
91. Hoshihiko   Maybe (.) different culture ((laughs lightly))

This time I was the one who reopened the CP. Although Hoshihiko had confirmed and had said that it "makes sense" (line 87), his facial expression led me to believe that he had not yet completely understood the task. I asked "so so?" (line 88) with a friendly smile encouraging an honest answer. I did not want him to feel embarrassed that the task instruction still did not make sense to him at this point. He again answered "almost" (line 89) which I took as his way of saying "no." I repeated his last comment with a change in prosody to rising intonation ("Almost?," line 90) as to mark it as a question and with a smile with the hope that Hoshihiko would not feel face-threatened, and that he would offer some new information that would bring light into the source of our misunderstanding. His reply and observation, "Maybe (.) [it's] different culture" (line 91), intrigued me. From my experience in intercultural interactions, speakers who often bring "culture" to the surface of a conversation do it so as a way to explain differences and to reason unfamiliar ways of thinking and doing.

Excerpt #4: "so we think same question" (30m36s)

98.	Teacher	So explain to me how Japanese would (.) answer or would think
99.		the answer
100.	Hoshihiko	(5.0) Answer Japanese?
101.	Teacher	Yeah
102.	Hoshihiko	People (.) um think that um bo::th question is we have to (.) need
103.		(.) 'in my opinion' they need 'in my opinion'
104.	Teacher	Okay
105.	Hoshihiko	so we think same question
106.	Teacher	O:::h I see. So any questions lead your opinion. Is that what you're
107.		saying?
108.	Hoshihiko	Mmm hmm ((voicing agreement))
109.	Teacher	Yeah? So:: ((writes on the whiteboard "what color is the girl's
110.		hood?" and "why is the girl's hood red?"))
111.		(20.0)
112.	Teacher	It would say:: ((points to the question on the whiteboard "what
113.		color is the girl's hood?"))
114.	Hoshihiko	Yes I understand that we can find out from textbook
115.	Teacher	Okay ((points to the question on the whiteboard "why is the girl's
116.		hood red?"))
117.	Hoshihiko	Yeah we need uh 'my opinion' our opinion

I reopened the CP again and asked Hoshihiko what he had meant by "different culture" (line 91). I asked him to "explain to me how [a] Japanese [person] would (.) answer" (line 98) these different types of questions. After a five-second pause, he replied requesting clarification ("(5.0) Answer Japanese?", line 100). Upon my confirmation ("Yeah", line 101), he explained that "[Japanese] People (.) um think that um bo::th question is we have to (.) need (.) 'in my opinion' they need 'in my opinion'" (lines 102-103) and that because of that "so we think same question" (line 105).

Hoshihiko's pronominal word choice in line 105 (i.e., we) stood out. I interpreted it as the justification of his belief that both knowledge-based and evaluative questions were the "same" (line 105) by including all Japanese people to back up his claim. The fact was that only he seemed to be having difficulties distinguishing between both types of questions and progressing with the task in a class with seven other Japanese students. Alternatively, he took on the role of spokesperson for him and his partner. An interesting observation in his attempt to be understood was his use and potential reliance on the formulaic sentence "in my opinion" (lines 103 and 117) to articulate and mark evaluative comments. His reliance suggests that without this phrase, Hoshihiko may have lacked the linguistic expertise to express that what he was stating was an opinion, rather than demonstrating understanding of the text. Hoshihiko's continual use of and reliance on formulaic language to guide his expression was what seemed to have been the source of our misunderstanding.

I had a feeling that we continued not to understand each other even though my comment in line 106 ("O:::h I see") portrayed the contrary. At that time, I felt like we were talking about two different things: (a) the adequacy of task interpretation, and (b) the adequacy of grammatical forms. In order to bring us together and work towards understanding each other, I framed the task again by writing the two questions I had previously used as examples (lines 78 and 80-81) on the whiteboard ("what color is the girl's hood?" and "why is the girl's hood red?", lines 109-110). My purpose in writing the questions on the whiteboard was two-fold. First, to support speech by reinforcing the spoken message. Second, to help Hoshihiko visualize the different grammatical structures present in these two types of questions (e.g. *what* versus *why*). Before I could refer to these differences, however, he claimed understanding the nature of both types of questions. For the knowledge-based question he stated, "Yes I understand that we can find out from textbook" (line 114); for the evaluative question, "Yeah we need uh 'my opinion' our opinion" (line 117).

Excerpt #5: "But why this answer is text" (32m34s)

124.	Teacher	((smiling)) Okay:: (.) But?
125.	Hoshihiko	((smiling)) But why this answer is text
126.	Teacher	Okay

127.	Hoshihiko	I think it's the same
128.	Teacher	Because okay because (.) how:: ((in 12.0 writes on a piece of
129.		paper "how did the girl answer the wolf?" and "why did the girl
130.		answer the wolf?")) How did she answer? She was not afraid so
131.		she answered politely and she gave information. In the text.
132.	Hoshihiko	Yes

However, I was not satisfied with Hoshihiko's claim of understanding, "Yes I understand that we can find out from textbook" (line 114). Again, there was something about his facial expression and posture that led me to believe the misunderstanding had not yet been resolved. My impression was that his claim to have understood the task did not necessarily mean that a process of understanding had taken place (Mondada, 2011). I was not sure whether his continued lack of understanding had to do with the task instruction per se or with something else. Therefore, I pursued, "((smiling)) Okay:: (.) But?" (line 124).

Hoshihiko's response-question "But why this answer is text" (line 125) confirmed my initial thoughts. On the one hand, he did indeed understand the difference between knowledge-based and evaluative questions and the source of their respective answers. However, he did not understand why I had initially assessed his and his partner's original question, "How did the girl answer the wolf?", as not being adequate for the task—after all, their question was grammatically accurate. He went on to say, "I think [both questions] it's the same" (line 127). I found it necessary to change my strategy once more.

Now that I was sure he had understood the different nature of both questions, I decided to focus on addressing why his and his partner's original question was inadequate for the purpose of the task and on providing a satisfactory alternative question. I wrote on a piece of paper their original question, "How did the girl answer the wolf?", and rewrote it replacing the first word in the sentence, *how*, with *why*. The question now read, "Why did the girl answer the wolf?" (lines 128 and 129). My goal in writing it down was to provide a visual cue that, although their original question may have been grammatically accurate, it did not meet the task goal. I read their original question aloud and modeled some of the possible answers, "She was not afraid so she answered politely and she gave information" (lines 130 and 131), highlighting that these answers could be found "in the text" (line 131). As I modeled potential answers, I accommodated my speech ("She answered politely," line 130 and "She gave information," line 131) to improve my chances of being understood—a strategy commonly used by language teachers to facilitate communication (Zhu Hua, 2014). Hoshihiko agreed ("Yes," line 132) and, rather than treating his agreement as a closure, I acted to further confirm his agreement and understanding ("Yes?," line 133).

Excerpt #6: "Do you think? I think ((smiling))" (33m05s)

133.	Teacher	Yes? How can you change (.) to ask opinion?
134.	Hoshihiko	So this question? ((points to the written down question "why did
135.		the girl answer the wolf?"))
136.	Teacher	Do you think? I think ((smiling)) Do you think?
137.	Hoshihiko	((smiling)) Yes yes okay

In order to overcome the previous gaps in understanding and move on with the task performance, I needed Hoshihiko to demonstrate that he did indeed understand why his and his partner's original question was not adequate for the purposes of the task. In Excerpt #6, the goal of the CP moved from task instruction and his ability to distinguish between the two questions (lines 114 and 117) to the (in)adequacy of their question's grammatical structure for the purpose of the task. I asked him, "How can you change [the question] (.) to ask opinion?" (line 133) and he replied, "So this question?" (line 134) pointing to the written question "Why did the girl answer the wolf?" (lines 134 and 135). I interpreted his display of understanding in line 134 not as a display of understanding, but as a display of doubt and of confirmation check because of its rising intonation. I, in turn, responded in a smiling, friendly, teasing manner ("Do you think? I think ((smiling)) Do you think?," line 136). Prosody here was essential to Hoshihiko's positive assessment of my comment (Gumperz, 1982). Also with a smile, he closed the CP claiming understanding, "Yes yes okay" (line 137).

After his last communicative act ("Yes yes okay", line 137), I noticed the class had become quiet, a sign that the other pairs had finished the task and were ready to review their answer-questions. My interaction with Hoshihiko had been obvious to the students. I was aware of that and I did not want students to get the impression that, because Hoshihiko had seemingly disagreed with me, he was being disrespectful according to traditional views of student/teacher relationship. Hence, I addressed the class and summarized what Hoshihiko and I had discussed up to that point. Next, I asked the students to write their two evaluative questions on the whiteboard for the class to see, and together we reviewed each question to make sure it was evaluative in nature and intelligible. Each pair then selected two evaluative questions created by another pair, discussed those questions, and shared their answers with the class.

Excerpt #7: 24 minutes later... (58m52s)

182.		((Teacher and Hoshihiko make eye contact with each other))
183.	Hoshihiko	I- I understand. This is-
184.	Teacher	-what's that?
185.	Hoshihiko	mistake grammar. Mis- grammar mis- okay I understand. I want to
186.		say ((writes down 'how should the girl have answered the wolf?'))
187.	Teacher	Yes!
188.	Hoshihiko	[Yea
189.	Teacher	[Very different!
190.	Hoshihiko	I want [to say
191.	Teacher	[Yes yes!
192.	Hoshihiko	Grammar mistake okay I understand
193.	Teacher	Very good!
194.	Hoshihiko	Okay [I understand
195.	Teacher	[Very good

After the students had completed the task of creating, sharing, and answering each other's evaluative questions, I began a new part of the lesson and explained another, unrelated task. Once I had explained this new task, the class became quiet as student-pairs engaged in it. Almost immediately after the class became quiet, Hoshihiko, who was sitting closest to my right (cf. Figure 6.1), and I made eye contact. The excerpt above (Excerpt #7) reflects the conversation we had following our eye contact, 24 minutes after Hoshihiko and I had last interacted (Excerpt #6).

Hoshihiko reopened the CP when he began to explicitly claim understanding and use the formulation "I- I understand" (line 83)—what he understood exactly I was unsure. I had not anticipated the reopening of the CP, and my communicative act, "What's that?" (line 184), reflected my puzzlement. Hoshihiko interpreted my reply as a request for clarification, which led him to attempt to describe what it was that he now understood. His self-repairs in line 185 ("mistake grammar. Mis- grammar mis-") seemed like he was struggling to explain it. He resorted to a method we had previously used when working towards mutual understanding through writing. He wrote down in his notebook, "How should the girl have answered the wolf?" (line 186). I immediately and excitedly understood what he meant ("Yes!", line 187). "How should the girl have answered the wolf?" (line 186) was right on target with the task of creating evaluative, not knowledge-based, questions. Indeed this question was "very different" (line 189) from his and his partner's original question, "How did the girl answer the wolf?"

Finally, we had understood each other. Our misunderstanding had ultimately been because of a "grammar mistake" (line 192), not because of the task instruction nor the difference between knowledge-based and evaluative questions. The fact that Hoshihiko determined that a "grammar mistake" (line 192) had been the source of our misunderstanding suggests that he was thinking the whole time during our previous CP about why his original question was inadequate for the task. Regrettably, I was not able to observe any signs of the exact moment when he came to such realization. Nevertheless, he waited for the appropriate time to reopen the CP and made eye contact with me before sharing his discovery.

Repeatedly Hoshihiko said, "I understand" (lines 183, 185, 192, and 194), and each time it had a different function which can be observed by looking closely at the previous and later communicative acts. In line 183, it served to reopen the CP while also claiming understanding. In line 185, it claimed understanding and prepared me for the expectation of demonstration of understanding. Finally, in line 192, it confirmed the understanding that had been previously demonstrated during the action of writing the task-adequate evaluative question. In line 194, it served to emphasize achievement of understanding and to close the CP.

I too signaled understanding. In line 187 ("Yes!"), I claimed understanding by positively assessing his previous communicative act. In line 189 ("[Very different!"], I demonstrated understanding by contrasting the original question ("How did the girl answer the wolf?") with the current question ("How should the girl have answered the wolf", line 186). In line 191 ("[Yes yes!"], I continued to display understanding enthusiastically. In line 193 ("Very good!"), I demonstrated understanding by again positively evaluating Hoshihiko's ultimate understanding of the task and grammatical differences involved. In line 195 ("[Very good"], I repeated my last communicative act while overlapping with his, as together we understood each other and concluded our interaction about this topic.

Excerpt #7 is the only excerpt throughout our CAT where overlapping speech was present. While turn-taking had been largely organized with little to no overlapping up to this point, now there was significant overlapping. From my experience in the language classroom, overlapping speech is often associated with either attempts to interrupt a speaker, displays of excessive agreement, or when emotions are intense. Perhaps the institutional classroom discourse had an influence on the structure of our earlier CP (Excerpts #1-6). However, as Hoshihiko and I drew closer to understanding, towards the end, our CP shifted. It shifted from enacting the institutional roles of teacher (asking questions and offering clarification) and student (being confused, requesting clarification) to that of just two individuals conversing, not necessarily speaking through the roles of teacher and student, because of the excitement to have finally understood each other.

Discussion

The conversational inferences (Gumperz, 1992) made by both Hoshihiko and I throughout this CAT are what guided the other's actions and turn-taking. We worked hard and continuously to understand the other's perspective and to express our own as we attempted—sometimes unsuccessfully—to make meanings understood. Like a dance, we moved between checking, claiming, and demonstrating our own and the other's (lack of) understanding, and the lines between our institutional roles became blurred as we drew closer to understanding each other. I was not just the teacher nor was Hoshihiko just a student. As the teacher, I was not the only one checking (lack of) understanding. As the student, Hoshihiko was not the only one claiming and demonstrating (lack of) understanding. In multiple moments, Hoshihiko checked my understanding just as I claimed and demonstrated my understandings of his communicative acts.

Hoshihiko's willingness to reopen the CP (Excerpt #7) and share his analysis was, ultimately, what resolved our misunderstanding. Had he not reinitiated the CP and shared his finding, I would not have been privy to the source of our misunderstanding ("grammar mistake," line 192). Such dynamics have implications for all teachers, but here I address the implications directly related to language teachers. Language teachers can encourage students to investigate the origins of lack of understanding, and continuously and authentically attempt to understand the source of students' lack of understanding. This in turn may help students feel validated and more comfortable to explore the potential causes of these misunderstandings. As students embark in such exploration, they may feel more willing and less hesitant to carry on, or reopen the CP, as Hoshihiko did.

Misunderstandings are a part of everyday life, and language teachers can support students as they navigate through the potentially face-threatening moments of misunderstandings by providing meaningful opportunities for them to practice strategies of checking, claiming, and demonstrating their own and others' (lack of) understanding. In addition, language teachers can ask honest, open-ended questions and welcome student-initiated topics. Language teachers can also encourage students to practice these strategies in a meaningful classroom environment where interactions and negotiations of understanding are dynamic and spontaneous. When students have such opportunities, we can support their pursuit of authentic and meaningful interaction, and better prepare them for misunderstandings that may occur both in and out of the classroom.

References

Crookes, G. V. (2013). *Critical ELT in action: Foundations, promises, praxis.* New York: Routledge. doi:10.1080/09500782.2013.80423

Guariento, W., & Morley, J. (2001). Text and task authenticity in the EFL classroom. *ELT Journal, 55*(4), 347-353. doi: 10.1093/elt/55.4.347

Gumperz, J. J. (1982). *Discourse strategies.* Cambridge, UK: Cambridge University Press.

Gumperz, J. J. (1992). Contextualization and understanding. In A. Duranti & C. Goodwin (Eds.), *Rethinking context: Language as an interactive phenomenon* (pp. 229-252). Cambridge, UK: Cambridge University Press.

Ishida, H. (2006). Learners' perception and interpretation of contextualization cues in spontaneous Japanese conversation: Back-channel cue< i> Uun</i>. *Journal of Pragmatics, 38*(11), 1943-1981. doi:10.1016/j.pragma.2005.08.004

Käänta, L. (2014). From noticing to initiating correction: students' epistemic displays in instructional interaction. *Journal of Pragmatics, 66,* 86-105. doi:10.1016/j.pragma.2014.02.010

Koole, T. (2010). Displays of epistemic access: Student responses to teacher explanations. *Research on Language and Social Interaction, 43*(2), 183-209. http://dx.doi.org/10.1080/08351811003737846

Koole, T., & Elbers, E. (2014). Responsiveness in teacher explanations: A conversation analytical perspective on scaffolding. *Linguistics and Education, 26,* 57-69. http://dx.doi.org/10.1016/j.linged.2014.02.001

Koschmann, T. (2011). Understanding understanding in action. *Journal of Pragmatics, 43*(2), 435-437. doi:10.1016/j.pragma.2010.08.016

Leal, P. (2015). Connecting reading and writing using children's literature in the university L2 classroom. *Reading in a Foreign Language, 27*(2), 199-218.

Linell, P. (2009). *Rethinking language, mind, and world dialogically: Interactional and contextual theories of human sense-making.* Greenwich, CT: Information Age Publishing. http://dx.doi.org/10.1111/j.1468-5914.1993.tb00236.x

Linell, P., & Marková, I. (1993). Acts in discourse: From monological speech acts to dialogical inter-acts. *Journal for the Theory of Social Behaviour, 23*(2), 173-195.

Macbeth, D. (2011). Understanding understanding as an instructional matter. *Journal of Pragmatics, 43*(2), 438-451. doi:10.1016/j.pragma.2008.12.006

Mondada, L. (2011). Understanding as an embodied, situated and sequential achievement in interaction. *Journal of Pragmatics, 43*(2), 542-552. doi:10.1016/j.pragma.2010.08.019

Ohta, A. S. (2001). *Second language acquisition processes in the classroom: Learning Japanese.* Mahwah, NJ: Lawrence Erlbaum.

Sacks, H. (1992). *Lectures on conversation.* Cambridge, MA: Blackwell.

Shor, I. (1993). Education is politics: Paulo Freire's critical pedagogy. In P. McLaren & P. Leonard (Eds.), *Paulo Freire: A critical encounter* (pp. 25-35). New York: Routledge.

Simonsen, B., Fairbanks, S., Briesch, A., Myers, D., & Sugai, G. (2008). Evidence-based practices in classroom management: Considerations for research to practice. *Education and Treatment of Children, 31*(3), 351-380.

Takahashi, T., & Beebe, L. M. (1987). The development of pragmatic competence by Japanese learners of English. *JALT Journal, 8*, 131-155.

Walsh, S. (2011). *Exploring classroom discourse: Language in action.* London: Routledge.

Zheng, D. (2012). Caring in the dynamics of design and languaging: Exploring second language learning in 3D virtual spaces. *Language Sciences, 34*(5), 543-558. http://dx.doi.org/10.1016/j.langsci.2012.03.010

Appendix 6
Transcript Conventions

[The point where overlapping talk starts

- word or utterance cut-off

(0.5) length of silence

(.) micro-pause

? rising intonation

, low-rising intonation, suggesting continuation

. falling intonation

! a rise stronger than a comma but weaker than a question mark

: lengthening of the preceding sound

… longer unfilled pause

(( )) transcriber's remarks of extralinguistic information

( ) best guess; unintelligible stretch

[...] some material of the original transcript has been omitted

CHAPTER 7

RESEARCHING COLLEGE COMMUNITY SERVICES ENGAGES ISOLATED FOREIGN-BORN ENGLISH LANGUAGE LEARNERS IN CAMPUS LIFE

Bettina P. Murray
John Jay College, City University of New York

Researchers maintain that foreign students in the United States suffer from feelings of isolation and would benefit from a sense of belonging to their college communities (Mustaffa & Illias, 2013). Therefore, it seems beneficial to provide students an environment that would foster a greater connection with their college organizations and community services. After all, engaging students in community service projects that stress cooperative learning is recommended by researchers (see Gillies & Ashman, 2003; Mason, 2006).

One of the main purposes of this study was to provide foreign-born English language learners (ELLs) with an increased knowledge of their college community and an opportunity to work together to improve their English language skills. The participants were from various cultural backgrounds and were familiar with the English language but had spent only a few years in the United States. The college ESL (English as a second language) program determined that these students needed further exposure to English in order to be successful with the college program. After conducting an initial survey, referred to in the study as the pre-intervention questionnaire, it became apparent that the ELLs were expressing a sense of isolation and a need to learn more about the college environment and the American society that surrounded them. Course goals were to immerse the student participants into college life and to assist them in their adjustment to the American college system.

Theoretical Framework

Researchers have maintained that foreign students in the United States suffer from feelings of isolation due to socio-cultural factors and adjustment issues pertaining to shyness or poor English-language ability (Cacioppo & Hawkley, 2009; Drake, 2014; Fischer, 2012; Mustaffa & Illias, 2013). International students have indicated that they wish to have more open intercultural experiences and would enjoy increased contact with native English-speaking students (Senyshyn, Warford, & Zhan, 2000; Ward, 2001). Bowman (2011) recommends intergroup dialogue, which he believes leads to civic growth. Ryan (2005) encourages small group interaction for international students. Other researchers maintain that through the use of intergroup dialogue both a greater sense of cooperation (Gillies & Ashman, 2003) and long-term friendships (Pettigrew, 1998) can be created. The research of Pettigrew and Tropp (2006) supports the theory that working in small racially mixed groups leads to greater reduction in prejudice.

In the mid-1980s Slavin and Karweit (1985) were proponents of cooperative learning. Slavin further developed his theories on this subject over the next three decades (Slavin, 1995, 2009, 2012; Slavin & Karweit, 1985). As does Bowman (2011), Slavin (1995) maintains that students make more friends and are more accepting of others if they can be coached to work cooperatively. He also points out that giving answers with explanations and taking one another's learning seriously is part of successful cooperative learning and should be fostered by the teacher. Slavin advocates cognitive theories of learning along with motivational theories (e.g., Webb, 2008) that support cooperative learning. He maintains that motivation to learn encourages cooperative behaviors that are intrinsic to learning (Slavin, 2009). In his review of research, Slavin (2012) provides studies that support his cooperative learning theories and makes suggestions as to how they might be applied in a classroom setting.

Mason (2006) corroborates the research of Slavin (1995) and maintains that cooperative learning encourages better inter-ethnic relations among students of varied cultural backgrounds. Mason's studies concluded that cooperative learning resulted in improvement in oral communication between students and increased competence in literary skills. Mason, like Slavin, cautions that the teacher's role is important, and it is the teacher who must keep the cooperative groups focused and be conscious that the goal of the ELLs is to improve their English language proficiency along with their writing skills.

Paris (2012) advocates a culturally relevant pedagogical approach that actively engages students in an area that is meaningful and pertinent to their lives and fosters learning and student participation in a democratic society. Ladson-Billings (1995) had originally written extensively about culturally relevant pedagogy. In his 2012 review of Ladson-Billings' research, Paris suggests a reassessment of the term culturally relevant pedagogy and offers instead the term "culturally sustaining pedagogy" (p. 97). Paris believes that an educational environment should present material that is meaningful to the students, as well as promote multilingualism and multiculturalism in a pluralistic society.

Participants

There were 56 participants in the study from diversified ethnic backgrounds. Information was provided to the professor by the college registrar giving the age and sex of the participants. The majority of these students (76%) were college freshmen, and the average age of the entire group was 20 years old. The remaining 24% of the students had recently reached sophomore status. They had been selected by the registrar to participate in college freshmen communication courses that were geared for ELLs because their college admission tests indicated that they needed additional development in the English language. Approximately 70% of the students had been previously designated as ELL students by their high schools on their college entrance applications. All 56 students who participated in the study agreed to do so. They signed a required consent form that was administered by the professor and her assistant and that had been approved by the college Internal Research Bureau. Further details about the students are provided in Appendix 7A.

Methodology

A pre-intervention questionnaire was administered to the students at the beginning of the semester by the researcher, who was a professor in the college communications department. This pre-intervention questionnaire asked the following questions:

Pre-Intervention Questionnaire
1. What country are you from and how long have you been in the United States?
2. What is your primary or first language (or languages)?
3. At this point, what particular challenges or problems do you think you are facing in the college system in the United States?

This questionnaire revealed the regions of origin of the participants, their primary languages, and the fact that they had been in the United States five years or less (see Appendix 7A).

At the end of the semester a second survey called the post-intervention questionnaire was administered to the students. Similar to the pre-intervention questionnaire, this questionnaire asked about the problems students thought they were facing at the end of the semester. This questionnaire was administered in order to see if students' responses had changed over the course of the semester. As part of this post-intervention questionnaire, students were also asked what their perceptions were concerning the community service project that their professor had assigned them.

Post-Intervention Questionnaire
1. At this point, what particular challenges or problems do you think you are facing in the college system in the United States?
2. What did you like about your community service class project?
3. What did you not like about your community service class project?
4. Did you join any new organizations or clubs after you were involved with your community service project or after you heard someone report on a community project?

The ELLs in this study focused on topics that illustrated how various individuals and ethnic groups, who were once considered "outsiders," found a way to achieve justice and to be accepted on an equal basis by the rest of the American population. An outsider was described as any individual or group of individuals who believed that they had not been accepted by the majority of the general population of the United States.

The 56 students in this course were divided by the registrar into four separate classes, which were called sections. Each section met for a three-month semester. The professor, who was also the researcher, divided each section into working groups of two to five. The professor made an attempt to mix the ethnic backgrounds of each group and disperse the population of students so that they were not working only with students from their own culture.

She then presented to and discussed with the students a list of available college clubs, services, and organizations. Students were required to choose a college service or organization and investigate it. They were also asked to interview a person employed at that organization. This activity in the study was to serve as an intervention or concrete plan to encourage the students to become involved with the college community. The majority of services, clubs, and organizations the students chose had offices or representatives directly on the campus. Some of the popular organizations interviewed by the students were The Writing Center, The Chinese American Organization, The Veterans' Club, Foreign Language and International Study Programs, and SEEK (Search for Education, Elevation, and Knowledge). SEEK refers to a higher education opportunity program at the senior colleges. Each student in every group had to conduct an interview with an employee or high-ranking member of the community organization that they chose to study. The professor provided an interview questionnaire to the students in order to make the interview process easier (see Appendix 7B). Students were then asked to write up their individual answers to each of the interview questions. The last step of this process was for students to report to the entire class, both orally and in writing, on the findings of the interview process. Each group of students was allotted 12 minutes to give a class presentation covering the findings of their interview and research on the organization.

Student comments on the pre-intervention questionnaire were the source of demographic information. They also provided information on what the students believed their challenges to be. The post-intervention questionnaire elicited comments about the students' reactions to the challenges they were experiencing and to their community service projects. The results of the questionnaires were tabulated and analyzed using a program formerly called Statistical Package for the Social Sciences, now known as SPSS Statistics v.23. This program was used to conduct frequency analyses. Chi-square tests were used to analyze responses to the pre- and post-intervention questions. Because of the larger numbers of Chinese and Latina/o students involved in the study, Chi-square tests were used specifically on the following variables: gender, Chinese background, and Latina/o background.

Results

The analysis of student responses to the pre-intervention questionnaire revealed that the students spoke 11 different primary or native languages. The two languages spoken by the greatest number of students were Mandarin and Spanish. Student responses also indicated the basic challenges that the students thought they were facing both at the beginning and at the end of the semester. These were generalized into two main areas of concern: (1) fluency of English expression, and (2) making friends.

The analysis of the student comments on the post-intervention questionnaire indicated that many students believed they had gained insights into the college community and about working with each other. Students also commented that they were feeling more at ease with their use of the English language and that they had gained confidence in dealing with students of different backgrounds. Many students, especially the males, stated that they were now going to be involved with the community organization or club that they had interviewed or that had been reported upon by other classmates.

Table 7.1
Differences between Male and Female Students on the Pre- and Post-Intervention Questions

Variable	Male (n = 37)		Female (n = 19)		χ^2 (df = 1)	p	Phi
	n	(%)	n	(%)			
Pre-Intervention							
Challenges with English	26	(70.3)	8	(42.1)	4.18	.04*	.273
Challenge Making Friends	19	(51.4)	2	(10.5)	8.93	.003*	.399
Post-Intervention							
Liked Interview Process	9	(24.3)	1	(5.3)	3.11	.08	.236
Liked Community Project	14	(37.8)	2	(10.5)	4.59	.03*	.286
Joined Club after Community Project	18	(48.6)	2	(10.5)	7.95	.005*	.377

Note. Phi coefficient is the effect size measure for these analyses and is interpreted as the percent of shared variability. Statistical significance is marked by an asterisk ($p < .05$)

The first variable to be analyzed was that of gender. Table 7.1 presents the variables for which there were significant differences by gender. Significantly more males (70.3%) than females (42.1%) reported challenges with English, as well as challenges with making friends (51.4% for males, 10.5% for females). Males also responded better than females to the intervention, showing greater liking of the interview process (24.3% versus 5.3%), liking the group work aspect of the community project (37.8% versus 10.5%), and more frequently joining a club after the community project (48.6% versus 10.5%). There was no statistical significance between gender and the other questions asked.

The second variable to be analyzed was pre- and post-intervention questionnaire questions with Chinese and non-Chinese students. Table 7.2 below presents the associations for which there were significant differences with pre- and post-questions with the students of Chinese or non-Chinese origin.

Table 7.2
Differences in Pre- and Post-Intervention Questions by Chinese Origins

Variable	Chinese ($n = 23$)		Non-Chinese ($n = 33$)		χ^2 (df = 1)	p	Phi
	n	(%)	n	(%)			
Pre-Intervention							
Challenge with English	20	87.0	14	42.4	11.29	.001*	.449
Challenge making Friends	12	52.2	9	27.3	3.59	.06	.253
Wants Non-Asian Friends	6	26.1	1	14.3	6.59	.01*	.343
Post-Intervention							
English Problems	16	69.6	12	36.4	5.97	.01*	.327
Improved in English	11	50.0	8	24.2	3.87	.049*	.265
Liked Community Project	23	100.0	29	90.6	2.28	.13	.204

Note. Phi coefficient is the effect size measure for these analyses and is interpreted as the percent of shared variability. Statistical significance is marked by an asterisk ($p < .05$)

At the time of the pre-intervention questionnaire, the Chinese students were significantly more likely to feel challenged with English (87.0%), challenged with making friends (52.2%), and more concerned about making non-Asian friends (26.1%) than were non-Chinese students (42.4%, 27.3%, and 14.3%, respectively). At the time the post-intervention questionnaire was given, the Chinese students reported a greater concern with English problems (69.6%) in spite of also reporting greater improvement in English (50.0%). Chinese students liked the community project (100%) and expressed enthusiasm about the group work, although not significantly more than the non-Chinese group.

The third variable to be analyzed was pre- and post-intervention questionnaire questions with Latina/o and non-Latina/o students. Table 7.3 below presents the Chi-square results for associations between pre- and post-intervention questionnaires and students of Latina/o and Non-Latina/o status.

Table 7.3
Differences between Latina/o and Non-Latina/o Students on Pre- and Post-Intervention Questions

Variable	Latina/o ($n = 12$)		Non-Latina/o ($n = 44$)		χ^2 (df = 1)	p	Phi
	n	(%)	n	(%)			
Pre-Intervention							
Challenge with English	3	25.0	31	70.5	8.17	.004*	-.382
Challenge Making Friends	3	25.0	18	40.9	1.02	.31	-.135
Post-Intervention							
English Problems	2	16.7	26	59.1	6.79	.009*	-.348
Improved in English	1	8.3	18	41.9	4.66	.03*	-.291
Liked Community Project	10	83.3	42	97.7	3.74	.053	-.261

Note. Phi coefficient is the effect size measure for these analyses and is interpreted as the percent of shared variability. Statistical significance is marked by an asterisk ($p < .05$)

Making friends presented a challenge to 25% of the Latina/o students. Significant differences were found between Latina/o students, with Latina/o students reporting fewer problems with English on both the pre-intervention questionnaire (25.0%) and the post-intervention questionnaire (16.7%) than non-Latina/o students (70.5% and 59.1%, respectively). Latina/o students also reported less improvement in English (8.3% versus 41.9%), which is consistent with them believing that they do not need improvement. Finally, Latina/o students, although showing a high proportion of students reporting that they liked the community project (83.3%), were less favorable about it than non-Latina/o students (97.7%).

Discussion

Table 7.1 presented the significant concern ($p = .04$) that the male students expressed over their problems expressing themselves in the English language and their ability to make friends ($p = .003$). These concerns may relate to the fact that they are now trying to adjust to American culture. As has been indicated in prior research (Hofstede, 2005), both Chinese and Latino males may feel more comfortable in a society where they are not encouraged to speak out and to assert themselves verbally. Hofstede (2001) maintains that the collectivist philosophy of the Asian population does not encourage individuals to put themselves forward aggressively but instead to work more within a group for what is perceived to be the best interest of the group. One of the problems of being interjected into American society, which is considered by many to be very individualistic (Fisher, 2012; Hofstede, 2001; Ngo, 2008), is that the American classroom culture encourages the individual to speak out and participate in discussions. As a result, a student who is more reticent may be viewed simply as not knowing the material. The fact that the male students in the study liked the group work involved in the community project ($p = .03$) and were the most likely to join a club after the community project ($p = .005$) is of interest, and it also supports the more collectivist philosophy described by Hofstede (2001; 2005). Out of a total of 56 students, 41% were Asian males (21 Chinese and two Korean). It is likely that the large number of male Asian students in this group affected the results of the outcomes of this aspect of the study.

This study supports the research of Bowman (2011), who maintains that working in a college situation that promotes diversity and encourages civic-minded activities fosters intercultural understanding and reduces the sense of isolation often felt by the foreign students who have come to study in the United States (Fisher, 2012).

The interest displayed by the males to participate in group activities suggests that they see membership in clubs and organizations as a way to make friends and reduce their feelings of isolation. David-Barrett et al. (2015) maintain that there is a fundamental difference between the sexes in their approaches to socialization and that men favor joining clubs and organizations where they can get together in groups and build larger more structured situations. It is of interest that the post-intervention questionnaire results revealed that after the male students had joined a community organization they no longer expressed anxiety about making friends. This matches the advice of Hong, Chen, and Hwang (2013), who advocate that learners should join an extracurricular club, because this as an opportunity for increased learning and peer collaboration.

Table 7.2 indicated that significant challenge was expressed by the Chinese students in the pre-intervention questionnaire. A majority of Chinese students (87.0%) believed they were deeply impaired by their lack of fluency in English. Several Chinese students believed it affected their grades in other courses and their ability to make friends in the United States. Some expressed that they felt "isolated" and were therefore only able to socialize with friends from their own country. Three of the Chinese students specifically stated that they wanted to make English-speaking American friends. Because this desire was only expressed in the post-intervention questionnaire by the Asian students, it was therefore included in Table 7.2 for analysis. There were six Chinese students and one Korean who said they wanted non-Asian friends. Although these students wanted to meet new friends who were not Asian, they kept company mostly with each other and seemed shy about socializing with the other different ethnic groups present in the class. The difficulty of moving from Chinese into English is well documented, as the alphabet and roots of the language are not similar to English (Drake, 2014; Hoosain, 1992; Ng, 2007; Ngo, 2008). The language barrier, in addition to cultural differences, most likely aggravated their adjustment situation to the United States (Rawlings & Sue, 2013), making their transition to American society more difficult.

The results in Table 7.3 suggest that the Latina/o students initially seemed to be more confident about their ability to communicate in English than the non-Latina/o students. They were significantly enthusiastic about the community project and stated they liked the group work and the opportunity to investigate the college services. The investigation of the community service by the various groups represented what Cammarota (2007) and Paris (2012) would recommend as a socially relevant curriculum, and the students in the Latina/o category responded especially well to the oral delivery aspect of their reports. This response might be consistent with their belief that they did not have English language problems as severe as those experienced by the non-Latina/o students. Their display of relative confidence in this area suggests that they were not feeling as high a level of isolation in this society as some of the students of other cultures. However, it is still noted that 25% of the Latina/o students stated that they had challenges with expressing themselves clearly in English on the pre-intervention questionnaire, and that 16.7% of the students still believed they had challenges expressing themselves in the English language at the time of the post-intervention questionnaire. On the post-intervention questionnaire, however, one student stated that he made improvement in his use of the English language. Overall, given the comments of the Latina/o students, it is apparent that they generally believed that they were having fewer problems with the English language than the non-Latina/o population and that they had an easier time making friends. It is unclear whether this might be due to the large number of Latina/o students at the college (approximately 40%) or in the urban environment where the college is located.

Limitations

There were several limitations to the present study. First, the nature of this research does not account for individual differences, as students were categorized into groups according to general regions of origin and according to the categories of what they viewed as their challenges. Second, these results were self-reported measures and perceptions students had of their own issues. The research of Chevalier, Gibbons, Thorpe, Snell, and Hoskins (2009) suggests that students' self-perception of their academic abilities may vary according to sex and background. Finally, the sample size of students of cultures other than those of Asian or Latina/o origin was small. Small sample size may affect the precision and differences in effect size (Slavin & Smith, 2009).

Implications and Suggestions for Future Study

In this study, the males had greater challenges with English language expression and liked the group work significantly more than the females. They joined more clubs or service organizations at a significant level. Taking these results into consideration, a future study might be conducted to further investigate these results and how they relate to male or female students in different settings and students of varied linguistic cultures.

The Chinese students expressed a particular interest in making English-speaking friends. These students indicated on the pre- and post-questionnaires that the English language was a significant challenge to them. Suggestions for future study might include creating a peer learning situation that has several English-speaking students who are quite fluent in English placed in each group. It is recommended that courses be designed to have more native English speakers in the class so that they could be placed in each group to enhance the peer learning experience. It would be advantageous to the groups of English language learners if they could be mixed in with students of different cultures and varying levels of English who were all trying to speak English so that they would not be in a situation where they would be more inclined to speak their native language. This might help reduce the problem that many students from the same background face, that is, they end up speaking their native language with each other and therefore spend less time getting to know students from other cultures.

It is also suggested that students be introduced to the group work as soon as possible and that they be encouraged to discuss their part of a project within their groups before presenting it orally in front of the entire class. In the current study, students spent too much time deciding which organization or community service to research in further detail. As the majority of the student participants liked the community project, it is suggested that representatives from various clubs and organizations come to the classroom and speak to the students briefly about their organizations so that students might be exposed earlier to a variety of options and start their research investigations and their group work earlier in the semester.

Scholarly Significance

The analysis of the student comments on the post-intervention questionnaire indicated that many students believed they improved their English acquisition and gained insights into the college community after working with each other to complete their community projects. After participating in a community project, 60% of the students joined a community service organization or a club. The group collaboration on the community service projects, supported by student comments, appeared to engage the students, help them expand their friendships, and reduce their sense of isolation. This study is supportive of culturally relevant pedagogy that promotes active participation and cooperative learning activities to reduce feelings of isolation in college ELLs.

References

Bowman, N. A. (2011). Promoting participation in a diverse democracy: A meta-analysis of college diversity experience and civic engagement. *Review of Educational Research, 81*(1), 29-68.

Cacioppo, J. T., & Hawkley, L. C. (2009). Perceived social isolation and cognition. *Trends in Cognitive Sciences, 13*(10), 447–454. doi:10.1016/j.tics.2009.06.005

Cammarota, J. (2007). A social justice approach to achievement: Guiding Latina/o students toward education attainment with a challenging, socially relevant curriculum. *Equity & Excellence in Education, 40*(1), 87-96. doi:10.1080/10665680601015113

Chevalier, A., Gibbons, S., Thorpe, A, Snell, M., & Hoskins, S. (2009). Students' academic self-perception. *Economics of Education Review, 28*(6), 716-727. doi:10.1016/j.econedurev.2009.06.007

David-Barrett, T., Rotkirch, A., Carney, J., Behncke Izquierdo, I., Krems, J. A., Townley, D., McDaniell, E., Byrne-Smith, A., & Dunbar, R. (2015). Women favour dyadic relationships, but men prefer clubs: Cross-cultural evidence from social networking. *PLOS ONE, 10*(3). Retrieved from http://journals.plos.org/plosone/article/asset?id=10.1371/journal.pone.0118329.PDF

Drake, A. (2014). The effect of community linguistic isolation on language-minority student achievement in high school. *Educational Researcher, 43*(7), 327-340. doi:10.3102/0013189X14547349

Fischer, K. (2012, June). Many foreign students are friendless in the U.S., study finds. *The Chronicle of Higher Education*, Retrieved from http://chronicle.com/article/Many-Foreign-Students-Find/132275/

Gillies, R. M., & Ashman, A. F. (2003). An historical review of the use of groups to promote socialization and learning. In R. M. Gillies & A. Ashman (Eds.), *Cooperative learning: The social and intellectual outcomes of learning in groups* (10th ed., pp. 1-19). London: Routledge.

Hofstede, G. (2001). *Cultures consequences: Comparing values, behaviors, institutions, and organizations across nations* (2nd ed.). Thousand Oaks, CA: Sage Publications.

Hofstede, G. (2005). *Cultures and organizations: Software of the mind* (3rd ed.). New York: McGraw-Hill.

Hong, J.-C., Chen, M.-Y., & Hwang, M.-Y. (2013). Vitalizing creative learning in science and technology through an extracurricular club: A perspective based on activity theory. *Thinking Skills and Creativity, 8*, 45–55. doi:10.1016/j.tsc.2012.06.001

Hoosain, R. (1992). Differential cerebral lateralization of Chinese-English bilingual functions. In R. J. Harris (Ed.), *Cognitive processing in bilinguals* (pp. 561–571). Amsterdam: Elsevier.

Ladson-Billings, G. (1995). Toward a theory of culturally relevant pedagogy. *American Educational Research Journal, 32*(3), 465-491. doi:10.3102/00028312032003465

Mason, K. (2006). Cooperative learning and second language acquisition in first-year composition: Opportunities for authentic communication among English language learners. *Teaching English in the Two Year College, 34*(1), 52-58.

Mustaffa, C. & Illias, M. (2013). Relationship between students' adjustment factors and cross cultural adjustment: A survey at the Northern University of Malaysia. *Intercultural Communication Studies, 22*, 279-299. Retrieved from http://www.uri.edu/iaics/content/2013v22n1/19Che%20Su%20Mustaffa%20&%20Munirah%20Ilias.pdf.

Ng, T. P. (2007). *Chinese culture, Western culture: Why must we learn from each other?* Lincoln, NE: iUniverse

Ngo, B. (2008). Beyond "culture clash" understandings of immigrant experiences. *Theory Into Practice, 47*(1), 4–11. doi:10.1080/00405840701764656

Paris, D. (2012). Culturally sustaining pedagogy: A needed change in stance, terminology, and practice. *Educational Researcher, 41*(3), 93–97. doi:10.3102/0013189X12441244

Pettigrew, T. F. (1998). Intergroup contact theory. *Annual Review of Psychology, 49*(1), 65-85. doi:10.1146/annurev.psych.49.1.65

Pettigrew, T. F., & Tropp, L. R. (2006). A meta-analytic test of intergroup contact theory. *Journal of Personality and Social Psychology, 90*(5), 751-783. doi:10.1037/0022-3514.90.5.751

Rawlings, M., & Sue, E. (2013). Preparedness of Chinese students for American culture and communicating in English. *Journal of International Students, 3*(1), 29-40. Retrieved from https://jistudents.files.wordpress.com/2012/07/4-preparedness-of-chinese-students.pdf

Ryan, J. (2005). Improving teaching and learning practices for international students: Implications for curriculum, pedagogy and assessment. In J. Ryan & J. Carroll (Eds.), *Teaching international students: Improving learning for all* (pp. 92-100). London: Routledge.

Senyshyn, R. M., Warford, M. K., & Zhan, J. (2000). Issues of adjustment to higher education: International students' perspectives. *International Education, 30*(1), 17. Retrieved from http://search.proquest.com/docview/1311677222?accountid=147304

Slavin, R. E. (1995). *Cooperative learning: Theory, research and practice* (2nd ed.). Boston: Allyn and Bacon.

Slavin, R. E. (2009). Cooperative learning: What makes group-work work?. In G. McCulloch & D. Crook (Eds.), *International Encyclopedia of Education* (pp. 161-178). Abingdon, UK: Routledge.

Slavin, R. E. (2012). *Educational psychology: Theory and practice* (10th ed.). New York: Pearson.

Slavin, R. E., & Karweit, N. L. (1985). Effects of whole-class, ability-grouped, and individualized instruction on mathematics achievement. *American Educational Research Journal 22*, 351-367. doi:10.3102/00028312022003351

Slavin, R. E., & Smith, D. (2009). The relationship between sample sizes and effect sizes in systematic reviews in education. *Educational Evaluation and Policy Analysis 31*, 500-506. doi:10.3102/0162373709352369

Ward, C. (2001). The impact of international students on domestic students and host institutions. *Education Counts,* 1-21. Retrieved from http://www.educationcounts.govt.nz/publications/international/14684

Webb, N. (2008). Learning in small groups. In T. L. Good (Ed.), *21st Century education: A reference handbook* (pp. 203-211). Thousand Oaks, CA: Sage.

Appendix 7A
Regions of Origin, Primary Languages, and Sex of Participants

Regions of Origin	Primary Languages	Male	Female	Total
Albania	Albanian	1	0	1
Bangladesh	Bangala	1	1	2
China	Chinese (Mandarin)	21	2	23
United States	English	3	2	5
West Africa	French & African Dialect	2	1	3
Greece	Greek	0	1	1
Korea	Korean	2	0	2
Uzbekistan	Persian	1	0	1
Poland	Polish	0	1	1
Russia	Russian	3	2	5
South America, Mexico, Dominican Republic, Puerto Rico	Spanish	3	9	12
Total		37	19	56

Appendix 7B
Interview Questionnaire for the College Community Service Project

These interview questions were provided by the teacher. Each student had to fill out his/her own questionnaire during the interview of the community service organization.

Questions to ask the Club or Academic Center Representative for your Group Project

1. What is the name of the representative you are interviewing? If there is more than one representative being interviewed, please write down everyone's name.
2. What is the interview date?
3. What is the goal of the club or organization?
4. How is the club or organization designed to the student?
5. How many people does the organization or club serve?
6. Is the group designed to help any particular age group?
7. What records or surveys does the club or organization have to show success?
8. What is required to become a member and what activities are involved related to the membership?
9. Are there particular requirements for the people who want to work at the organization or club?
10. How do you get your funding for the organization or club?
11. Do members contribute to the organization or club?
12. What recommendations for the future would you have for the organization or club that you looked at and studied?

CHAPTER 8

TESTING THE GROUNDS OF RECIPROCITY AND MULTILINGUALISM:
Forays into Writing Collaborations among L2 and L1 Writers

Mary Jeannot
John Eliason
Gonzaga University

Imagine a writing program administrator (WPA) taking a job at a university where multilingual students accounted for a significant percentage of the overall population. Picture what it would be like for *all* students in such an environment. Laden with authentic and immediate opportunities to engage with people from diverse cultural, linguistic, and educational backgrounds, monolingual and multilingual students alike could experience a university of language capacious and provocative. No Babel or nirvana, but a place and space worth inhabiting. This setting, for one of the co-authors of this paper (John), *is* an imagined one, because he works at an institution with a majority of the student population constituting traditional college-aged domestic US students. Many have studied a second language, but most are monolingual.

What questions should a WPA or any teacher of writing pose in this common learning environment in US colleges and universities? What questions will best serve the majority of students but not at the expense of the minority population of multilingual writers and speakers? How should a writing curriculum attempt to account for the tensions and possibilities presented by the ever-growing global reality of multilingualism, even as that curriculum is required to provide a "core" experience for students who have signed up for a monolingual-dominant liberal arts education? Where will engagement with multilingualism occur if not through such a core, if not in concert with the minority population of students who have perhaps lived an experience of isolation among often disinterested or simply unwitting monolingual students and faculty?

Answers to such questions occur in fleeting thoughts about the need to expand English as a Second Language (ESL) programs and the possibilities for promoting enhanced and extensive community outreach to multilingual populations beyond campus. But these thoughts simply cannot result in structural imperatives to support both majority and minority populations; regrettably, problems of scale and other practical constraints often prevent exhaustive outreach for the several hundreds or even thousands of students per semester who find themselves taking a required first-year writing course in US institutions of higher education. To acknowledge and then attempt to move past such challenges requires assistance, theory, and expertise. Many fine graduate programs exist in Writing Studies (here intended as an umbrella term for all sorts of writing-specific fields such as composition, rhetoric, writing across the curriculum, and writing centers), and in most cases training in second language (L2) writing is available; but for a large portion of WPAs and writing faculty, it makes sense to reach across campus for inside expertise.

This advocacy for collaboration acknowledges that the writing specialists working with first-language (L1) writers may have studied and taught ESL composition and taken sociolinguistics seminars in graduate school (as John did). Even so, such experiences will not suffice as a means of responding to a prevalent and pressing need for more cultural and linguistic complexity for all students. WPAs, who have been informed by L2 writing experts in Writing Studies, their own field, sense both the contributions made by multilinguals and their advocates (e.g., TESOL [Teachers of English to Speakers of Other Languages] affiliates). The L1 writing specialists also sense the urgency, the movement, to adapt to accommodating the growing number of multilinguals on college campuses. Atkinson et al. (2015) traced the lineage of this trend:

> L2 writing scholars at CCCC have been working for decades to develop resources and strategies for supporting writing teachers and program administrators in working more effectively with L2 writers. Because of the growing diversity of higher education, L2 writing specialists have called for all writing researchers, instructors, and administrators to have training in working with L2 writers. (p. 383)

With the history of L2 writers in mind, and a shared sense of mission, this same director sought out colleagues in the English Language Center (ESL and TESOL programs) at his home institution. John's colleagues there responded well to his initial inquiries, and positive communication was established through meetings, cross-cultural composition courses that combined domestic and international students, and several presentations at ESL and writing conferences. Even so, we (co-authors Mary and John) came to realize it was time to explore curricular avenues that might lead to replicable models for student exchange across wider multi-disciplinary terrains. We wanted to be clear in our commitment that whatever we established would privilege not only cross-cultural, cross-linguistic understanding in general but also an awareness specifically concerning the expansiveness of multilingualism in the twenty-first century. Our promise was to expand our conversations and acknowledge our collective expertise as lifelong students, teachers and researchers of language and culture. Reciprocity became our mantra to lead us in sustaining this promise for students, colleagues, and for us.

This focus on reciprocity in learning through cross-cultural collaborations has led to curricular opportunities created through co-planning efforts by writing faculty and ESL faculty. Before describing our project and its manifestations to date, however, we need to go back two decades, where Fox (1994) captured in a single question one of the most important dilemmas of academic ESL programs that prepare non-native English speakers for matriculation into the university: Does the university change to accommodate ESL students or do ESL students change to meet "world-class" standards (p. 107)? Despite Fox's own deep-seated feelings about the university's need for wide-ranging reform on macro-institutional and micro-instructional levels, she ultimately sided with the students who, in order to graduate, "cannot wait," "must get along," "know what they need to succeed," "need to learn what the rules are," and "conform" (p. 108). In a similar predictive vein, nearly two decades ago, Matsuda (1999) outlined the problems facing composition studies in which he noted the absence of L2 writing theories and the lack of conversation between the two disciplines, thus further underscoring the need for WPAs to lead by example.

Both Fox and Matsuda, along with scores of other ESL and TESOL professionals, have a firsthand view of a multilingual world that anticipates a complicated multilingual future—one that necessitates new partnerships, collaborations and frameworks, expands its notions of language, literacy, and culture; and reconfigures standards, classrooms, and curricula. ESL and TESOL specialists such as Mary know that on the one hand, non-English speaking students need preparation for the visible and invisible demands they will face in United States academic classrooms. Such faculty are conflicted, on the other hand, when students unquestionably and uncritically conform to dominant (i.e., "standard," "native," and "normal") ways of thinking, speaking, and writing English. ESL and TESOL professionals sit in the middle of this conundrum that has permeated the discipline because the field itself is quintessentially heterogeneous and out of necessity—and often by design—interdisciplinary. Are professionals in ESL and TESOL gatekeepers or iconoclasts? Colonialists promoting linguistic imperialism and English hegemony or critical activists? Should Mary and her disciplinary colleagues teach English in Sub-Saharan Africa or learn African languages? Precisely what kinds of assistance should ESL and TESOL experts provide a writing program administrator or anyone else on campus who expresses a desire for help in navigating an intensifying multilingual landscape?

As co-authors of this paper, we look toward possible responses to this question of navigation by investigating collaborative structures that bring together US domestic and international students in ways that make explicit reciprocity in learning and that encourage cross-linguistic and cultural understanding. Our persistent collaboration is framed, in part, as an acknowledgment of the habits of mind listed in *The Framework for Success in Post-Secondary Writing* (CWPA, NCTE, NWP, 2014): curiosity, openness, engagement, creativity, persistence, responsibility, flexibility, and metacognition. All such habits strike us as integral to student success. In particular, we highlight in the following pages some of the ways our two semester-long partnerships involving US domestic and international students in multimodal, multilingual learning environments helped to align us with the aspirations articulated in the *Framework*. We offer a multi-tiered assignment sequence designed to promote reciprocity and collaboration in learning and teaching. We hope to provide a foundation for sustained and creative initiatives for writing pedagogies that take into account peoples, languages, and cultures. In so doing, we seek to make a modest contribution to ongoing discussions in language studies regarding the concepts of "comprehensibility" and "incomprehensibility"—recognizing first that these two ideas are not opposing or competing forces, that they are not binaries, and that, finally, both have potential for enriching students' experiences with language and thus with one another.

Second Language Acquisition for the Twenty-First Century
Much of the current literature in fields of applied linguistics and social sciences (well represented by multilinguals) criticizes monolingualism not only as paradigmatic but also for its epistemologies which have set up target language and target structures—usually English—as a default for researching second language acquisition (May, 2013; Ortega, 2013). To date, many of us in ESL and TESOL, but also other faculty across the curriculum, have been guilty of viewing second languages as "failed approximations to the yardstick of native language systems" (Ortega, 2013, p. 2). Klein, for example, concluded in an address that "among the various disciplines investigating the manifold manifestations of human language capacity, Second Language Acquisition (SLA) researchers are the 'bottom dwellers in language sciences' thanks to our preoccupation with one target language or 'target deviation perspective'" (p. 2). Indeed, a prevailing native (English) speaker fallacy (Phillipson, 2012) has unwittingly misled many research agendas in ESL and TESOL. For example, SLA has traditionally used as their formative data, language from monolingual children as comparison data for bi/multilingual adults using their second. As Cook (1992) aptly wrote, "That non-natives are continually held up against what they cannot be is not only a proclamation for doom, but is tautologically circular" (as cited in Ortega, 2013, p. 16). Cook's following statement should help to frame new models for understanding multilingualism in its own right:

> Any theory about the acquisition of languages by ordinary human beings has to account for the fact that many of them acquire two languages simultaneously from the beginning, and that many others acquire one or more languages consecutively at a later time. (p. 24)

Research in bi/multilingualism has demonstrated that a bi/multilingual's competence is not merely the state of "dual monolingualism" or the sum of two discrete monolingual competencies conjoined. Language systems do not function as two independent systems in the brain. Rather, "bi/multilingual competence is a complex process *integrating* knowledge of two or more languages and is thus 'qualitatively different from monolingual competence'" (Ortega, 2013, p. 15). Without the dichotomies our field has traditionally adhered to, SLA researchers have a new direction for research. Multilinguals (i.e., people often referred to as non-native English speakers) who outnumber monolinguals (Lee, 2012) have been multilingual long before TESOL popularized through disciplinary focus a set of terms that includes globalism, multilingualism, and English as a second language teaching. Moreover, as Flores (2014) points out, *au currant* multilingual pedagogies are not the unique property of Europeans (or Americans), as EU countries ride the wave of technological innovations, economic and linguistic border crossing, and experience what could be framed as a dose of post-colonial payback.

These realizations about second language acquisition (SLA) compel us to ask how they apply to our local context. That is, the multilingual international students and the domestic monolingual US students mirror, on a small scale, some of the challenges facing cultures and nations and groups of language speakers throughout the world who are striving to adjust to economic globalism and the fast pace of change it propels. In our view, older models of institutional monolingual stasis deserve much closer scrutiny and have a responsibility for making adjustments in higher education. The pedagogies a veteran writing program administrator could have encountered in graduate study, for example, might have emphasized rhetorical awareness and dexterity, but so, too, might that person's exposure to language study have emphasized the importance of exposing all students to "Standard English" or the complexities found in English as an International Language, English as a Lingua Franca, or World Englishes. While we still advocate for such exposure, in the contemporary setting of higher education, we cannot imagine a writing program where multilingualism would not warrant significant attention in the curriculum, in faculty development, and in discussions about assessment. A monolingual model upon which so many language courses (including writing courses) are built is holding monolingual as well as multilingual students back from experiencing connections that complicate student assumptions about language and power.

As Fox (1994) notes, institutional shifts are at the heart of what would constitute productive change for monolingual and multilingual university students. Our position moves in a different direction, too, however, as we see models advocating for the university to adjust to ESL student needs as only one part of what is necessary to respond to the changing climate of higher education. More important is a paradigm shift for how educators treat and guide monolingual US domestic students. For example, we must refigure our ideas about partnerships between multilingual and monolingual students and resist the available narratives that situate the US domestic students as helpers with English (especially grammar) and culture brokers for mainstream culture. While those roles are important and such efforts should be sustained, we observed in ourselves and our students a dissatisfaction with such partnerships and therefore sought to explore possible means of making sure that the multilingual students gave as much support as they received. What follows represents two of our efforts in this regard.

General Description of Two Projects

In Fall 2013, we experimented with two partnerships: the first involving English 395 (The Teaching of Writing) students and ESL international students from ESL 107 (Advanced Academic Writing), and the second in Spring 2015, in which we built in an ongoing collaboration that brought students from ESL 106 (Academic Reading and Communication) with English 200 (Multimodal Composition). All of this work we did for the purpose of designing structures that Writing Programs along with TESOL programs (and other) faculty might emulate/copy/refine for their own collaborative purposes. In addition, the net effect is that we are building stronger administrative bridges between the Writing Program and the English Language Center (where the ESL and TESOL programs are housed); those bridges of support enhance everyone's awareness of language on micro and macro levels, from how tacit presuppositions disappear in foregrounded dependent clauses (see Gee, 2014) to the question of ownership of language found in scholarship on nativity and English. The themes in this paper represent some of the main topics in college writing programs, including multilingualism, multimodality, multiple literacies, and the futures of English and the teaching of writing. These themes can be connected with no difficulty to a dynamic conversation relevant to anyone teaching writing in higher education. TESOL faculty and faculty and administrators in college-level writing programs are in unique positions to build and maintain longstanding professional partnerships. Our hope is that the following descriptive account of our own exploratory journey will provide ideas and inspiration for others who share our interest in testing the grounds for reciprocity in learning through L2 and L1 collaboration.

Research Perspectives

As we have pointed out, our most important goal was to provide for our students sustained, creative, and meaningful opportunities for cross-cultural exchanges rooted in the subject matter of our respective courses: reading, writing, and speaking in the case of the international students, and writing of various kinds for the US students. Though we have experimented with a range of such exchanges, we describe in the following pages notable moments, assignment structures, and reflections from two specific classroom collaborations. Our design for this exploratory foray into L2 and L1 collaborations draws from principles and practices found in *in situ* classroom-based research. We privilege the idea that reflection on one's pedagogy can yield insights that, when reframed with theory and resituated in the scholarship of our disciplines, can yield evidence to inform institutional conversations around the importance of cross-cultural exchange. Also animating our work are our attempts (not always achieved) to include our students in every aspect of the research process, something we pursue in order to reformulate and adjust our teaching, curricula and philosophies, and, in this case, to accommodate the variety of multilingual epistemologies found in our classrooms. (Ultimately, this research ecology would invite graduate students to participate.) At the very least, our inquiry—largely inspired by participant-observer and ethnographic research methodologies—has led us to investigate our classroom languages and cultures where all of us take turns as knowers and learners in a dynamic process of knowledge gathering.

The students from the two collaborative projects described here are from two distinctive contexts and cultures within our private 4-year institution. Both groups are invested in their academic futures, are highly motivated to succeed, and can afford to study at our university (a point that will be taken up in future projects). Some of the multilingual students described in this paper will continue on at the university and view this opportunity to engage with US students as academically enriching, especially since most of them for a variety of reasons not covered in this paper perceive themselves to lack what North American academics might refer to as "critical thinking skills." In our first project (*Thinking and Writing about Writing with Writers*) there were 19 multilingual students from six different countries who were fully enrolled ESL students at the university taking 20+ hours of academic English in all "skill" areas (i.e., oral and written academic communication) and 20 Americans from different regions throughout the United States who were English majors enrolled in English 395: The Teaching of Writers. In our second collaboration (*Reciprocity in Multilingual and Multimodal Pedagogy*) there were 16 ESL students, again full time ESL students, from five different countries and 11 US students, 8 of whom were first year students. The two classes we joined together for the length of one semester were Upper-Intermediate Academic Reading ESL and English 200: Multimodal Composition.

Our data sources for both projects consist of the following: short reflection papers from ESL students and US students at various intervals during the collaboration, ESL student writing with written responses from US students, revised drafts with US student comments, and Mary's (ESL teacher) written comments on revised drafts. We used the same classroom-based data in our second project, but because of the multimodal composition focus of English 200, we expanded our collection of artifacts to include student podcasts and documentaries we had archived on a shared digital space within our institution's learning management system.

Our goal for this chapter was to identify a point of departure for our collaboration and to gather selected emic perspectives on what students say and what they write. Our observations reported are collections of interpretations from both the students and from instructors. In this sense, we are not reporting hard evidence or proof but rather our reflections on experiments in institutional collaborations in which we believe others might identify ideas for their own work. We are not inclined to impose our sense of finality or theoretical inventions on the project. We are hopeful that our collection of impressions and first-cut analyses are descriptive of our explorations; they certainly should not be read as research "findings." Our claims are mostly anchored in our collaborative processes, in-depth experience as writing teachers across cultures and languages, and our emic and etic awareness and thus explanatory power of academic cultures. This is not, in other words, guess work or hyper analysis. We have in mind and want to avoid the pitfalls of writers whose frameworks are theoretically rich but whose data is desperate, too eager to map onto short-lived and one-off experiences elaborate theories in the name of experimenting with, for example, multilingual genres, or even something as practically challenging as *translingualism*. We have found that meaningful experiences take time and require modest steps. Our project and our observations are meant to be descriptive, and our emerging theories are driven by real, sustained, and sustainable practices.

Description of Project 1

Our first project was limited to two face-to-face meetings with international students in an advanced ESL writing class taught by Mary and upper-division undergraduate students from the U.S. who were enrolled in a course John was teaching titled The Teaching of Writing. The international students were asked to respond to an Edward Hall quotation from their course reading text, *American Ways*. The quotation is appropriate especially for framing our project ethnographically; that is, our classrooms form cultures and sub-cultures, our students are potential cultural informants, and all cultures—including our classrooms—can be observed, interpreted, and critiqued from etic and emic perspectives. Predictably, most students can tell us what they do, but they cannot tell us why they do it. They cannot tell us why they dress the way they do, why they stay quiet when they do, or why they respond to authoritative texts the way they do. In other words, in many regards, most young students, international or otherwise, do not make good cultural informants. While both groups of students are sophisticated with some advanced academic writing skills in one or more language, many have not had practice thinking about or articulating a more nuanced understanding from what might be considered *ineffable* emic practices from an etic point of view. Thus the reason we find Hall's (2014) perspective useful as an entrée for our work:

> Culture hides much more than it reveals, and strangely enough what it hides, it hides most effectively from its own participants. Years of study have convinced me that the real job is not to understand foreign cultures but to understand our own. (p. 1)

After the students completed their first drafts, Mary provided the English 395 students with a short crash course in SLA, a vital aspect to the success of the overall course, but much underplayed, due in part to the compressed time of the project. We felt it was important for the English 395 students to also have a sense of how language works in their own lives, to introduce them (some for their first time) to critical linguistic/discourse analysis that would help unearth tacit normalizing practices found not only in our local words but also our own university curricula. With this lack of training in mind, we ensured that the crash course involved relatively in-depth analysis of two writing samples, one from a "native" English speaking writer, an 8 year-old Catholic-educated (by nuns) American writer using standard English (Mary's first story in childhood); and the other from a Saudi Arabian male in his first semester of ESL in the western United States. We asked a series of questions as to the identity of the authors based on a variety of linguistic features (e.g., pragmatic, discourse, syntax, morphology). Two outcomes are usually achieved by this exercise. First, for most of the students, this is their first time to consider that the field of SLA may be of use not only for working with multilinguals, but for other aspects of their schooling—since the content of what we learn and teach is mediated through language, and in fact, depending on one's major, languages that can be as obfuscating as a foreign language.

Even foreign and English language majors are not required to take a course in SLA, where useful communication tools and concepts such as language transfer, negotiation of meaning, scaffolding, and error (in a broad sense) analysis and feedback might enhance their own first and second language competence. Students are often surprised to learn about language transfer: that much can be gained by knowing something about a student's first language (L1) in order to assess his performance in his second language (L2). A humorous example illustrating this point comes from an Arabic student's unusual spelling of the word *because*, which he uses seven different times in a one-page journal entry. After the students get over their shock of seeing it spelled seven different ways *("But because is such an easy word and its one of the most commonly used. Doesn't he get lots of exposure to it?")*, we ask students why this ESL student is capable of so many creative renditions of such a common word (rather than *Why can't he get this common word right?)*. We follow this mini lesson with a short discussion of the vowel systems and diacritic markers (used to signal a vowel sound) in Arabic and compare that language with the comparatively idiosyncratic orthographic system of Standard English. By the time we have finished identifying several other cognitive, linguistic, and cultural features of both writing samples, the students are ready to "forgive" the L2 errors, acknowledge (because of the errors) the rapid language progress the L2 student has made, differentiate between an L1 error and an L2 error, and discuss broader underlying sociopolitical discourse features (Gee, 2014). With this minimal level of training, students are well poised to resist the temptation to mark every grammar mistake (especially article and preposition errors) and to recognize the vital role a first language plays. One final background task that we assign to our students is a reflection paper on Fox's (1994) reading that we refer to in the beginning of this paper. Despite some earlier criticism by Kubota (1999) that Fox essentializes, we have used Fox's straightforward, user-friendly chapter to introduce non-TESOL faculty and advanced writing students to the basic tenets of SLA. The following list includes the main ideas students addressed in their reflections on the articles assigned to them:

- Introduction to tensions surrounding multilingualism;
- Exposure to idea of communication styles as different rather than good or poor;
- Opportunity to question their own assumptions about language use and notions of "standard English";
- Occasion to cultivate a sense of linguistic and cultural empathy;
- Introduction to idea that culture and language differences affect writing.

While we believe that all students at the university would benefit from a course that investigates more rigorously our discourse routines—quotidian, ordinary, or "exotic"—we also believe that the students are better equipped to respond to an ESL student's paper with a heightened awareness of a multilingual student's development and progress.

Project 1: Initial Observations and Responses
Even though one of the key themes to advancing any discussion of multilingual pedagogy should deal with definition and treatment of "errors," space limits us from covering in more explicit detail how each discipline views and treats the vast and colorful array of errors, from morphological to pragmatic, from monolingual to multilingual. Suffice it to say that any seasoned writing teacher has a sense of the style of "errors" she wishes to call attention to. Of the tensions that surface in both projects, the concept of coherence is perhaps the most problematic: what strikes one as coherent in one's culture might obfuscate in another. Similarly, what may appear to be coherent in an ESL paper to a seasoned ESL teacher may be painfully

"incomprehensible" to an audience of monolingual English-speaking students in the U.S. Individuals as well as cultures have their own continuum for what constitutes an acceptable amount of ambiguity; many decisions are based on time, space, and other contextual vagaries. Consider the range of possible grades assigned, for example, when even the most experienced writing teachers gather to norm an exit exam. Finally, while good writers and teachers of writing also encourage accuracy and precision, a discussion of precision itself should foreshadow what Canagarajah (2013) refers to as "performative competence," a competence not characterized by mental models or propositional content, nor "the *what*," but rather the "*how* of communication" (p. 174). Linguistic achievements—cognitive, grammatical, strategic, social—are thus "shaped by locally situated performance" (p. 174).

A simple example might help to shed light on our discussion here. One of the more "talented" writers from Korea begins his paper with the following sentient idea: "Culture is smelly," to which the Writing 395 student asked for more clarity by asking *how so?* Accordingly, in his second draft, the writer "corrects:" *culture is smelly because it is invisible and intangible.* He received favorable feedback from the writing student for his clarity and editing. Mary's personal knowledge of the multilingual student's abilities, however, posed a challenge to this "correction," which in Mary's mind is both coherent and comprehensible. Mary suggested that he keep *"culture is smelly"* as a simple sentence and that he follow with the commentary that would evoke the more elusive yet ubiquitous nature of culture rather than the malodourous one. The explanatory power of the conjunction *because* is where the English major and Mary disagreed. First, this simple rhetorical move provided a basis for a substantive conversation regarding feedback for both audiences. As numerous authors have pointed out, depending on one's point of view, Asian writing is "writer friendly" while English, from the West, is "reader friendly." This perhaps oversimplified example points to some intriguing possibilities regarding student Jong Bae's performative competence. In subsequent conversations with both his English major editor and me, Jong Bae—who, along with all of the rest of our students elected to not have us use pseudonyms—was able to elucidate his reasons for his lack of specificity, his tendency to hint at ideas rather than stating them outright as many Korean writers will do. He explained to his American partner that he perceives the "error" as his fault, meaning his mistake; he has committed a rhetorical blunder that should be corrected, much like the idea that he is responsible for language "barriers" that need to be overcome. Somehow the circuitous routes he takes to establish a thesis (if there is one) is wrong. His conversation illuminated further underlying beliefs related to rhetorical awareness, audience, purpose and function of the written text, and even conflicting definitions of self-reliance—a topic they had been exploring in their ESL academic reading course. This example counts as one of many simple, yet powerful, examples demonstrating not only the *extra steps* a multilingual student must take to make himself "competent" or "comprehensible" regarding the "what" but also for showing the conflicting advice and feedback one receives as a multilingual performer-writer.

Since our major focus for this paper is to describe and reflect upon our second collaborative project involving our students, space prohibits from attending here to some of the micro analytic linguistic detail that the above example involves. Overall, the feedback for the course was overwhelmingly positive, with many students commenting on the necessity for *all* students at our university to have this kind of experience. Several of the US students wrote that in the four years that they had been in college, this was their first meaningful exchange with an international student.

Description of Project 2

The second multi-tiered project brought together two groups of students: (Academic English Reading—105/106 ESL and English 200, Multimodal Composition). As we mentioned earlier, there were 16 ESL students from 5 different countries. Eight of the 11 students in English 200 were in their first year of college, and the other three were seniors. None of the 11 students identified as bi- or multilingual, yet all had experience in studying a language besides their native English. Several of the US domestic monolingual students cited extensive experience with multilingual speakers and writers, but that experience, when explored in more detail, was revealed to consist mostly through their contact with peers in ethnically and linguistically diverse high schools in urban and suburban areas. Most of the English 200 students had little-to-no experience engaging with international students, especially in an educational setting.

Assignment 1: Building the Foundation
In the first weeks of class, the ESL students were, per the ESL curriculum, working on traditional micro and macro reading skills and strategies (e.g., decoding, building vocabulary, practicing comprehension, and using contextual cues). Knowing that our collaboration was imminent, Mary put special emphasis on inferencing skills as a way to create a bridge to what our US domestic students and instructors would refer to as critical thinking. Using a variety of genres (e.g., short stories, culturally relevant images, poetry), she emphasized the importance of "reading between the lines" and "connecting the dots." When the students gained some confidence in their abilities to "read into" texts, we introduced the idea of textual literacy and reading images. For the US students in English 200, Project 1 for the course was a researched argumentative essay. A reading was assigned on whether students listen to one another, with the purpose being to help the English 200 students start to think about their own approaches to listening, especially when they may have initial difficulty in understanding what another person may be trying to express. The students completed a letter to the author of the assigned article. This assignment was to promote critical reading skills and sharpen the students' skills at responding to writing, something they would be doing with international students' work.

As an additional means of helping the students prepare for their collaboration, they were asked to exercise information literacy skills by searching for and collecting information about the diversity of the student population at our university and its environs. Search strategies and sources were discussed, in keeping with course-related student learning outcomes, but a principal purpose also aligned with the goal we had for both the domestic and international students: work together and share insights about language and culture. Toward that end, the English 200 students were asked to do a cursory search "preparing" them for cross-cultural, cross-linguistic encounters. The students then wrote letters addressing the Gonzaga Study Abroad website and its advice to students. Again, the purpose of these mini-reading assignments and informal writing prompts were to invite students into our ongoing conversation about what it means to work with people not typical to their own backgrounds.

The next assignment in this portfolio of writing that constituted Project 1 was a request for a one-page letter to international students at our university.

The English 200 students offered advice, based on their reading about cross-cultural engagement, for how international students at their own institution might navigate some of the cross cultural encounters they are having or likely to have at Gonzaga and in Spokane. To facilitate a more robust exchange, we also assigned to the English 200 students a second letter assignment, one in which they would imagine themselves visiting their international partner's country for the first time—what would they want to know? The motivation for this inquiry connects to an overarching interest the instructors have in emphasizing reciprocal rather than one-sided benefit in the cross-cultural encounters between the two groups of learners. Our goals were not constrained to the two classes we had brought together, and we were explicit about this point with our students, noting in one message, "We will continue to expand upon this cross-cultural discussion in the days to come, with an eye toward improving awareness on our campus for both international students and those from the U.S." The two student groups meet for a collaborative session and discussed the letters and questions.

To promote student reflection in English 200, the instructor posted the following assignment that served as the concluding stage of Project 1:

> Write a letter to Dr. Jeannot in which you explain your cross-cultural/linguistic encounter. As you draft and revise, draw specific examples from the *cultural differences and similarities* chart you filled out and ensuing discussion with your international partner. Bring those examples to bear as you explain to Dr. Jeannot what you learned through this process. Also consider addressing what you found of particular interest, what you wished could have gone differently, and/or what you would like to see happen the next time you come together with the international students in her course. Please include anything else you feel compelled to add regarding the lead-up to our meeting as well as the cross cultural encounter itself. In other words, include those ideas and examples that you find worth writing about and sharing.

Assignment 2: Sharing and Writing About Images

The reflection letters from the students in English 200 emphasized their eagerness to continue collaborating with their international partners. Given the emphasis on multimodal composing, John and Mary developed a text + image assignment for Project 2. This unit started with reading assignments keyed to promoting student understanding about critical evaluation of images. What the US students gained from the cross-cultural collaboration they had experienced in the Project 1 assignment cycle served as an excellent lead-in for the current unit focused on "reading" images as texts. This is because the diverse backgrounds of the L2 members—situated as primary audience members for the US students' work—necessitated that L1 domestic students elaborate upon their interpretations of images. For additional orientation, we required the US students to peruse selected image-rich websites and come to class prepared to discuss at least two samples of the photojournalism (but not the photography or the video) they found. The informal assignment within Project 2 also requested that students find at least two examples of writing blended with images, and be prepared to showcase the examples in the next class session. These text + image examples could be from any source, on any topic of interest to students.

Students were then asked to gather at least two images that caught their attention from everyday life and be prepared to "read" (analyze) them for the class, using the tips on analyzing images that they had gleaned from the resources they had found on that topic. The goal was for students to practice developing an analysis of images that would be accessible and informative for both the L1 and L2 audiences. We wanted the unit to enhance all students' abilities in interpreting images and identifying what they found to be significant or provocative. The next step entailed having US students in English 200 move beyond the general practice of analyzing the intersections of text and images and graduate to selecting a particular image that was important to them and their international partners. We suggested that the US students find an image that corresponds to some of the themes (e.g., social, faith, family) that emerged following a structured discussion with the international students.

The English 200 students were given license to choose whatever image they liked, but were also reminded to keep in mind their diverse audiences. In other words, if it seemed inflammatory (particularly given many of the current stereotypes about the Middle East, for example), they should avoid it. Not wanting to stray far from traditional writing, we assigned another piece of informal writing: "Write at least one well-crafted reflection that provides some context for what the image means to you and why you chose it. Be ready to share your writing in class. In the process of writing this one-page document, you might want to refer to the resources you found on how to read images." An ongoing goal in this unit was to keep all of the students "close to the texts," meaning both the image and the text within or captions under it, but also the resource texts students had identified during their searches for tips on how to analyze images.

In this way, the unit invited students to read, write, and analyze critically. The formal stage of Project 2 in English 200 consisted of students composing a multimodal presentation that combined texts (theirs and their international partners') + images (also their own and the written work of their partners'). In the assignment parameters, we reiterated this point: "Your Project 2 will entail your assemblage, your focused efforts to bring together texts + images in a meaningful way for a primary defined audience." We then asked the English 200 students to prepare a 2-minute overview presentation of their text + image slide shows which they subsequently presented to the international students over the course of two face-to-face class sessions. We then all turned our attention to a third formal project.

Assignment 3: Meaningful and Creative Reciprocity
For Project 3 in English 200, we asked students to expand their multimodal composing and create a podcast. This would allow them to move from text + image to a project rooted in an exploration of text + sound. This foray into the sonic landscape of composing also capitalized on the developing relationships between the US and international students. The instructions were intentionally broad:

> You are not required to make Project 3 an explicit argument, but you do need to present a 3-5-minute audio story that has a narrative arc or main organizing principle with which listeners can identify. In other words, you need to build a project that, if not an actual argument, at least takes a stand or follows a particular line of intellectual exploration.

This line of inquiry involved further collaboration with the international students with the English 200 students integrating international student voices into their podcasts. Overall, the students adeptly blended the multilingual sounds into their recordings, and they generally felt no need to edit out what they earlier might have reflexively considered to be "incomprehensible" language intended for a monolingual audience. That is, we became aware of the US students' growing ability to understand the international students as legitimate speakers of English, despite the variety of accents or their heretofore assumptions about clarity or comprehensibility. For the most part, the topics of the interviews revolved around family and education themes, with all students noting cultural similarities and differences.

Assignment 4: Up Close
Until the fourth and final assignment for the project, we had felt a notable absence of anything the two authors would refer to as creative or meaningful reciprocity. The international students were needed for the success of the English 200 projects that explored text + image and text + sound, but the American students were not serving as high stakes cultural and linguistic informants for the international students. One might readily imagine the following scenario: American student has an assignment, say in a 101 Sociology course that requires her to locate the ESL students on campus. The imaginary conversation could be, "I am supposed to find out what your religion is and how you practice it. Then, I need to identify your struggles with Academic English based on some these ideas from our reading." After a friendly fifty minutes (a class period) of questions and the answers, the American student could perhaps go off to write a paper that, by quoting the Thai student enough, ends up earning an A for the assignment rubric which required three quotes from the international student. This hypothetical-yet-familiar exchange is predominately one-sided. So while the domestic monolingual student may have made contact with a multilingual student, practiced her interviewing skills, and completed the requisite reading, the assumption is still that the entire exchange would take place in English with very little thought given to the multilingual aspect of the exchange. The multilinguals are perennial guests even in a space that has been designated as theirs. At the outset, the international students in such collaborative scenarios are positioned as the researched, and the domestic students are presented as the researchers. Furthermore, there is the subtle, but certainly not innocuous, perception that the undergraduate Americans have the "real" assignment. What makes this brand of "global engagement" especially misguided is a pervasive idea that the international student is the carrier of culture and language difference, but the American is not.

For Project 4 in English 200, then, we were determined to represent a different, richer collaboration between the two student groups. We assigned the US students to write, video, and present a brief documentary project that would require them to reflect upon and synthesize the semester of cross-cultural experiences with the international students. This assignment would therefore require the English 200 students to explore intersections of text + image + sound + video, as well as to work in more depth with their international partners. To begin this process, English 200 students researched and viewed at least one short documentary on a topic of their choice, taking notes on how the documentarians present their story, the technical aspects, and the language employed. Not having much or any formal prior experience with such work required the students to search for resources on how to make short documentaries. They looked on the open web and in subscription databases for advice and helpful reminders that would assist them in getting a strong start. We introduced mini-exercises (e.g., create a 45-second "warm-up" documentary) to reinforce early in the assignment the many challenges associated with writing and taking video as documentarians. A key focal point for Project 4 was for students to draw from their resources on making documentaries and begin to assume their roles as deliberate and rhetorically savvy composers working with diverse informant-partners from other countries and different language backgrounds. After feedback and more discussion of the possible approaches afforded them, the English 200 students began to take on their main documentary projects. Three weeks passed quickly as face-to-face English 200 class sessions were dedicated to multimodal studio time for peer review, mini technology workshops, and project management. Outside class time, more writing, producing, and presenting occurred, and some of this process involved both groups of students since this final phase of the project stipulated that English 200 students must include their international partners in the documentaries, at least to the degree the international students were comfortable.

At the same time that the English 200 students were working on their projects, the 106 ESL students began writing and producing their own newscast reports highlighting scenes from an American short story, a culminating project that integrates academic reading as well as written and spoken communication. Similar to the English 200 students, the projects, led by ESL faculty member Sandra Bancroft-Billings, required outside class time, writing, producing, and presenting (all in their second or third language). The project stipulated that students must include their US domestic partners in the documentaries. We encouraged and expected the American students to be informants on any number of subjects or skills: themes in literature, filming, editing, idioms and slang, broadcasting, pronunciation assistance, popular American cultural motifs, and so on. With the assessment criteria well established, the students were granted complete autonomy over the intellectual content of their broadcast. By the time we reached this fourth stage of the project in which students had met several times, they were at ease with each other, a fact that helped them all face the unavoidable burden (or, we argued, the opportunity) of the ambiguity inherent in such projects. Equally important, both groups of students now had unconstrained access to rich context and content as well as linguistic and cultural knowledge on which to build either their multimodal documentary or their news broadcast. In other words, the multimodal, multilingual, multicultural backbone of the projects are grounded in—not imposed on—the goals we highlighted earlier from the *Framework for Success in Postsecondary Writing*: curiosity, openness, engagement, creativity, persistence, responsibility, flexibility, and metacognition.

Now having enjoyed meaningful contact with international students on campus, most of the monolingual domestic students in this project are quick to discuss "communication barriers," and they usually do so in the form of mentioning their own linguistic "obstacles" to overcome. Even though they recognize the value of the assignment, language is still considered a barrier. It would follow, then, that if everyone were able to communicate according to English speaking, norms, barriers, and obstacles would not exist. By that logic, non-Science majors might do well to forego their science requirements based on the idea that science discourses with their requisite vernacular and idiom create barriers to learning and slow down the overall educational (consumption) experience. In this paper, we have tried to take the view that language differences are conduits for exploring, at the very least, cultural differences, and that uncomfortable linguistic exchanges induce the intended or unintended lessons on ambiguity, flexibility, and creativity.

The tasks for this second collaboration between the US and international students were invented, scripted, documented, and edited to include multiple genres, all of which were collected as portfolio artifacts for assessment. Just as each task became increasingly complex, so, too, did each phase. Predictably, perhaps, this sequenced approach demanded more rigorous focus and depth from both sets of students. Each layer also contributed to each student's relative effectiveness as a multimodal and multilingual writer, presenter, and reader. Within the sequence, as each layer intensified in complexity, the collaboration itself became increasingly student-centered. For example, in some cases, the content was driven by the English 200 participants and in other cases, the multilingual students. These back and forth, push-pull configurations in turn influenced the assessments and the process of clarifying desired outcomes for future projects.

Concluding Remarks: Was It Worth It?

We conclude by invoking one of the more memorable insights from two of the English 200 students. In their Project 4 documentary—an analysis of the entire process of collaborating with international partners—they provide a 30-second stretch delineating a long list of course requirements and a pervasive ambiguity: "Nothing was ever consistent due to our collaboration with the ESL program. Was it worth the required time and effort? Of course it was."

Yet despite our efforts to create a reciprocal multilingual collaboration, such projects pose a number of challenges. For those of us who work with multilinguals on a regular basis, we anticipate the usual complaints, the first being that international students need to have the subject matter "diluted," "dumbed-down," or translated. In an institution that does not serve many international students, the need to shift the point of view is not critical. If it were, we would need to shift priorities in terms of what we label academic, and what we label academic success. Just as the nature of writing will change, so will the nature of multimodality performances change with an increased emphasis on "performative competence" (Canagarajah, 2013). For example, while the Project 3 audio quality and Project 4 video quality suffered as a result of the multimodal students having less studio time for refining their authoring skills with the technological affordances, judging by the content of the documentaries, the quality and time-consuming international "engagement" bespoke a quality of authentic interaction that heretofore may not have been experienced by any of the English 200 students in their entire lives.

Having the students meet four times, plus additional faculty time for planning, poses problems for everyone who has time constraints. Below, we have highlighted areas that presented challenges we would not necessarily eliminate but prioritize differently next time:

- Coordination with other faculty required extra time for course planning;
- Multimodal projects often take more time than traditional compositions;
- Collaborations between student groups means less studio time for composing;
- Guest speakers from the other group means less direct instruction by faculty;
- Faculty can face fatigue/resistance from students because of project complexity;
- Some students and faculty can assert a "dilution" of conventional "language teaching" (and argue not enough time is spent on English language skills);
- Working with other students, to some, doesn't "look like" or constitute legitimate reading activities (for a course in Reading);
- Partnerships of these types can lead to productive and unproductive tensions on what could be described as the incomprehensibility/comprehensibility continuum.

In documenting some initial insights from two collaborations across disciplines as we have, our goal was to provide a glimpse into what might be achieved if faculty across disciplines are willing to suspend their judgments regarding linguistic and perhaps even cultural comprehensibility. As writing teachers of contemporary multilinguals, we do in fact aspire to the lofty goals of the *translingual* classroom, which challenges the static view of language and writing, privileges the view of multiple languages as resources, and calls for a more agentive use of various language resources in constructing and negotiating meaning, identity, and even larger ideological conditions (Atkinson et al., 2015, p. 384).

Our forays into what we characterize as a sort of multimodal-multilingual reciprocity in learning represents, from two faculty and four sets of students, both a modest point of departure and praxis and an entry point for further conversations. Given our current context and the challenges we have described, if we are going to continue, on the faculty level, there needs to be willingness to abandon the to-some-degree-antiquated notions about what constitutes academic content and concomitant academic literacy, particularly for those disciplines whose content is foreshadowed by genuine global engagement—which, regardless of our current subject positions, eventually will include us all.

References

Atkinson, D., Crusan, D., Matsuda, P. K., Ortmeier-Hooper, C., Ruecker, T., Simpson, S., & Tardy, C. (2015). Clarifying the relationship between L2 writing and translingual writing: An open letter to writing studies editors and organization leaders. *College English, 77*(4), 383-386. Retrieved from http://www.ncte.org/library/NCTEFiles/Resources/Journals/CE/0774-mar2015/CE0774Clarifying.pdf

Canagarajah, S. (2006). Toward a writing pedagogy of shuttling between languages: Learning from multilingual writers. *College English, 6*, 589-604. doi:10.2307/25472177

Canagarajah, S. (2014a). Theorizing a competence for translingual practice at the contact zone. In S. May (Ed.), *The multilingual turn: Implications for SLA, TESOL, and bilingual education* (pp. 78-102). New York: Routledge.

Canagarajah, S. (2014b). Negotiating translingual literacy: An enactment. *Research in the Teaching of English, 1*, 40-64.

Council of Writing Program Administrators (CWPA), National Council of Teachers of English (NCTE), & National Writing Project (NWP). (2011). Framework for success in postsecondary writing. Retrieved from http://wpacouncil.org/files/framework-for-success-postsecondary-writing.pdf

Cruz-Ferreira, M. (2010). *Multilinguals are...?* London: Battlebridge.

Flores, N. (2013). The unexamined relationship between neoliberalism and pluralingualism: A cautionary tale. *TESOL Quarterly, 3*, 500-520. doi:10.1002/tesq.114

Fox, H. (1994). *Listening to the world: Cultural issues in academic writing*. Urbana, IL: NCTE.

Gee, J. (2014). *Introduction to discourse analysis*. New York: Routledge.

Hall, E. (2014). Epigraph. In M. Kearny-Datesman, J. Crandall, & E. Kearny (Eds.), *American ways: An introduction to American culture* (4th ed., p. 1). New York: Pearson.

Kubota, R. (1999). Japanese culture constructed by discourses: Implications for applied linguistics research and ELT. *TESOL Quarterly, 1*, 9-35. doi:10.2307/3588189

Lee, J. H. (2012). Implications for language diversity in instruction in the context of target language classrooms: Development of a preliminary model of the effectiveness of teacher code-switching. *English Teaching: Practice and Critique, 4*, 137-160.

Matsuda, P. K. (1999). Composition studies and ESL writing: A disciplinary division of labor. *College Composition and Communication, 4*, 699-721. doi:10.2307/358488

May, S. (2013). *The multilingual turn: Implications for SLA, TESOL and Bilingual Education*. New York: Routledge.

Ortega, L. (2013). SLA for the 21st century: Disciplinary progress, transdisciplinary relevance and the bi/multilingual turn. *Language Learning: A Journal of Research in Language Studies, s1*, 1-24. doi:10.1111/j.1467-9922.2012.00735.x

Phillipson, R. (2011). English: From British Empire to corporate empire. *Sociolinguistic Studies, 3*, 441-464. doi:10.1558/sols.v5i3.441

CHAPTER 9

HISPANIC SETTLEMENT IN RURAL SETTINGS:
The Role of Language in Adaptation

María Cristina Montoya
Ho Hon Leung
State University of New York at Oneonta

Recent census data (U.S. Census Bureau, 2010) and recent studies indicate that increasing numbers of immigrants, including Hispanic immigrants, are settling in some non-metropolitan counties and rural America (Wortham et al., 2013; see for example De Haymes & Kilty, 2007; Donato, 2007; Jones, 2008). Similar to the "push and pull factors" in transnational migration (Massey, 1993), immigrants are pulled into non-traditional gateway cities for reasons such as employment opportunities, community safety, affordable housing, and reunions with family and friends (see Flores et al., 2015). This new trend of migration to rural America is expected to continue. Since the Hispanic population comprises the nation's largest racial minority, 55 million or 17% of the total population, and the immigrants of this group make up almost half (1.15 million) of the total immigrant population (2.36 million) between 2013 and 2014 (U.S. Census Bureau, 2015), it is imperative to continue to document not only their immigration experience in general, but also their particular experience in less-urban areas. While there are rich research studies about the Hispanic immigrant experiences in more urban settings, very little empirical research has been conducted about their settlement experience in more rural areas. This research attempts to fill the gap in the literature about the rural experience.

The term "Hispanic" is used throughout the current study according to the description of this term by the United States Census Bureau, and includes persons of Mexican, Puerto Rican, Cuban, South and Central American descent, or other Spanish culture regardless of race. In addition, the term is used to clarify that all participants are unified by the use of Spanish as a native or heritage language.

Literature Review

Lin (1998) categorizes cities like New York, Houston, Miami, and Los Angeles as immigration gateway cities. Not only do most of the immigrants who come to the U.S. land in these gateway cities, but they also settle in these metropolitan areas. There are some good reasons for immigrants to settle in urban places. One of them is that they can find more support in their respective ethnic communities. Immigrants in the past settled in cities and formed communities in which they established organizations to meet the needs related to settlement in the host country. Although this trend continues today, recent research and census data suggest that more immigrants are choosing to settle in small towns and rural areas of the U.S., and sometimes these immigrants arrive in these new settlement areas bypassing gateway cities (Jentsch & Simard, 2009; Jones, 2008; Logan et al., 2002). This preference to settle in rural areas is not only observed among Hispanics, but also among the Chinese and Asian Indian communities (Leung, 2007; Leung & Mohammed, 2004). It becomes intriguing to investigate what factors would pull these immigrants to move, settle, and adapt to smaller places, if their ethnic network is most likely to be weak due to lack of ethnic enclaves. Such enclaves provide necessary resources, including heritage speech communities.

The Hispanic population is an ethnically and culturally diverse group. They come from various countries in Central and South America, with more than sixty percent of the group arriving from Mexico (Reimers, 2005, p. 125). Brief demographic characteristics of some major groups from the Hispanic population included in this study follow. First, populations of Mexican immigrants are currently changing demographic patterns as they move to more rural areas and states where there was not a significant presence in the past; they keep moving through a complex network of family and friends while fueling the economies of entire towns (Guevarra, 2013; Vecchione, 2009). Mexican immigrants present a complex history of settlement in the north as explored by Torres-Rouff (2013), and that history continues today with a population that does not stop moving across the border (Mines & Massey, 1985; Spener, 2004), and throughout urban and rural areas within the U.S. Among Hispanic immigrants, Mexicans are the top guest workers who have been present in many seasonal businesses, particularly agricultural sectors.

The settlement process of immigrants draws scholars' attention because it is important to the well-being of not only the immigrants themselves, but also the host communities. Studies examine immigrant settlement in terms of the experience of learning about the receiving country (Khoir & Koronios, 2015), integrating into the housing market and economy (Wei & Teixeira, 2014), and establishing a home in their settled communities as a sign of permanent settlement (Chiang & Leung, 2011).

Massey (1986) examined the process of settlement of Mexican migrants to the U.S. in three phases: the initial "sojourner phase," the "transitional phase," and the final "settlement phase." In the final phase, Massey argued that after the migrants live in the U.S., they "come to see themselves as residents of the host society. They have been joined by wives and children, and they have developed widespread contact with people and institutions in and out of the immigrant enclaves" (p. 671).

Studies indicate that the process of settling in the host country is filled with different types of challenges. One of the major challenges is racism (Cohen & Chavez, 2013; Hanna & Ortega, 2016). The racism could be a result of racist laws, discriminatory procedures, and acts of prejudice that prevent immigrants, Hispanic immigrants included, from having equal access to job markets (Pager, Bonikowski, & Western, 2009), housing (De la Roca, Ellen, & O'Regan, 2014), health and social services (Hall et al., 2015), and schooling (McGlynn, 2015). These challenges pose barriers to immigrants achieving the "American dream" (see Huntington, 2004). Undocumented Hispanic migrants suffer additional hardship because they lack the protections deriving from legal status. Immigrant children and adolescents face challenges similar to those of their parents. Studies also highlight multiple challenges associated with acculturation, as well as language acquisition and retention (Kang et al., 2014; Rumberger et al., 2009).

In addition to resources available in the mainstream society, many immigrants tend to make good use of those in their ethnic enclaves to help deal with the challenges. Ethnic enclaves are an urban phenomenon, where immigrants benefit from its enclave economy, social networks, and familiar cultural and linguistic environment (Portes, 1987). Furthermore, given both historical and recent trends, churches play a vital role in immigrant settlement. In addition to providing formal programs and informal support to help immigrants settle and integrate, churches have a strong tradition of participating in community building (Janzen et al., 2014). In particular, Hispanic immigrants benefit from the rapid rise of Catholic parishes with Hispanic ministry (Ospino, 2014).

The purpose of this study is to investigate the settlement experience of Hispanic migrants who arrived and settled in a rural town in a large state in the Northeast of the United States. Given the different geographic, social, and economic nature of small towns where ethnic enclaves and immigrant infrastructure are missing, this study seeks specific answers in 1) what attracted these migrants to this small town; 2) what challenges these migrants face; 3) what their coping strategies are; and 4) what role the acquisition of English and Spanish plays in the settling process.

Research Methods

The Current Study

The current research is a collaborative interdisciplinary task. It involved student researchers from a course in Advanced Spanish Conversation with a service-learning component taught three times during the spring semesters of 2012 and 2013, and the fall semester of 2014.

The data collected from the interaction with the Hispanic community was part of a larger academic project based on experiential learning in the context of social science and second language and culture education. The faculty researchers trained students to conduct interviews. College students were invited to conduct the research as part of applied learning practices based on service-learning pedagogy. This approach is useful in communities where immigrant and college student populations co-exist because it provides mutual service for actions that seek to improve community welfare. Students learn by interacting with community members, and people in the community receive services for their families that aid their integration into the larger mainstream society. This kind of practice is not unique to the current researched town. A similar example of this practice was implemented by Long (2003).

Participants, Researchers, and Data Collection
Data were collected in various forms; there was a total of 20 formal interviews and casual conversations with other immigrants at social gatherings. Recruitment of the interviewees started before the semester began. Contacts were made initially by the Hispanic professor with non-probability sampling strategies that included haphazard, purposive, and snowball. Haphazard and purposive strategies are ways to identify willing participants who meet the requirements of the purpose of the study. Only those who identified themselves as immigrants who live in small towns from Hispanic background were recruited. The snowball sampling strategy refers to a technique to recruit new interviewees through those who have previously agreed to participate in the project.

When the school term started, one family was assigned to one student in the course. Informed consent was obtained from the adult interviewees. The Institutional Review Board also approved interviews with children when their parents were present. In some cases, parents talked while their children were present, and some interviews consisted of only one adult reporting about his or her family settlement experience. Throughout the semester, the students provided tutoring service to the children or taught English as a second language to the adults while preparing for research methods and data collection in the classroom. A faculty member from Sociology trained the students to conduct in-depth ethnographic interviews and field observations. The other professor from Foreign Languages who was fluent in speaking Spanish guided the students with the specific service-learning task. The students had opportunities to familiarize themselves with the interviewees' culture of origin and immigrant experience. The foreign language professor served as a bridge between each student and family to allow trust to be developed, and encouraged the participants to talk freely about their immigrant experiences and concerns during their settlement process. Other students were placed to volunteer at the adult education school that provided free English as a Second Language classes. One-on-one interviews were conducted in this setting. The data collected by the college students were used for their class projects and for the analysis of this paper.

Other data were collected by direct observation and interaction with children in the afterschool tutoring, and at the end-of-the-semester celebration with the Hispanic community and the college students. After one semester of data collection, and before a second semester of the same practice, a formal community gathering was organized in a central location of the town in order to integrate other non-Hispanic community members, the other college in town, and the Hispanic immigrants, including professionals working at the colleges. The purpose of this gathering was to express specific needs from community members and the kind of collaboration required among all groups. This meeting allowed researchers to specifically observe language attitudes and take note of existing obstacles preventing the Hispanic community from feeling welcomed in the larger community.

Sections of the interviews were transcribed by the student interviewers, as well as by two student research assistants recruited later in the process. The privacy of the participants and confidentiality was strictly observed. The information that could be used to identify the participants was not revealed to the student research assistants, and there was a document for protecting confidentiality signed by each college student involved. The Center for Social Responsibility and Community in the college was involved in this procedure to assure that students taking part in the course and research were clear about their responsibilities. Before the actual interviews started, the immigrant participants were orally informed about the procedures to protect their privacy and confidentiality. When they signed the informed consent letter, their signatures indicated that they agreed and understood their rights and were assured of their privacy.

The data was analyzed inductively and categorized according to themes in the research: settlement, challenges, adaptation experiences, and the role of language in the course of living in rural settings. The analysis focused on their common experiences and their specific challenges across the various ethnic groups according to level of education, professional skills, immigrant status, and marital status.

The Background of the Town

The rural town researched for the current study is located in a large state in the Northeast of the United States between two major urban areas. It is surrounded by small hills and an agricultural landscape. The total population of the county is 62,259, and 13,901 reside in the town (U.S. Census Bureau, 2010). The town is central for the commerce of the region, providing for the socio-economic needs of surrounding areas. Two colleges, two health networks, and local retailers provide services to its residents. The Hispanic residents in the town increased from 3.6% (475) in 2000 to 5.9% (825) in 2010 (U.S. Census Bureau, 2000, 2010). The majority of Hispanics in the area come from Puerto Rico, followed by Mexico and other Spanish-speaking countries.

There are similarities among the Hispanic residents, yet the cultural and linguistic characteristics of each racial and ethnic group differ from each other. Their settlement patterns and experiences differ due to each group's unique political, economic, educational, social, and cultural backgrounds. This was observed among Hispanic immigrants in this town, who are very heterogeneous and differ in educational level, place of origin, and legal documented status.

Some of the Hispanic members come to work in the service industry of the town that includes many restaurants and hotels. In addition to serving the residents and the college students when school is in session, the demand for these services is particularly high in the summer months for tourists and summer events. The low-skill workers, who tend to be males, usually come by themselves and establish a relationship with restaurant owners. Once they become more settled, they bring their family, followed by other male friends or relatives who also seek work at other kitchens in the town's restaurants. There is a diverse population of single men that live a more nomadic lifestyle by moving around the rural areas in the state as jobs become available.

The low-skill female population finds jobs at various hotels, and also has developed a network with the professional population of the town, such as medical doctors and college employees who need cleaning services. Seasonal cleaning positions are available every summer as sport camps open in the nearby town every year. These opportunities become another source of income for these women. These specific families and individuals who fill the service needs of the town may come from rural or suburban places in their original countries, but most of them have experienced living in big cities at some point of their journey to the United States. Some participants in this study are originally from Oaxaca, Monterey, and Veracruz. They reported that during their journey to the U.S. they stayed in places like Mexico City and Tijuana for some time before they decided to cross the border.

The South American immigrants come from various countries of origin such as Panama, Colombia, Peru, Argentina, Uruguay, Venezuela, and

Ecuador. Some of them tend to be more skilled and educated immigrants who come without any previous family or friend network in town. Some of these professionals arrive single and others bring spouses and children with them or start families in the town.

Lastly, one particular group that deserves special attention is from the Caribbean. The Caribbean population represents a majority of Hispanics in town: 2.5% of Puerto Rican origin and 0.3% of Cuban origin (U.S. Census Bureau, 2010); this group has the longest residential period in the town, since there has been a steady migration from the surrounding metropolitan areas to the rural parts of the Northeast region. These Puerto Ricans are not newcomers into the U.S. from the island; they are usually third and fourth generations of immigrants, moving north and away from urban environments.

In addition to the regular Hispanic residents, some Hispanic college students who come to earn their undergraduate degrees only stay in town during the academic year. A particular group of Hispanic college students come mostly from Mexico. This group comes to the state college from various agricultural regions in the state through an educational opportunity agricultural program. Other Hispanic college students come from the metropolitan areas, and their countries of origin are mostly the Dominican Republic, Puerto Rico, Colombia, Ecuador, and occasionally Spain.

Due to the small percentage of Hispanics in the county (5.6%), there are no clusters of a particular country of origin. The interviewees vary in place of origin, education level, English proficiency, Spanish variety, professional skills, and jobs held. Of the interviewees, there are 5 Mexican families with children, who arrived in the town childless within the last 16 years and started a family in rural areas of the state. These families work in the service industry, the men in the kitchens of the many restaurants in town, and the women in housekeeping jobs. In addition to these families with low-skill workers, there is a group of single men mostly from Mexico and El Salvador who stay in town as restaurant jobs are available. The low-skill workers had limited English proficiency at the time of arrival and four out of the five families came directly from the west coast. Others came from surrounding cities and made several stops at other urban places before landing in this town. Several in this group are undocumented. The other group consists of three Caribbean families that came into the area from metropolitan urban settings. They were drawn by a job opportunity. This group was fluent in two languages at time of arrival; some even speak English as their dominant language. Most of the members in this group were already US citizens. Lastly, there was a group of South Americans, and some Spaniards, with a diverse educational background. Some of them were highly educated and came to teach at one of the colleges in the town. Some arrived childless and started a family in town; others remained childless. English is not a barrier for the group of college professionals. Their career is to teach and research in various fields. Some of them spend months on conducting research and writing elsewhere during college breaks. Other South Americans who have legal status but are not highly educated work in various small manufacturing or agricultural industries in the surrounding rural areas.

Results

Pulling Factors to Rural Areas

At first, immigrants are attracted to this rural town because of job opportunities and affordability of better housing, short commuting time from home to work, accessibility of local markets, and safe environments to raise families. The group expressed that they found tranquility and opportunities for education in this rural town. They also reported that the accommodating social environment helped them deal with common challenges for immigrants such as employment, housing, health care, transportation, English fluency, and risk of deportation; all of this becomes easier to manage in this small town analyzed in the current study. One of the longest residents, a male from Mexico, married with two children born in town, a low-skill worker holding two jobs at a Pizzeria and a hotel kitchen, who settled in this town 16 years ago, expressed how different life was in this town compared to Los Angeles, where he initially settled. He expressed feeling safer in this rural area:

> *Pues en Los Ángeles yo manejaba vehículo pero sin licencia y la policía te quita el carro si no tiene licencia y ellos me quitaron varios pero lo necesitaba porque alguna vez trabajaba lejos y tenía que transportarme. Yo estaba cansado porque me estaban quitando los carros y en el dos mil yo vine a este pueblito con una hermana de ella.*
>
> [Then in Los Angeles, I used to drive without a license and the police take away your car if you don't have a license, and they took several cars from me, but I needed them because sometimes I worked far from home, and I had to

commute. I was tired of losing my cars and in the year 2000, I came to this small town with her sister.]

Regardless of place of origin, all immigrants with families were attracted to this small rural town because they were seeking better places to raise their children and wanted to leave the harsh urban environments where gangs, drugs, and street conflicts may have affected their children. Two Puerto Rican families interviewed were particularly attracted to the rural town because of the opportunities available for higher education for their children:

Yo vivía en Brooklyn, allá llegué de Puerto Rico cuando era más *joven y me casé y tuve tres hijos, pero criar los muchachos en la ciudad era difícil y antes que me crecieran más, me los traje para acá, conseguí trabajo en la escuela y ahora mis muchachos van a la universidad.* (female, elementary school special education assistant)
[I used to live in Brooklyn. I arrived there from Puerto Rico when I was younger, and I got married and had three sons. But raising family in the city was difficult and before they grew more, I brought them here. I got a job at a school and now my boys go to college.]

This Puerto Rican group is more proficient in English than in Spanish. This allows them to integrate into the community rapidly. They are all US citizens; therefore finding jobs is not usually a challenge. They participate in all of the social and educational opportunities in the town. They tend not to rely on a Hispanic network because they can associate with the English speaking population.

All the South American interviewees are either green card holders or nationalized citizens. The types of their jobs correlate with their levels of education. Some Colombians are found working at the horse ranches in the area. They find this work similar to the farming lifestyle they used to have in the Andean region of their country of origin. Other Colombians with a longer immigrant trajectory in the U.S. and better socioeconomic mobility left urban areas and came to the rural seeking cheaper real estate. These more well-off immigrants take advantage of the rental industry offered in this area due to the large residential student population and the baseball camps. They earn a living by seasonally renting to students and to tourists' families in the summer. A Colombian female with more than 30 years living in the U.S. owns a rental property next to her own home in a beautiful landscape ten minutes away from the baseball camps expressed her feelings:

> *Ay mamita, la vida por aquí es muy sola, yo extraño la ciudad, pero por aquí es donde está la platica cuando llegan todos estos muchachos a jugar béisbol.*
> [Ay dear, life here is very lonely, I miss the city, but here is where the money is when all these kids come to play baseball.]

Several professionals also arrived in town. Some were single and came with work visas sponsored by the colleges. Others hold green cards due to previous family petitions, or were born in the U.S. They are a group of highly educated first generation of Hispanics. They hold doctoral degrees and settled in the area because of teaching opportunities in this particular rural town with two colleges present. These Hispanic professionals are from various country of origins: Mexico, Guatemala, Cuba, Puerto Rico, Costa Rica, Colombia, Venezuela, Peru, Uruguay, and Argentina.

Challenges

After examining the motives for settling in this rural town, it is necessary to lay out the challenges that these Hispanic immigrants face in the course of adapting and integrating into the larger rural community. Difficulties range from harsh long cold winters and low paying jobs to extended working schedules, discrimination based on race in a mostly white town, and provincial lifestyles. Some of the interviewees expressed that one of their challenges is their undocumented immigrant status, which puts them at a disadvantage when negotiating salaries or earning raises. Employers take advantage of their vulnerable situation and pay them low wages. This is usually the case among low-skill male workers who are forced to find better paying jobs at restaurants' kitchens. They have little choice but to compete for cheap labor during the busy academic year and summer tourist seasons which crowd their restaurants with customers. While males are looking for better paying employment there are periods of male unemployment, and during this transition their wives help support the family with their more stable housekeeping work. The following testimony is from a Mexican mother with three children, one just born at the time of the interview. The eldest daughter crossed the border with them, and the other two were born in the U.S.:

> *Aquí no somos ricos, pero al menos no vivimos en una casa de palitos como en México. Mi esposo vive muy aburrido y diciendo que se va a volver pa' México,*

pero yo le digo que yo no me voy. Aquí tenemos una casita para nosotros y los niños van a la escuela.
[Here we are not rich, but at least we do not live in a house made of sticks like in Mexico. My husband is bored and says that he is going to go back to Mexico, but I tell him that I am not leaving. Here we have a little house for ourselves and our children go to school.]

Hispanic male adaptation into the rural setting may present challenges that are different from the female experience. For example, there is a lack of public places for males to gather with friends to talk and drink as they may have been used to in their places of origin. Another factor affecting males is the empowerment that women experience in the household while in the U.S.; they earn money to support the family and at times find better paying jobs than their husbands (see also Paris Pombo, 2006).

Other challenges are the weather in the region and weather-related issues. Since most of them come from warmer regions in Central and South America, they find the harsher winter challenging to which to adjust. They remain mostly indoors during winter months, and the change of weather also changes the dynamics of the town's economy. There are fewer housekeeping jobs in the winter. This situation reduces income for the families with lower educational levels, and they have to pay high heating bills. Their commuting to work becomes more difficult and they have to rely on public transportation instead of biking. This becomes an additional burden for them due to their lower income in the winters. Women with young children also feel more challenged when going to markets and to work. A particular challenge comes with the mothers going to doctors' appointments with their young children when the weather could be below zero Fahrenheit for consecutive days.

Another expressed difficulty is the lack of family time during the weekends for the low-skill workers. Frequently, men work long shifts on Saturdays and Sundays leaving the wife and the children in the house. Days off for fathers, if they have any, are usually during weekdays when the children are at school and mothers at work. Often in the evenings the mothers are alone with their children assisting them with homework and cooking dinner while the fathers are still at work. For these mothers with low educational levels, it becomes difficult to assist their children with homework and understand the schools' assessment procedures. Communication between school and families is difficult for this particular group. Therefore these Hispanic children develop independence very soon due to their parents' struggle to engage in their education and deal with limited family time. Women in this group also expressed that this struggle could make them feel lonely at times, without family closeness and a female network when survival pressures become oppressive.

A major challenge experienced by all rural immigrants, regardless of their origin or educational level, is isolation from their own ethnic groups. This isolation limits the opportunities for cultural interaction and strengthening ethnic ties. Also, isolation becomes especially difficult for those who arrive and remain single in the area. Some consider leaving the area because of this reason. Higher educated and professional immigrants do not have the same challenges in navigating the large dominant community. However, if they remain single and childless, they have fewer opportunities to integrate into the life of the town.

Isolation is not an issue for those who have been long-term US residents and who already are the second and third generations of the family in the U.S. The Puerto Ricans are a group in this case. They stated that their main struggle is not isolation as they have integrated into the community. However, their challenge is to deal with racial and socioeconomic discrimination. This group is viewed by the traditionally white local population as a "city problem" reaching upstate. This challenge was disclosed by a young couple of second generation Puerto Ricans who moved into the town with two small children and one to be born at the time of the interview. The mother of the family, who does not speak Spanish, expressed her feelings:

There are more city people up here, my family is moving up here too, and the locals see us as a problem, but we are just looking for safer places, I just feel safer here.

Dark-skinned Puerto Ricans and others from the Caribbean are often associated with the African American population by the white people in town. This Spanish-speaking group experiences discrimination similar to that suffered by African Americans in this mostly white town. There has been a history of racial profiling by law enforcement officers who focus more on this population, viewing them as potential troublemakers. Dark-skinned college students have also suffered from police profiling, which leads the public safety officers from the universities to work with local police officers, including state police, to handle cases of racial discrimination. It is important to clarify that individuals with more indigenous Caribbean appearance do not suffer the same racial profiling. Because of their mixed ethnicities and lighter skin color, they are associated with immigrants who come from more remote places to work in the agricultural or service industries. This group is never seen in clusters in public places because they mainly work inside the restaurants, hotels, or private houses and are rarely visible to the public. Their race is not viewed in the same way as the blackness of the individuals who usually moved from the urban metropolitan areas of the north-eastern coast. The urban immigrants with darker skin color and English proficiency are more integrated into the economy and social life of the town and become more visible publicly. One of the Dominican families interviewed came to the area because of a professional job opportunity in a manufacturing company. They were a professional couple, both engineers; however, it became difficult for the wife and the only daughter to adapt to the lifestyle of the small town. They did not have access to products and ethnic community life, and often felt different when navigating the public space and at school because of their darker skin. In addition, the husband had to cope with racism experienced in the workplace. This educated man, dark-skinned, fluent although with a marked accent, confounded the employees who were under his supervision. The man finally relocated within his company into a larger city where he felt valued in his management position regardless of his ethnicity and race. Dominican immigrant residents found that not many first generation immigrants find rural life attractive. This population relies strongly on the connection with the enclave in a nearby urban area (see also Sagás, 2013). Among all groups it was observed that Dominican families prefer the urban or suburban environments with strong ethnic connections and the availability of fresh produce from their home country, as expressed by one of the mothers:

> Yo la verdad, yo no me adapto. Este yo lo hago y de vez en cuando nos juntamos un grupo de latinos. Este ahí cuando nos juntamos me siento un poquito mejor. Pero en los días normales de fin de semana para mi es pesado. Este estar separada de mi gente, yo digo mi gente. Lo que yo digo mi gente son este los latinos, no importa de donde sea, porque es que la cultura es diferente.
> [Honestly, I can't get used to it. I try and sometimes we get together with a group of Latin people. When we get together, I feel a little better, but during normal days on weekends, it is hectic for me. Being separated from my people, I say "my

people" that are Latin, it does not matter where they come from because the culture here is different.]

Adapting and Settling into the Town
Advantages in the Town

One important factor that distinguishes this rural town from other towns is the existence of two higher education institutions. These universities attract a diverse population into the area, with particular purposes and needs. The co-existence of traditional rural residents with young college students, educated retired professionals, and current employees who may come from urban areas or places outside of the U.S. breeds all kinds of needs and interactions. Colleges use the local community for applied learning practices with their students; furthermore, families and children are served by the various programs initiated by different disciplines: nursing, education, human ecology, sociology, foreign languages…etc. There is also the city school district servicing the children in the community and the adults with special educational needs such as English as a Second Language, or high school equivalency (GED) programs. Professionals in the field of education often work closely with the colleges fulfilling mutual needs. During some academic semesters when the service-learning courses are offered, the college students serve as bridges for families to interact and to integrate with school personnel.

Throughout the year, many immigrants benefit from the job opportunities offered by the service industry such as hotels, restaurants, and summer camp programs. These business sectors constantly recruit low-skill laborers when college students return in the fall and the spring and tourists come in the summer. Some immigrants have remained for more than five years and begun to settle down due to work availability, less competition for jobs among immigrants, and the possibility of saving more money since life is more affordable than in urban locations. Earnings are enough for them to survive in the town and to send money back to their home countries, as one of the single, low-skill immigrants expressed:

> …el pueblo es tranquilo y el trabajo está cerca, todo es más barato, entonces hay que hacerle la lucha. (Central American immigrant, single, male)
> [The town is calm and the job is close by, and everything is cheaper, so it is worth the struggle.]

Legal status provides an advantage to the immigrants who have it: it affords them the capital to seek better job opportunities. The undocumented low-skill workers remain at the restaurants and in private housekeeping. Their mobility is low. However, documented low-skill workers have opportunities to find permanent or better-paying work at hotels, retail businesses such as Walmart Super Center, Home Depot, and some manufacturing industries around the area where they also find a home. In other words, their legal immigration status allows them to move to where resources are:

> *Nosotros vinimos aquí primero a vivir a una finca, pero estábamos encerrados allá y dependíamos mucho de los patrones. Entonces decidimos dejar ese trabajo y venirnos pa'l pueblo. Aquí encontramos trabajo cerquita de la casa y podemos caminar o tomar el bus y hacer la compra.* (female, mother, Mexican origin)
> [We arrived here first to live on a farm, but we felt captive there, and we depended too much on our boss. Then we decided to leave that job and come to the town. Here we found work close to our house, and we can walk or take the bus and go shopping.]

On the contrary, the educators interviewed have to "go away" to find what they need. Although the college educators expressed that they experience a welcoming environment while working on campus and that their children are well served by the public schools, their children cannot enjoy a culturally diverse environment as urban-raised children can. These educators claim that they often feel trapped in a provincial life style. They need to travel away with their children to experience multiculturalism elsewhere. This situation is not experienced only by Hispanics, but also by other non-Hispanic professionals who are brought to work in the education and health sector from more urban areas of the U.S. Therefore, they frequently leave town during academic breaks or vacations. This was particularly stated by one of the college professors with children:

> *Hay una buena educación aquí para los hijos, aunque los maestros a veces no entienden nuestro idioma y nuestra cultura, me siento como que tengo que explicarle a todo el mundo de dónde vengo y mis hijos no encuentran mucha diversidad cultural entre la gente del pueblo, entonces cuando se puede nos vamos a visitar la familia o a pasear por la ciudad.*
> [There is good education here for our children, although teachers sometimes do

not understand our language and culture. I feel like I have to explain to everyone where I come from, and my children do not find much diversity among the town people, so whenever we can, we go to visit family and take trips to the city.]

The temporary Hispanic college students who come from the metropolitan areas offer another interesting case. These young adults first arrive in the town to pursue a college degree. Upon spending four years of their lives in a less crowded area and finding rent more affordable and opportunities to integrate themselves in the economies of this rural setting, they claim that going back to the city where they were raised is not a priority anymore. They integrate easily and can make a living outside the city. One of their strategies to adapt to a more isolated area away from their cultural and linguistic roots is that some of them purposefully seek Hispanics in town through the service-learning opportunities; as a result, they can identify with their culture and feel welcome. This was expressed by a young Dominican college student in his junior year:

Yo vivo en una casa grande con mi novia y hasta tengo mi perro, me falta un año pa' terminar el college, pero no me dan ganas de volverme pa' la ciudad, aquí no hay tanta gente y eso me gusta. Ehh, pero no hay mucho latino, pero hay veces que conozco unos por el trabajo pa' mis clases y luego ellos hacen fiesta o comida y me gusta ir.
[I live in a big house with my girlfriend and I even have my dog, I still have one more year in college, but I don't feel like going back to the city, there are not many people here and I like that. Ehh but there are not many Latin people, but there are times that I meet some when doing my work for class, and then they throw a celebration or cook food and I like to go.]

There have been community meetings and service-learning closure celebrations that have served as a strategy for community empowerment. Immigrants are invited to participate and express their needs in public meetings, which were sponsored by the higher education institutions. This revealed a very unique support in this rural setting for integration. After these gatherings between the Hispanic community at large and the college students, people are starting to participate more often in linguistic and cultural exchanges. Officials from the city, the school district, the commission of human rights of the town, and the colleges' administrators are currently engaged in conversations regarding the possibility of creating a multi-ethnic community center and a cooperative where these immigrant groups can interact, bring ethnic products and educate the rural larger community in multiculturalism and multilingualism. This action may be unique to the work initiated in this town due to the presence of higher education institutions.

Religious Congregations and Schools as a Source of Hispanic Network
Many immigrant groups rely on their religious organizations as a system of support. The churches themselves are already a well-established network where resources can be mobilized to help the settlement of immigrant groups, and Hispanic groups are not exceptional in this regard. The Hispanic immigrant groups are commonly bounded not only by the Spanish they speak, but also their Catholicism. Yet Christian congregations in this particular town do not work as well as those in urban settings where Spanish-speaking congregations can be easily found. Spanish-speaking congregations are especially comforting for those who lack English proficiency, and for those who wish to associate more with congregations organized by the people from the same country of origin. Cultural bonding can be established more easily. However, in a predominately English speaking town, Hispanic immigrants find no religious service in Spanish; therefore, they are not particularly attracted to one congregation. As Hispanic immigrants develop their proficiency in English, they integrate into diverse churches of various Christian denominations. Their active participation in spiritual practices depends on their jobs, the free time they have, as well as whether there are children in the family. Some families find some religious networks that are more pertinent to their needs. Since the town itself is a cluster type of social networks in relation to work or school connections for example, immigrants may find comfort if they meet other attendees who come from the families of their children's schoolmates.

As was mentioned before, the heterogeneous Hispanic immigrant groups in this small town have varied needs and adaptation strategies. In general, they feel welcomed by the public school personnel. Parents are invited to take the opportunity to learn English as a Second Language (ESL) at the adult education program offered by the school district. The adult education program, unstructured in terms of curriculum and proficiency levels, becomes extremely important as a departure point for integration and construction of a social network. Various immigrants, not only Hispanics, continue to attend the adult ESL classes, not only for the improvement of their English, but also to have something to do and somebody to talk to about anything during their day off from work. The fact that there are not so many Hispanics in town forces them to communicate in English. The immigrants see this as positive, as a way to survive and advance in this country. Ironically, this English educational opportunity for adults becomes the source of a Spanish language network used to fulfill a need for a language community enclave. They can locate other Spanish-speaking fellows in these English classes.

Role of Languages in Settling
The role of English and Spanish in the adaptation process is identified as important to the Hispanic immigrants' settlement. First, many residents who were born and raised in town have never left the area. This group often sees the presence of other languages and the arrival of immigrants who speak other languages as a drastic change in their communities; thus their attitudes toward a multi-lingual community may not always be as positive. Some immigrant families, and the Hispanic college students, feel that they have to face some obstacles when using Spanish in public and encouraging their young generations to maintain their heritage language. The isolation from other Spanish speaking groups and the need to communicate in English for daily survival limit the opportunity to use the heritage language. This difficulty was expressed during one of the interviews with a Mexican mother:

> *La hija me contesta más en español, pero este muchacho no me quiere hablar español, maestra por favor consígame un estudiante del college de México para que me le enseñe y le hable en español.*
> [My daughter answers me more in Spanish, but this boy doesn't want to talk to me in Spanish. Please, teacher (addressing to the interviewer who is a Spanish-speaking professor at the college), get me a college student from Mexico to teach and talk to him in Spanish.]

Children often grow up with passive bilingualism in Spanish; their comprehension is greater than their speaking fluency. Children's speaking fluency in Spanish increases as relatives from home countries come to visit, and Spanish usage may be encouraged at home. There are also single adults who rent a room from some of the immigrant families. This allows for more

Spanish spoken by adults surrounding the child. When Hispanic college students serve the immigrant children, then there is a positive message passed onto these children about speaking Spanish as a heritage language. In addition, Hispanic families with a steady income often include satellite TV services in their budget that allow them to have multiple channels in Spanish and stay connected to the homeland remotely. Therefore, some children are exposed to Spanish media, mostly adult television shows, such as soap operas or news. All of this input helps develop passive bilingualism.

Furthermore, not only do some immigrant parents actively seek out other Spanish-speaking students who can help maintain the heritage language for their children, but also highly educated non-Hispanic professionals who have the same desire. Students and professionals who seek to improve their Spanish skills see the Spanish-speaking community as a resource to enhance their language fluency. In this unique situation, immigrants, college students, and professionals who hold a positive attitude towards the use of other languages are happy to develop a network where Spanish can be used with comfort and confidence.

The school district and the two colleges provide an atmosphere where multi-language use is welcome and encouraged. The Hispanic immigrant families with small children benefit from these institutions. When these immigrants seek help related to language needs and find resources available for them, they develop a sense of belonging to the community. At the same time, when college students volunteer at the English language adult education program, the encounter generates more opportunities for the immigrants to get individual attention. They can tell their stories and ask questions that will eventually help them navigate within the community. In the same manner, through the service-learning activities, these immigrants observe a genuine interest from the students who are willing to learn Spanish and practice communicative skills with them. A proof of this integration sentiment was noted during a community gathering in December 2012. The Hispanic community and other non-Hispanic community leaders were invited to the meeting. The two colleges were involved in bringing together various academic departments and their students from Foreign Languages, Sociology, Education, Nursing, and Africana and Latino Studies. The meeting intended to open a forum where various members of the community, including the Hispanic families as well as the college students, could express their needs. A highlight of the meeting was the need for linguistic exchange in Spanish. Intriguingly, the members of the Hispanic community offered themselves as Spanish teachers and conversational partners for the college students, rather than demanding English language assistance. Obviously the Hispanic community perceived themselves at this meeting more as resource for the overall community than an obligation.

Furthermore, Hispanic children in this town feel unique and different from the mainstream students in the public school system. This rural town only offers public education. Regardless of their socioeconomic or cultural backgrounds, all children attend the public schools in town. Hispanic children grow up with two languages: one private and one public. In this particular rural town, school personnel show great support for and interest in the immigrant language. Participants interviewed stated that teachers often try to enhance their communication with parents by trying themselves to use some Spanish or seeking a bilingual speaker to serve as a bridge. In the case of the families, the language broker's responsibility among children was observed mostly among the low-education level group (see Martinez et al., 2009, for details of the role of a Language Broker).

Parents' involvement varied according to the amount of hours each of them work, free time, and opportunities to get involved with school, and the involvement also depended on who was responsible for picking up the children at the end of the school day. It was also found that in this town, parents often do not necessarily have to rely only on their children as language brokers because there is support of professional staff from the schools, the colleges, and the educated people in the community who serve as a bridge for these families' needs in regard to their children's education. In addition, these immigrants in general feel more prompted to use their English skills for daily survival and school is one location for this usage.

One group that deserves a different analysis in regard to language use is the Puerto Ricans. They present a different experience with language interaction. The two Puerto Rican families interviewed are second and third generation with many years of residency in the U.S. The language shift began before arriving in the rural community. Therefore recovering and maintaining the heritage language becomes more difficult for them than for the other Hispanics. Puerto Ricans stated that people discriminated against them for two reasons: their country of origin, and coming from the U.S. metropolitan areas. This situation pressures the children at times to shift into English entirely. However, in the case of one family with three boys brought into the small town by their parents seeking a better living place, the experience of passive bilingualism and growing up bicultural has presented new opportunities for them. The eldest, with more Spanish oral skills, found a job in one of the big stores in town that required at least one bilingual sales associate. His heritage and oral proficiency in Spanish made him competitive to obtain the job. The other two boys with less oral fluency and passive bilingualism enrolled in the public college and felt the need to associate with other Hispanics in an environment where this population is small. They joined Latino-recognized fraternities and provided service for the community as is required of all recognized Greek life on campus. They also took elementary Spanish courses at the college to become more proficient and to fulfill their language requirement.

The second Puerto Rican family interviewed is a second-generation young couple. They arrived in this rural town with an almost complete shift into English already. They had two small children and one more coming at the time of the interview. Life was becoming too difficult for them to maintain a family of five; therefore, they decided that one of the parents would return to college and complete a degree for opening more opportunities. The young father started a college career with government assistance and decided to take up two majors, one of these being Spanish. He started recovering his heritage language in an intermediate course where he used his passive bilingualism and slowly learned the grammatical aspects of the language as well as increasing his vocabulary. Currently, he is in his last year at college and working at one of the local banks where he uses Spanish purposely as he encounters Hispanic customers.

The young Hispanic college students arriving in this town to pursue a college degree frequently experience the need to connect to their Hispanic heritage; however, they find it difficult in a rural town where most of the population is white and English speaking. While taking courses in Spanish, they are invited to take part in service-learning activities, which take place in the larger community. All these community practices invigorate Spanish language maintenance and develop social networks that assist the immigrant families in their rural settlement experience as well as developing Spanish recovery among young adult college students and generating a sense of social responsibility. This study's current findings in the use of Spanish as a heritage language prove the point made by Rivera-Mills (2012) when she states that Spanish is taking a different path from previous immigrant languages in the U.S., and that more research is needed with a distinct approach (see Beaudrie & Fairclough, 2012).

This particular service-learning practice between the college courses and the community in town facilitates in the development of community networks that generate interest in preserving or recovering Spanish as a heritage language. This provides a warm Spanish-speaking environment where these immigrants feel comfortable to settle in. Even if they have to overcome barriers in using English, the help is available. Overall, the welcoming presence of the schools and colleges helps the immigrants with whichever language is needed for various purposes. This situation helps the settlement of the immigrants who have an opportunity to develop their roots in this town.

Discussion and Conclusion

Census data constantly reveals a steady increase of Hispanic population not only in the country as a whole, but also in non-metropolitan areas. It becomes necessary to observe trends in movement and settlement that may transform localities. We started with the question concerning the motives that drive these Hispanic immigrants to move to rural areas and found the main answers to be: affordability for all, regardless of education level, legal documentation or marital status; and for those with families, the tranquility offered by the town, the family-friendly environment, and the existing higher education institutions present an irresistible attraction to settle and raise a family in this rural town.

The relocation of Hispanics into the north central region of this state in the US Northeast and particularly in rural areas happens because of increased work opportunities and more affordable cost of living, which has become difficult to find in crowded urban places where competition for jobs is greater and the cost of real estate is higher. Participants expressed that raising their children in a small setting is easier and that there are more opportunities for their children to become involved in extracurricular activities that may be affordable for some Hispanic families. Affordability was one of the factors reported as a strong pull factor. Later as they navigate the town, they find that the presence of higher education institutions and the support from schools offered by local community leaders become reasons for settling in town.

The current study suggests that the sentiment of permanent settlement is directly connected to the networks they construct in contact with the overall population and community leaders. These networks allow the Hispanic immigrants to find jobs, to buy houses regardless of their undocumented status, and to find opportunities for their children to grow up safely. Children develop confidence and independence in an environment like a small, rural community, where it is easy to have personal space, walk home from school, go to parks, rivers, and lakes, and participate in afterschool sports available for them in this town. They feel that the town provides a family-oriented environment for people with children.

For the immigrants who remain single in this rural town, affordability is their main driving factor. Life is difficult anyway in isolation, but these individuals share homes with other immigrants with families. They are surrounded by the immigrant family networking connections and often take advantage of these contacts to change jobs and find places that rent rooms, as well as to use the tutoring services provided by the college students. These single individuals then give back sometimes by supervising the children when parents are working. The small Hispanic population encourages intragroup connection that facilitates mutual help for daily survival.

Our second research inquiry was to observe the role of the languages in rural settings, and it was found that community support is not only necessary for the newcomers to feel welcome, but also to perceive a positive language attitude for Spanish use and maintenance. School leaders become key persons for the integration of Hispanic immigrants, and it was revealed that the presence of the higher education institutions in this rural setting becomes helpful for the settlement of Hispanic immigrants and encouragement of Spanish maintenance as a heritage language. The fact that the public college offers service-learning projects gives the message that somebody is caring for their success in the community. Adults with families may find it difficult to pass their language to their children; however, the connection between the Hispanic college students tutoring Hispanic children motivates these second generation Hispanic children to maintain their heritage language. The success of children in this group heavily depends on the concerned school personnel and the aid they may receive from college student volunteers.

In sum, heritage language use within rural environments is particular to each family's experience. The increase of the Hispanic population nationally, their attachment to language as an important identity factor, their need for oral proficiency in order to communicate with extended family, and the children's roles as linguistic and cultural brokers for their Hispanic parents have served as integrative motivators for second and third generations of Hispanics to recover or maintain Spanish as a heritage language. The general perception that Spanish is used very actively in the United States encourages parents to pass their language on to their children, and Hispanic parents report being more conscious about the language spoken at home and the demands and experiences they provide for their children to help them develop proficiency and be more than passive bilinguals. Language maintenance strategies may be fulfilling cultural values and identity construction as a result of a greater support from the majority who may see bilingualism as positive (see examples in Montoya, 2009; 2015). Although more research is needed in rural settings in order to discover how languages are used privately and what strategies parents use to pass their language on to US-born children, we have found in this study that community networks are necessary to maintain heritage languages even in places where opportunities to use the these languages are reduced. In turn, the retention of heritage language creates a larger Spanish speaking community in which the immigrants feel comfortable.

In conclusion, the current study indicates that settlement and adaptation experienced by Hispanic rural immigrants differ based on two factors: their documented status and level of education. These two factors mark the challenges experienced by the immigrants who decide to move to rural settings. The two higher education institutions are sources for high-skill employment, which requires professors with advanced knowledge of Spanish language and culture, and promotes the use of Spanish among Hispanic immigrant families residing in town through the service-learning opportunities. This interaction invigorates networks that require the use of Spanish. This reality is unique to this town, and it may not be present in other rural towns in the area. The role of heritage languages in the settlement and adaptation experience may be distinctly lived in urban versus rural settings. It was perceived in this study that maintaining cultural and linguistic identity becomes positive as Hispanic immigrants see themselves as unique individuals and are encouraged to contribute to the cultural diversity of the town. In the presence of highly educated immigrants along with less educated others, proficiency in Spanish constitutes a resource for advanced educational practices required by the colleges in this town. This makes the immigrant settlement experience exceptional and more positive. More comparative studies are needed throughout the rural United States in order to discover the particular conditions that would determine in what ways rurality poses challenges or offers comfort to Hispanic immigrants.

References

Beaudrie, S. M., & Fairclough, M. (Eds.). (2012). *Spanish as a heritage language in the United States: The state of the field.* Washington, DC: Georgetown University Press.

Chiang, S., & Leung, H. H. (2011). Making a home in US rural towns: The significations of home for Chinese immigrants' work, family, and settlement in local communities. *Community, Work & Family, 14*(4), 469-486. doi:10.1080/13668803.2011.574871

Cohen, J. H., & Chavez, N. M. (2013). Latino immigrants, discrimination and reception in Columbus, Ohio. *International Migration, 51*(2), 24-31. doi:10.1111/imig.12032

De Haymes, M. M., & Kilty, K. M. (2007). Latino population growth, characteristics, and settlement trends: Implications for social work education in a dynamic political climate. *Journal of Social Work Education, 43*(1), 101-116. doi:10.5175/JSWE.2007.200400493

De la Roca, J., Ellen, I. G., & O'Regan, K. M. (2014). Race and neighborhoods in the 21st century: What does segregation mean today? *Regional Science and Urban Economics, 47*(SI: Tribute to John Quigley), 138-151. doi:10.1016/j.regsciurbeco.2013.09.006

Donato, K. Y. (2007). Recent immigrant settlement in the nonmetropolitan United States: Evidence from internal census data. *Rural Sociology, 72*(4), 537-559. doi:10.1526/003601107782638666

Flores, L. Y., May, S. F., Jeanetta, S., Saunders, L., Valdivia, C., Arévalo Avalos, M. R., & Martínez, D. (2015). Latina/o immigrant integration in the rural Midwest: Host community resident and immigrant perspectives. *Journal of Latina/o Psychology, 3*(1), 23-39. doi:10.1037/lat0000029

Guevarra, R. P. Jr. (2013). Mexicans and Mexican Americans, 1940-Present. In E. R. Barkan (Ed.), *Immigrants in American history: Arrival, adaptation, and integration* (pp. 1119 -1133). Santa Barbara, CA: ABC-CLIO, LLC.

Hall, W. J., Chapman, M. V., Lee, K. M., Merino, Y. M., Thomas, T. W., Payne, B. K., & Coyne-Beasley, T. (2015). Implicit racial/ethnic bias among health care professionals and its influence on health care outcomes: A systematic review. *American Journal of Public Health, 105*(12), e60-76. doi:10.2105/AJPH.2015.302903

Hanna, A. V., & Ortega, D. M. (2016). Salir adelante [Perseverance]: Lessons from the Mexican immigrant experience. *Journal of Social Work, 16*(1), 47-65. doi:10.1177/1468017314560301

Huntington, S. P. (2004). The Hispanic challenge. *Foreign Policy, 141*, 30-45.

Janzen, R., Stobbe, A., Dejean, F., & Ochocka, J. (2014). The role of churches in immigrant settlement. *Canadian Diversity, 11*(1), 86-95.

Jentsch, B., & Simard, M. (2009). *International migration and rural areas: Cross-national perspectives.* Surrey, UK: Ashgate Publishing.

Jones, R. C. (Ed.). (2008). *Immigrants outside megalopolis.* New York: Lexington Books.

Kang, H. H., Haddad, E., Chen, C., & Greenberger, E. (2014). Limited English proficiency and socioemotional well-being among Asian and Hispanic children from immigrant families. *Early Education & Development, 25*(6), 915-931. doi:1 0.1080/10409289.2014.883664

Khoir, S., Du, J. T., & Koronios, A. (2015). Linking everyday information behavior and Asian immigrant settlement processes: Towards a conceptual framework. *Australian Academic & Research Libraries, 46*(2), 86-100. doi:10.1080/0004862 3.2015.1024303

Leung, H. H. (2007). Roads less taken: The settlement of Chinese immigrants in small towns. *Asian and Pacific Migration Journal, 16*(1), 101-120.

Leung, H. H., & Mohammad, F. (2004). *Asian Indians in small town: Settling or struggling?* Unpublished manuscript.

Lin, J. (1998). Globalization and the revalorizing of ethic places in immigration gateway cities. *Urban Affairs Review, 34*(2), 313-339. doi:10.1177/107808749803400206

Logan, J. E., Alba, R. D., Zhang, W. (2002). Immigrant enclaves and ethnic communities in New York and Los Angeles. *American Sociological Review, 67*(2), 299-322.

Long, D. R. (2003). Spanish in the community students reflect on Hispanic cultures in the United States. *Foreign Language Annals, 36*(2), 223-232. doi: 10.1111/ j.1944-9720.2003.tb01472.x

Martinez, C. R., McClure, H. H., & Eddy, J. M. (2009). Language brokering contexts and behavioral and emotional adjustment among Latino parents and adolescents. *Journal of Early Adolescence, 29*(1), 71-98. doi: 10.1177/0272431608324477

Massey, D. S. (1986). The settlement process among Mexican migrants to the United States. *American Sociological Review, 51*, 670-684.

Massey, D. S., Arango, J., Hugo, G., Kouaouci, A., Pellegrino, A., & Taylor, J. E. (1993). Theories of international migration: A review and appraisal. *Population and Development Review, 19*(3), 431-466.

McGlynn, A. P. (2015). Black males and Latinos: Aspiration, achievement, and equity. *Education Digest, 80*(5), 57-60. doi:10.1080/00131881.2012.710089

Mines, R., & Massey, D. (1985). Patterns of migration to the United States from two Mexican communities. *Latin American Research Review, 20*(2), 104-123.

Montoya, M. C. (2009). Maintenance of Spanish as a heritage language in a global world. In H. H. Leung, M. Hendley, R. Compton, & B. Haley (Eds.), *Imagining globalization: Language, identities and boundaries* (pp. 63-84). New York: Palgrave Macmillan/St. Martin's Press.

Montoya, M. C. (Ed). (2015). *Mi vida en los Estados Unidos* [My life in the United States]. New York: El Pozo.

Ospino, H. (2014, May 18). The church's changing face. *Our Sunday Visitor.* pp. 9-12.

Pager, D., Bonikowski, B., & Western, B. (2009). Discrimination in a low-wage labor market: A field experiment. *American Sociological Review, 74*(5), 777-799. doi:10.1177/000312240907400505

Paris Pombo, M. D. (2006) Transiciones de género y etnicidad: las mujeres triquis en el Valle de Salinas [Transitions of gender and ethnicity: Triqui women in the Salinas Valley]. In I. Wehr (Ed.), *Un continente en movimiento. Migraciones en América Latina* [A continent in movement: Migration in Latin America] (pp.131-142) Madrid: Iberoamericana/Vervuert.

Pfeffer, M. J., & Parra, P. A. (2004/2005). *Immigrants and the community rural New York initiative.* Retrieved from http://www.acsf.cornell.edu/Assets/ACSF/docs/events/policy/20100924-11-2004-immigrants_community.pdf

Portes, A. (1987). The social origins of the Cuban enclave economy of Miami. *Sociological Perspectives, 30*(4), 340-372. doi: 10.2307/1389209

Reimers, D. M. (2005). *Other immigrants: The global origins of the American people.* New York: New York University Press.

Rivera-Mills, S. V. (2012). Spanish heritage language maintenance: Its legacy and its future. In S. M. Beaudrie & M. Fairclough (Eds.), *Spanish as a heritage language in the United States: The state of the field* (pp. 21-42). Washington, DC: Georgetown University Press.

Rumberger, R. W., Lee, J. S., & Wiley, T. G. (2009). *The education of language minority immigrants in the United States.* Bristol, UK: Multilingual Matters.

Sagás, E. (2013). Dominicans and Dominican Americans, 1940-Present. In E. R. Barkan (Ed.), *Immigrants in American history: Arrival, adaptation, and integration* (pp. 881-890). Santa Barbara, CA: ABC-CLIO, LLC.

Spener, D. (2004). Mexican migrant-smuggling: A cross-border cottage industry. *Journal of International Migration and Integration, 5*(3), 295-320. doi: 10.1007/s12134-004-1016-8

Torres-Rouff, D. S. (2013). Mexicans and Mexican Americans, 1870-1940. In E. R. Barkan (Ed.), *Immigrants in American history: Arrival, adaptation, and integration* (pp. 507-520). Santa Barbara, CA: ABC-CLIO, LLC.

United States Census Bureau. (2000). *Profile of general demographic characteristics by geographic area.* Retrieved from http://censtats.census.gov/data/NY/1603654881.pdf?cssp=SERP

United States Census Bureau. (2010). *Profile of general population and housing characteristics: 2010.* Retrieved from http://quickfacts.census.gov/qfd/states/36/3654881.html?cssp=SERP

United States Census Bureau. (2015). Newsroom: Hispanic heritage month. Profile America Facts for Features: cb15-ff.18. Washington, DC: U.S. Department of Commerce. Retrieved from https://www.census.gov/newsroom/facts-for-features/2015/cb15-ff18.html

Vecchione, J. (2009). Bienvenidos a Fleischmanns-An Immigrant Community in Rural America. [Youtube video]. Retrieved from http://www.youtube.com/watch?v=qALS_-krAEA

Wei, L., & Teixeira, C. (2014). *The housing and economic experiences of immigrants in US and Canadian cities.* Toronto: University of Toronto Press.

Wortham, S., Clonan-Roy, K., Link, H., & Martínez, C. (2013). Scattered challenges, singular solutions: The new Latino diaspora, the surging Hispanic and Latino population across the country has brought new. *Phi Delta Kappan, 94*(6), 14-19. doi: 10.1177/003172171309400604

CHAPTER 10

CRITICAL ANALYSIS OF NATION-BUILDING AND MAINTENANCE THROUGH DISCOURSE: *Transition in Slovenia*

Anton Vegel
Kent State University

By considering the "reality" of a nation-state as an imagined community that is not inherently dependent on the make-up of its population, and policy creation as a discursive process with ideological values and goals, our view of national issues can ultimately be that of constructed reality. Such constructions can work towards justifying and legitimizing public and political discourse regardless of their actual reflection of reality by utilizing invisible and imagined resources, such as symbolic power and historical revisionism (Bourdieu, 1991; Luthar & Sazu, 2012). Particularly, transition countries are often predisposed to the implications of ethnic nationalism and romantic nationalist ideology due to their contingent desires, which often out-group a portion of the population through exclusionary attitudes and action (Cox, 2005; Raijman, Davidov, Schmidt, & Hochman, 2008). Such conditions ultimately challenge the believed permanence of fundamental human rights as well as the fixed notions of society, community, nation, and ethnicity (Maybin, 2013).

Slovenia, as a transition state, specifically, shows evidence of nationalist ideology in public and political discourse that does not reflect their state reality. I would like to show how discourse has been relevant in Slovenia (a) in its nation-building, through the creation of its first global atlas and the development of exclusive and autonomous toponymy, while spatially repositioning itself towards Europe and away from the Balkans; and (b) in its national maintenance, through the promotion of ethnic nationalist ideology in opposition to state realities by textually diverting responsibility of particular minorities and refugees that contrast with historical revisionist goals (Lindstrom, 2003; Urbanc, Fridl, Kladnik, & Perko, 2006).

Background

Slovenia is a particularly relevant research context due to its recent independence and current transition. Slovenia seceded from Yugoslavia in 1991 and gained national independence before other constituent states. Slovenia also gained membership to the European Union (EU) and the North Atlantic Treaty Organization (NATO), showing a relatively quick move towards Europe and away from the Balkans (Lindstrom, 2003; Wachtel, 1998). Before this move, the Spring of Nations had emphasized language questions and promoted language to equal status of national questions. As a result, while developing their national question, the Slovenian state relied on language as a centralizing tool for their unity and was ultimately able to develop its national idea through linguistic isolation and autonomy from Yugoslavia and Serbian cultural hegemony (Dolenc, 2006; Jesenšek, 2010).

However, Slovenia's national contingent aim was clearly challenged as it joined the Yugoslavian union, and its linguistic questions were challenged as it determined how to cultivate Slovenian language while facing the economic capital associated with German or the unity associated with Serbian and Croatian (Rogel, 1994; Roter, 2003; Wachtel, 1998). Despite these challenges, Slovenia reached its national contingent aim by seceding from Yugoslavia, although national and linguistic questions still exist in post-communist Slovenia (Wachtel, 1998).

From what has been presented, two important details about Slovenia are important to consider:

1. Due to its size and because it's autonomous goals were ultimately unrealizable for centuries, Slovenia is said to maintain evidence of smallness. A distinct root of this notion might be related to Slovenia's historical inferiority under the Habsburg Monarchy and Yugoslavia (Erjavec, 2008; Rogel, 1994; Roter, 2003).
2. Slovenian language was largely the most significant homogeneous tool promoting its national identity (Roter, 2003).

The following reported data show a sample from 1981 to 1987 regarding whether Slovenians felt that immigrants endangered employment or language. Initially, employment was believed to be more endangered than language (1981-1982, employment: 33%, language: 28%). However, closer to 1991, opinions changed (1986, employment: 33%, language: 39%; 1987, language: over 65%). Slovenians increasingly came to believe that language was more endangered than employment (Roter, 2003). The data of immigrant fear can also be seen to correlate with the arrival of immigrants and Slovenian independence in 1991. Slovenia's subordination to Yugoslavia marked the greatest influx of immigrants from greater Yugoslavia, particularly between 1971 and 1990 (Žitnik, 2008).

Considering this relationship, opinions of Slovenia language endangerment follow a framework of perceived threat. Perceived threat, as described by Raijman, Davidov, Schmidt, and Hochman (2008), can "mediate the relationship between national attachments and discriminatory attitudes, and operate as a catalyst for the emergence of ethnic exclusionism" (p. 200). This is seen in Slovenia's inclusion and exclusion initiatives related to Europe, the Balkans, and ex-Yugoslavian immigrants, further emphasizing that in transition countries out-groups are often denied rights (Cox, 2005; Roter, 2003).

Minority Issues

Frameworks. Bourdieu (1991) illustrates that political action not only aims to but also has the power to make and unmake groups according to dominant interests and that it is symbolic power that constructs the legitimacy of reality. This power also reiterates and manipulates our understanding of the world and is particularly relevant it contexts of ethnic and regional ideology. Slovenia's lack of defined borders before joining Yugoslavia and the border negotiations between Italy, Hungary, and Austria present opportunities for this struggle. Furthermore, these symbolic productions provide a critical view of policy as a discursive process that is a vehicle for ideologically-charged values from motivated stakeholders (Stevens, 2009). This view is crucial because policies' overt and covert goals can deviate from each other and can therefore promote nationalist ideology under the guise of attending to state reality demanding a deeper investment in the deconstruction of these goals (Kymlica & Grin, 2003).

In consideration of the "reality" of a nation-state as an imagined community that is not inherently dependent on the make-up of its population, two statements by Roter (2003) illuminate the view that Slovenian policy creation (and the general policy motivation of nation-states) is motivated by its attendance to national ideology versus state reality:

1. "The fact that nothing was done to accommodate various aspects of the heterogeneous ethnic reality of Slovenia seems to be predominantly related to the emphasis ... to protect the Slovenian nation" (p. 235), and
2. "[they] preserve their identity on the one hand, and not knowing (or not wanting to know) how to address the growing numbers of ethnic minorities that do not fit into the carefully crafted concept of national minority" (pp. 235-236).

Furthermore, even when particular rights are provided to target groups as welfare initiatives, they are not always accessible to the target groups. Williams (2011) explains that through neo-liberal practice, when minorities are free from government control, it can not be inherently deduced that they will have access to their rights and that even a more overt empowerment of rights might actually result in covert regulation.

In another view, Raijman, Davidov, Schmidt, and Hochman (2008) relate the membership status provided to immigrants to chauvinism, patriotism, and the perception of threat. Specifically, perception of threat has been detailed as an element of Slovenian perception towards non-immigrant minorities through public opinion and as a result further provides support for the notion of Slovenian smallness while detailing its contribution to ethnic exclusionism. Additionally, two theoretical explanations describe these exclusionary attitudes towards migrants: "the first stresses the role of national attachments in explaining discrimination against out-group populations; the second stresses the role of perceptions of competition on the socio-economic level on exclusionary attitudes towards migrants" (p. 198). These frameworks can be seen reflected in Slovenia's detachment from the Balkan regions (and populations), as well as their attendance to non-indigenous immigrants (and refugees).

To analyze the Slovenia context, critical discourse analysis (CDA) was utilized. CDA is concerned with issues of inequality and domination that are maintained, reiterated, and reproduced through discourse (contributing to social reproduction). CDA thus suggests a deconstruction of discourse that is beyond the implicit level or presupposition. This approach is in turn necessary when attempting to understand sociolinguistic and sociocultural issues (Bijeikiene, 2008; Durant, 1998; van Dijk, 2001, 2009). The critical goals of CDA further attempt to answer questions regarding (in the concern of sociolinguistics) the social consequences of misunderstanding and misrepresenting speech patterns as socially determined and (in sociocultural issues) the naturalization process of ideologies and their maintenance (Fairclough, 1995). Although social reproduction cannot be considered inherently negative, the uncritical reproduction of dominant ideologies that perpetuate stigmatized and marginalized status threatens fundamental and basic human rights (Edwards, 2003).

Ultimately, by perceiving public and political discourse as a discursive process inherently injected with ideological values with overt and covert goals, a critical deconstruction of this process is necessary. This study approaches discourse analysis through meaning (i.e., the message that is inherently ideologically charged with a target trajectory), interaction (i.e., the reaction or reproduction of ideology), and cognition (i.e., how the uptake of discourse shapes or reiterates ideologies or acts as a mediator between ideology and reification) to deconstruct the discursive processes relevant to nation-building and maintenance (van Dijk, 2009). The influence that discourse ultimately has over the reproduction of ideology and thus social reproduction suggests how important critically analyzing discourse and its productions can be to illuminate the maintenance of ideologies.

Following van Dijk's suggestions, the literature review (see below) will attempt to (a) contribute to the understanding and the solution of serious social problems, especially those that are caused or exacerbated by public text and talk, (b) be defined in terms of international human rights, and (c) take into account the interests, the expertise, and the resistance of those groups that are the victims of discursive injustice and its consequences.

The following articles were accumulated in part as an attempt to develop a context model for analysis. The articles help to develop context by providing a spatiotemporal setting, which is post-Yugoslavian Slovenia currently in a physical and ideological context between the Balkans and Europe. This includes (a) participants with identities, roles, and relationships (i.e., citizens and politicians), (b) goals (i.e., trajectories), (c) knowledge and ideologies (i.e., background), as well as (d) current on-going social action related to the context (i.e., recent publications and public records).

Minorities. Two points are initially important for detailing the discursive representations of minorities in Slovenia. The first point is that the Slovenian government distinguishes between autochthonous and non-autochthonous minorities. By doing this Slovenia overtly and covertly works to protect ethnically Slovenian minorities in Italy and Hungary. The second point is the situation of the "erased" and other post-Yugoslavian minority issues regarding statelessness and refugees.

The distinction made between the autochthonous and the non-autochthonous minorities in Slovenia is largely contingent on whether or not the individuals came from the former Yugoslavian constituent states. Cabada (2011) details three minority types that were considered throughout 1992 in constitutional debates (as they are still referenced today). The term autochthonous is used for Italian and Hungarian minorities, while the term non-autochthonous is used for all other minorities other than Roma who are considered an ethnic minority. One striking point is that according to Žitnik (2008) the terms autochthonous and non-autochthonous have not been clearly defined in any Slovenian legal text, which makes it very easy to include and exclude particular minorities. Mandelc and Učakar (2011) also note that because of the terms' arbitrary nature, they have been removed from use in EU documents for the purpose of differentiating national and ethnic minorities, yet Slovenia remains an exception. In addition, despite the Council of Europe's Commissioner for Human Rights suggesting to abolish the distinction of autochthonous and non-autochthonous national minorities in 2003, nothing had been reformed. Furthermore, despite the terms' differentiation between minorities from pre-Yugoslavia and post-Yugoslavia, it is not representative of those who were present in Slovenia during Slovenian independence but who lost their citizenship afterwards (Gosselin, 2003; Mandelc & Učakar, 2011).

Although the largest autochthonous minorities are Italians and Hungarians, they only make up approximately 0.4% of the population while nearly 90% of all immigrants are from the former Yugoslavian constituent states, making up the non-autochthonous minority. It can be seen that despite the heterogeneous elements that are present in Slovenia, it is still believed to be a mono-culture at the public and state levels (Žitnik, 2008). This point is further emphasized by analyzing the cultural budget granted to the specific minorities. There is disparity here as well, as Žitnik also relates that Italians alone receive more than 300 times more for their cultural activities per capita than immigrants from the former Yugoslavian constituent states. This cultural attendance can be seen in Article 64, which protects the autochthonous minorities' rights to education in their own languages, and yet it is not guaranteed to new minorities, again re-emphasizing that even at the state level, these non-autochthonous minorities are misrepresented (Mandelc & Učakar, 2011).

In further detail of minorities' rights in media outlets, Gosselin (2003) identifies that because Italians and Hungarians are granted well-defined rights and because new minorities are not positioned as an official minority, there is a great imbalance in access to resources such as media funding for symbolic outlets. Consequently, because of this inequality in access and because such outlets contribute to group identity and membership, the deliberate exclusionary maintenance of these media outlets can be seen as a power struggle between the romantic homogenous national ideology of Slovenia and the heterogeneous reality of the state (Gosselin, 2003; Mandelc & Učakar, 2011; Žitnik, 2008).

Lastly, the following case study reiterates that Slovenia, being in transition status, attends to ideology versus state reality while illuminating the memory act and historical revisionism process still present in the attendance to minority issues (Luthar & Sazu, 2012). Mandelc and Učakar (2011) directly relate Slovenia's move towards democracy and ultimately nation-building and Europeanization as contributing to the "erasure" of close to 25,000 people from the permanent resident register during the citizen registration that marked Slovenian independence. This incident emphasizes what Mandelc and Učakar (2011) call a perforated or deficient democracy.

This issue, despite having occurred during Slovenia's process of restructuring in the early 1990s, is still relevant and can be seen in the 2012 European Court of Human Rights court case, *Kurić and Others v. Slovenia*, which was published as a press release in 2014. According to the press release, "the applicants belong to a group of persons known as the 'erased', who on 26 February 1992 lost their status as permanent residents following Slovenia's declaration of independence in 1991" (The European Court of Human Rights,

Council of Europe, 2014, p. 1). Ultimately, the court found that, parallel to the applicants' complaints, Slovenia had unjustifiably deprived the residents of the legal status as permanent residents of Slovenia.

This case specifically reiterates that much of the proceedings towards the erased have been bottom-up, as stateless individuals must take responsibility for their position. Fundamentally, this action is connected to how national discourse effects our perception of human rights and how citizenship and the populations of a state are not inherently congruent (Mandelc & Učakar, 2011; Maybin, 2013), while simultaneously emphasizing the need of Maybin's (2013) insistence on destabilizing "the fixed notion of 'society', 'community', 'nation' and 'ethnicity'" (p. 548).

Literature and Discourse
Discourse Frameworks

In addition to considering how perceptions of reality are constructed and perpetuated through symbolic power, Chilton and Lakoff's (1995) work particularly emphasizes that metaphors can conceal and reduce details of reality and that understanding them is critical to truly understand what they conceal. Metaphors that are most relevant to understand the maintenance of national ideology have been selected and compared to national ideological maintenance in Slovenia. The following metaphors will be utilized in this analysis: state-as-person metaphor, body metaphor, spatialization metaphor of movement, balance of power metaphor, and container metaphor. These are further detailed below.

The state-as-person metaphor is described by three generalizations:

1. an isolated individual, pitted against all others;
2. a socially cooperative and responsible autonomous individual; or
3. a member of a collective in which individual identity is secondary, or entirely submerged.

Slovenia in particular seems to struggle between the first two identities. The first emphasizes smallness and perception of threat. The second illustrates Slovenia's independence as a historically autonomous region and state and yet its necessary attendance to EU and NATO initiatives as a functioning member. Additionally, Chilton and Lakoff (1995) describe that a metaphor of a person further necessitates a metaphor of a body that "can grow, mature, decline, be healthy, be developed, underdeveloped, weak, strong, diseased" (p. 40) or even in Slovenia's case be young, small, and at times, exhausted. A body metaphor can then also embody disease, which is referenced as "a major part of the new ... nation-state mode of thinking" (p. 44). Spatialization is also applied metaphorically in terms of motion, as it can be seen in Slovenia's physical movement away from the Balkans and towards Europe. Furthermore, the balance of the power metaphor "removes any notion of human will" (p. 51), which can ultimately provide power towards covert initiatives by diverting any direct responsibility. Lastly, a container metaphor suggests that, as a container, its contents can get out "by leakage, spillage, boiling over ... and ... 'penetrate' the secure containers of other states" (p. 53), while the house metaphor (similar to the person metaphor) can identify domestic matters and foreign matters as well as safety and security.

Nation-Building
According to Luthar and Sazu (2012), historical revisionism is aimed at "reclaiming the 'true' history" (p. 886) and legitimizing what is believed to be symbolic by radically reinterpreting the past. They also remark that in Slovenia's post-socialist, post-communist, post-Yugoslavian era, "besides textbooks, a whole range of other texts—ranging from monuments to historical, political, and media discourses—are being mobilized" (p. 886) for this purpose. These processes have been seen in Slovenia as a tool to maintain a monocultural idealization in public opinion and political discourse (Roter, 2003; Žitnik, 2008).

In the pre-Slovenian state regions, Slovenian was constructed as a discrete language from the other South Slavic languages through grammatical developments, its establishment in schools and administrations, and its foundation with newspaper publications in the early and mid-nineteenth century (Rogel, 1994). Furthermore, Slovenia had the highest literacy rates, primary school attendance, and periodical publications compared to the Yugoslavian constituent states as well as the Yugoslavian average (Dolenc, 2006). In addition, the creation of maps has been essential to the process of nation-state idealization, and particularly in the Slovenian case. Urbanc, Fridl, Kladnik, and Perko (2006) describe this process of developing linguistic and ideological autonomy in Slovenia by analyzing the creation of the first Slovenian atlas, the Atlant (Kearns & Berg, 2009; Urbanc, Fridl, Kladnik, & Perko, 2006).

By accepting maps as texts with text trajectories or constructed productions that do not purely mirror objective realities it can be seen that maps have communicative value and contain hidden social foundations created by dedicated intellectual efforts that embody the imagined community of the map-makers, which then reach the map users (Urbanc, Fridl, Kladnik, & Perko, 2006). Furthermore, although toponyms appear to be ideologically innocent, they are in fact ideologically charged, and because of the implicitness in which they are accepted, they often appear as meaningless marks, despite the deliberateness in their creation (Vuolteenaho & Berg, 2009). Particularly for Slovenia, the creation of the Atlant was momentous, as Urbanc, Fridl, Kladnik, and Perko (2006) state, because of its ability to develop a self-image as well as a global identity and legitimize Slovenian as capable of "scientific and cultural creativity of the highest order" (p. 266), which is seen in its ideological attendance and movement towards Europeanization and away from Balkanization.

Maintenance

Implications of Europeanization. Erjavec (2008) presents a dichotomous view of Slovenia's entrance into the EU by presenting headlines and interviews of Slovenian and Carinthian elites. In this review, the headlines of various publications will be presented with a summary of Erjavec's critical discourse analysis while applying Chilton and Lakoff's (1995) metaphors and Maybin's (2013) sociolinguistic research recommendations.

Erjavec (2008) provides two propositions. The first is that Slovenia is welcome in the EU, which can be seen, in referring to Slovenia's acceptance into the EU, with the use of words such as "historic moment," "historic period," and "historic day," sensationally describing the admission. The second is that Carinthia/Austria and Slovenia are (or became) borderless, friendly, and unified, which is expressed by words such as "unity," "borderlessness," and "friendship" (p. 41). Erjavec (2008) then shows how these propositions are (and were) expressed and reproduced textually in headlines and verbally through interviews of political leaders. Selected headlines are presented below for analysis.

Group 1.
A. "Slovenia: Welcome to the EU"[1]

B. "Europe: All under one roof"[2]
C. "Cordially Welcome"[3]
D. "Welcome to Europe"[4]
E. "Slovenia: The lost daughter has returned home"[5]
F. "Carinthia is celebrating with its new neighbor!" (p. 41-42)[6]

Headlines B, E, and F most clearly represent the use of the state-as-person metaphor along with other embodied metaphorical implications. Headline B assumes that the constituent states of the EU are people who all live in the same home, "under one roof," which can therefore delineate the home metaphor notions of domestic and foreign, as those under EU membership are one family, and those without membership are outside of the genealogy, creating a timeless notion of community and society. Headline E also shows the use of the state-as-person metaphor as well as the spatialization metaphor, which suggests that Slovenia physically returned home while also suggesting family membership like Headline B, but further suggesting a subordinate connotation "daughter" (contrasting chauvinism and patriarchal culture). Furthermore, the spatialization metaphor "returned" suggests what is shown in Lindstrom (2003), with Slovenia's movement away from Balkanization. Headline F from the Carinthian/Austrian perspective shows use of the person-as-state metaphor, house metaphor, and spatialization metaphor of a neighbor. The house and spatialization metaphor suggests the notion of community or neighborhood that can further reference safety and security.

Interestingly, however, Erjavec (2008) mentions that home is not always referencing warm intention from the Carinthians/Austrians, as Slovenia's return to Europe also expresses a return to the Habsburg Monarchy where pre-Slovenian regions were inferior for centuries. This notion can be further seen in the following.

Group 2.
G. "Slovenia as an exemplary student, which fulfilled all of the tasks from Brussels in a diligent and precise fashion"[7]
H. "New EU-citizens are the dream of every manager: they are motivated, well educated, diligent and poorly paid"[8]
I. "Their (Slovenian/former communist countries) economy is the hope for our (Carinthian/Austrian/Western European) economy, because it represents economic growth and has cheap work force" (p. 43)[9]

This subordinate view of Slovenia can be traced to early Yugoslavia with the stereotype that "the Serbs rule, the Croats debate, and the Slovenes work" (Vodopivec, 1994, p. 31). However, a different perspective is shown in Lindstrom (2003). In line with Headline E and other interview responses from Erjavec (2008), the token "returned" is used to indicate that while not in Europe, Slovenia and Croatia certainly did not identify with the Balkans, which accomplished a necessary goal for them to enter the EU, that is, distancing themselves from the Balkans and Yugoslavia (Lindstrom, 2003).

As the Carinthia/Austrian discourse focusing on Slovenia suggests (at the very least) an unsophisticated and subordinate southern neighbor, Slovenian discourse on the Balkans suggests a "primitive, lazy, intolerant" (Lindstrom, 2003, p. 317) southern neighbor. Both of these examples follow a framework of chauvinistically differentiating identity by othering the subordinate group and further illuminating attendance to ethnic nationalism and romantic nationalist ideology through exclusion (Lindstrom, 2003; Raijman, Davidov, Schmidt, & Hochman, 2008). Carinthia/Austria, as seen in Headlines G, H, and I, considers the possibility of internal growth through the subjugation of Slovenia's EU membership, thus emphasizing Slovenia's subordinate status as a "student" or "cheap work force." Slovenia, on the other hand was able to strengthen its image as superior and European by essentializing the Balkans as the other.

Lastly, the discourse strategy of othering was also used immediately after Slovenia's declaration of independence by then-President Milan Kuèan, who stated that "as a nation which for more than one thousand years has been integrally involved in the development of Europe, we should like to be reintegrated into the best of the European tradition" (Lindstrom, 2003, p. 317). However, this statement ignores Slovenia's autonomous motivations rejecting Germanization (Thaler, 2013). This motivation highlights, within the discourse, Chilton and Lakoff's (1995) third generalization of a person state metaphor, "a member of a collective in which individual identity is secondary, or entirely submerged" (p. 40), as a means of appearing less hostile or autonomous, which the first two identity generalizations suggest.

Legitimization and representation. The following excerpts detail the analysis of Horvat, Verschueren, and Žagar (2001) and Vezovnik (2013) as well as their further relation to Chilton and Lakoff's (1994) metaphors, Roter's

(2003) notion of Slovenian smallness, and Raijman, Davidov, Schmidt, and Hochman's (2008) details of chauvinism, patriotism, and the perception of threat regarding discourse on the legitimization and representation of particular minorities in Slovenia.

Horvat, Verschueren, and Žagar's (2001) article, "The Pragmatics of Legitimation the Rhetoric of Refugee Policies in Slovenia," details the discourse of transcribed parliamentary meeting records, public record reports, transcribed speeches, and collections of news clippings, focusing on the one-year period from April 1992 to March 1993 regarding the process of Slovenian refugee policy legitimization. The following discourse samples represent support for an overarching trend of ambiguity in policy discourse.

> Group 3.
> J. [...] refugee tide that has already swamped our moral obligations and capabilities of economically exhausted Slovenia calls for new measures despite the infinite readiness [of Slovenia] to do everything within its capacities (p. 19)[10]
> K. [...] the refugees who could be potential criminal offenders [...] will influence the distrust of foreigners about safety (p. 24)[11]

Horvat, Verschueren, and Žagar (2001) describe Excerpt J as utilizing the metaphor of an "uncontrolled natural force" with the use of "tide" and "swamped," which suggests that the refugees are a problem whose future damage should be avoided. In addition, by stating that Slovenia is "economically exhausted" it argues that there is nothing Slovenia can do to help. The use of "exhausted" also utilizes the state-as-person metaphor and in the process relieves the policy makers of the responsibility of solving or improving the refugee issues by misrepresenting the actors involved in the doing process. Furthermore, Excerpt K only references the potential that the refugees can be criminal offenders, yet the claim is not supported by reported past acts. This flawed claim succeeds by weakening the claim through modality (i.e., by using "could be") but still emphasizing that "the distrust of foreigners about safety" is a real issue.

Vezovnik (2013) further illuminates shifts in discourse regarding the erased as the attempts to protect and promote human rights moved to discourse that ultimately victimized the erased and led to a lack of positive action. In utilizing Laclau's (2005) operation (i.e., logic of naming) in support of analyzing the process of the representations provided, Vezovnik (2013) ultimately finds that the representation of the erased was essentially reduced to victim-centric discourse that discouraged attendance to their fundamental human rights.

Group 4.
L. [...] erasing 30,000 people [...], in a society that is not ashamed of its democratic values, cannot happen. This would, however, be a fall into barbarism, which is practiced over there in the Balkans (p. 614)[12]
M. The Constitutional Court then ordered a simple solution to the problem of the Erased, but the Slovenian politics, just prior to joining the European Union, began to solve it in a Balkan way. With a high degree of intolerance, unilateral interpretations, and also xenophobia. (p. 615)[13]
N. [T]he spare change of political games" (p. 618)[14]
O. As those "who are expected to be like a dish disappearing from the political menu" (p. 619)[15]
P. As "a train from some time now put on the second track" (p. 619)[16]

Example L relates democratic regression to barbarism in the Balkans. Further othering is expressed in the spatialization metaphor "over there," which positions Slovenia and the Balkans as physically separated. Vezovnik (2013) details Example N as describing the erased as victims, yet, in this representation, there is no call for political action, and further "political games" and the game metaphor suggests that there must be players, designers, or even actors, yet these are not identified, and instead, they are only described with the adjective "political," leaving any kind of accountability vague and indeterminable (Chilton & Lakoff, 1995; Vezovnik, 2013). Example O shows how the erased are related to an objective "dish," and the political issue is associated with a menu, emphasizing a temporary issue. When related to the container metaphor as a dish item that can be physically taken off of a menu, the statement may even imply that once the dish or issue has been taken off or removed from the menu or political agenda it cannot return, masking the issue's permanence. Excerpt P, similar to Excerpt O, suggests that the erased issue is not important anymore. This problem of importance, despite the positive intentions, may be due to the ambiguity and failure of the spatialization metaphor. For example, putting something on a second track may not innately indicate that it is in a deficient position, traveling towards an inferior destination, or in any other inherently different spatial reality than it was in on the first track. This ambiguity may be further due to a tracks spatial parallelism, which ultimately weakens the attempt to show the subject in a deficient state in the political agenda.

Group 3 and Group 4 show how discourse in Slovenia has been particularly salient in regard to legitimizing and providing representation to particular minorities, specifically ones that do not match the ethnic nationalist goals of Europeanization.

Conclusion

Ultimately, this study shows that discourse and the discursive process is inherently injected with ideological values with overt and covert goals and is especially relevant in nation-building and maintenance that does not always reflect state reality by using Slovenia as a case study. Through Slovenia's position as a small transition state manipulated by notions of chauvinism, patriotism, and perception of threat, symbolic power, historical revisionism, and particular metaphors were utilized to strategically make and unmake groups through discourse (Bourdieu, 1991; Chilton & Lakoff, 1995; Raijman, Davidov, Schmidt, & Hochman, 2008; Roter, 2003; Stevens, 2009). It is shown that discourse has been relevant in nation-building as Slovenia developed linguistic and ideological autonomy through the creation of its first global atlas and the development of exclusive and autonomous toponymy while spatially repositioning itself towards Europe and away from the Balkans. It is also shown through CDA that discourse has been relevant in national maintenance as Slovenia has further maintained its national idea through the promotion of ethnic nationalist ideology in opposition to state reality by ideologically repositioning itself towards Europe through Europeanization and by textually diverting responsibility of particular minorities and refugees that contrast with these goals (Lindstrom, 2003; Urbanc, Fridl, Kladnik, & Perko, 2006). Illuminating these goals deconstructs the romantic and timeless notions of society, community, nation, and ethnicity by showing how they can be maintained without honestly representing the reality of a state (Maybin, 2013).

Notes

1. (2004, April 25) Kärtner Tageszeitung
2. (2004, May 1) Kleine Zeitung

3. (2004, April 28) Kärtner Woche
4. (2004, April 11) Neue Kronen Zeitung
5. (2004, April 25) Kärter Tageszeitung
6. (2004, April 29) Neue Kronen Zeitung
7. (2004, May 11) Wiener Zeitung
8. (2004, May 1) Kurier
9. (2004, April 30) Kleine Zeitung
10. (1992, April 28) Delo
11. (1992, April 29) Dnevnik
12. (2003, March 1) Večer
13. (2004, February 3) Delo
14. (2007, November 3) Večer
15. (2003, December 27) Delo
16. (2003, November 8) Delo

References

Bijeikiene, V. (2008). Critical discourse analysis: An overview and appraisal. *Respectus Philologicus, 13*(18), 104-113. Retrieved from http://www.rephi.khf.vu.lt/en/

Bourdieu, P. (1991). *Language and symbolic power.* Cambridge, UK: Polity Press.

Cabada, L. (2011). Typology of Slovene minorities and differences in their status and rights. *The Annual of Language & Politics and Politics of Identity, 5,* 23-40. Retrieved from www.alppi.eu

Chilton, P., & Lakoff, G. (1995). Foreign policy by metaphor. *Language and Peace,* 37-59. Retrieved from http://georgelakoff.com/writings/

Cox, J. (2005). *Slovenia: Evolving loyalties.* London: Routledge.

Dolenc, E. (2006). Comparative analysis of cultural development statistics: The case of the first Yugoslavia. *East European Quarterly, 39*(4), 465-489. Retrieved from https://www.questia.com/

Durant, A. (1998). Aspectos problematicos del significado: analisis critico del discurso [Critical discourse analysis and social engagement] (P. Tena, Trans.). In M. L. Rojo & R. Whittaker (Eds.), *Poder decir o el poder de los discursos* [Power-speak or the power o discourse] (pp. 121-147). Madrid: Arrecife Producciones.

Edwards, J. (2003). Contextualizing language rights. *Journal of Human Rights, 2*(4), 551-571. doi:10.1080/1475483032000137138

Erjavec, K. (2008). Discourse on the admission of Slovenia to the European Union: Internal colonialism. *Journal of Multicultural Discourse, 3*(1), 36-52. doi:10.1080/17447140802153527

The European Court of Human Rights, Council of Europe. (2014). Question of pecuniary damage decided in Grand Chamber judgment concerning the issue of "erased" people in Slovenia [Press release]. Retrieved from http://hub.coe.int/web/coe-portal/home

Fairclough, N. (1995). *Critical discourse analysis: The critical study of language.* London: Longman.
Gosselin, T. (2003). Minority media in Hungary and Slovenia: Comparative assessment. Ljubljana, Slovenia: *Peace Institute.* Retrieved from http://www.mirovni-institut.si/Main/Index/en/
Horvat, M., Verschueren, J., & Žagar, I. (2001). *The pragmatics of legitimation the rhetoric of refugee policy in Slovenia* (2nd ed., Media Watch). Retrieved from http://mediawatch.mirovni-institut.si/eng/the_pragmatics_of_legitimation.pdf
Jesenšek, M. (2010). Slovene standard language between the centre and the periphery. *Studia Slavica Hung, 55*(2), 279-287. doi:10.1556/SSlav.55.2010.2.13
Kearns, R. A., & Berg, L. (2009). Proclaiming place: Towards a geography of place name pronunciation. In L. Berg & J. Vuolteenaho (Eds.), *Critical toponymies: The contested politics of place naming* (pp. 153-178). Burlington, VT: Ashgate Publishing Company.
Kymlica, W., & Grin, F. (2003). Assessing the politics of diversity in transition countries. In F. Daftary & F. Grin (Eds.), *Nation-building, ethnicity and language politics in transition countries* (pp. 1-27). Budapest, Hungary: Local government and public service reform initiative. Retrieved from http://www.ecmi.de/uploads/tx_lfpubdb/ECMI-Vol-II.pdf
Laclau, E. (2005). *On populist reason.* New York: Verso.
Lindstrom, N. (2003). Between Europe and the Balkans: Mapping Slovenia and Croatia's "return to Europe" in the 1990s. *Dialectical Anthropology, 27*(2-3), 313-329. doi:10.1023/B:DIAL.0000006189.45297.9e
Luthar, O., & Sazu, Z. (2012). Forgetting does (not) hurt. Historical revisionism in post-socialist Slovenia. *Nationalities Papers, 41*(6), 882-892. doi:10.1080/00905992.2012.743510
Mandelc, D., & Učakar, T. (2011). Perforated democracy: Disintegrating state-building, Europeanization and the erased of Slovenia. *Revija Za Sociologiju, 41*(1), 27-49. doi:10.5613/rzs.41.1.3
Maybin, J. (2013). Working towards a more complete sociolinguistics. *Journal of Sociolinguistics, 17*(4), 547-555. doi:10.1111/josl.12047
Raijman, R., Davidov, E., Schmidt, P., & Hochman, O. (2008). What does a nation owe non-citizens? National attachments, perception of threat and attitudes towards granting citizenship rights in a comparative perspective. *International Journal of Comparative Sociology, 49*(2-3), 195-220. doi:10.1177/0020715208088912
Rogel, C. (1994). In the beginning: The Slovenes from seventh century to 1945. In J. Benderly & E. Kraft (Eds.), *Independent Slovenia: Origins, movements, prospects* (pp. 3-21). New York: St. Martin's Press.
Roter, P. (2003). Language issues in the context of Slovenian smallness. In F. Daftary & F. Grin (Eds.), *Nation-building, ethnicity and language politics in transition countries* (pp. 213-238). Budapest, Hungary: Local government and public

service reform initiative. Retrieved from http://www.ecmi.de/uploads/tx_lfpubdb/ECMI-Vol-II.pdf

Stevens, L. P. (2009). Maps to interrupt a pathology: Immigrant populations and education. *Critical Inquiry in Language Studies, 6(1-2)*, 1-14. doi:10.1080/15427580802679245

Thaler, P. (2013). The discourse of historical legitimization: A comparative examination of southern Jutland and the Slovenian language area. *Nationalities Papers, 40*(1), 1-22. doi:10.1080/00905992.2011.633077

Urbanc, M., Fridl, J., Kladnik, D., & Perko, D. (2006). Atlant and the Slovene national consciousness in the second half of the 19th century. *Acta Geographica Slovenica, 46*(2), 251-283. doi:10.3986/AGS46204

van Dijk, T. (2001). Critical discourse analysis. In D. Tannen, D. Schiffrin, & H. Hamilton (Eds.), *Handbook of Discourse Analysis* (pp. 352-371). Oxford: Blackwell.

van Dijk, T. (2009). Critical discourse studies: A sociocognitive approach. In R. Wodak & M. Meyer (Eds.), *Methods of critical discourse analysis* (pp. 62-85). London: Sage.

Vezovnik, A. (2013). Representational discourses on the erased of Slovenia from human rights to humanitarian victimization. *Journal of Language and Politics, 12*(2), 606-625. doi:10.1075/jlp.12.2.01tho

Vodopivec, P. (1994). Seven decades of unconfronted incongruities: The Slovenes and Yugoslavia. In J. Bendery & E. Kraft (Eds.), *Independent Slovenia: Origins, movements, prospects* (pp. 23-46). New York: St. Martin's Press.

Vuolteenaho, J., & Berg, L. (2009). Towards critical toponymies. In L. Berg & J. Vuolteenaho (Eds.), *Critical toponymies: The contested politics of place naming* (pp. 1-18). Burlington, VT: Ashgate Publishing Company.

Wachtel, A. (1998). *Making a nation, breaking a nation: Literature and cultural politics in Yugoslavia*. Stanford, CA: Stanford University Press.

Williams, C. (2011). Paradigm shifts, geostrategic considerations and minority initiatives. *Journal of Ethnic Studies, 66*, 8-23. Retrieved from http://cat.inist.fr/?aModele=afficheN&cpsidt=25336156

Žitnik, J. (2008). Statistical facts are human fates: Unequal citizens in Slovenia. *Journal of Ethnic and Migration Studies, 34*(1), 77-94. doi:10.1080/13691830701708775

CHAPTER 11

THE BENEFITS OF PLAY-BASED LEARNING IN A NATIVE AMERICAN COMMUNITY

Thomas M. Hill, Jr.
University of New Mexico

Introduction

In the post No Child Left Behind educational climate, great attention was focused on how schools are deficient in standardized test performance, how legislation is outdated and insensitive, and how educators are not meeting student needs. Rarely discussed was what can be done to assist students to develop and grow in a society that education has yet to catch up to, both socially and academically.

Most educators that I have worked and studied with have taken a different approach to the traditional "skill and drill" method of instruction. Rather than focus on what the students are lacking, they choose to focus their instruction on their student's strengths, which often attempts to remove the social stigma that comes from high stakes, standards based testing (Hollingworth, 2009).

A consistent flaw with scholastic testing is that it is used to determine school and teacher effectiveness, and financial funding. It is an ineffective form of evaluation for many communities that exist outside of the cultural mainstream. The National Center for Educational Statistics in a 2004 report (as cited in Major & O'Brien, 2005) states that compared to Anglo counterparts, Native American students perform lower on standardized tests across all grade levels and all subject areas.

This is due in large part to the focus of these tests on instruction and assessment using Standard English only and do not acknowledge the needs and abilities of students from diverse language backgrounds (Hollingworth, 2009). For many groups outside of the mainstream culture, schools and curricula do not acknowledge their diverse cultural and linguistic background, removing a key tenant of their educational philosophy at the risk of including non-culturally relevant materials (Brayboy, 2005).

Since the first official Native American Education Policy of 1790, schools have been used as a tool and the institution to undertake the task of assimilation of Native peoples and the eradication of their language and culture (Rehyner & Eder, 2004; Tiller, 2000). For many Native American communities, it has been an ongoing struggle to make mainstream education relevant since first contact from outside explorers and settlers.

Today, these policies are no longer in place, but schools in Native American communities continue to provide inadequate academic instruction and there seems to be little desire to match the performance of Native American students to their mainstream counterparts (Sleeter, 2001). One factor that is influencing this lagging education is that many teachers do not possess adequate knowledge on Native American culture nor are they trained for specific or additional skills to teach in these types of communities (Rehyner & Eder, 2004). Currently, the use of inappropriate curricula and assessment continue to burden Native American students, which not only prevents them from succeeding academically, but also hinders their development and understanding of their place in society.

The number of Native American students that drop out of high school is staggering. For example, according to a 2008 report on a class of students in New Mexico in 2005, 54.7% of Native American high school students dropped out before graduation (New Mexico Voices for Children, n.d.). This is above the national average of 49.4% for Native American Students and above the average of 7% for all students (National Center for Education Statistics, n.d.). In the district where this research was conducted, dropout rates for the 2011 5-year cohort were 31.9% according to the New Mexico Public Education Department (n.d.).

What is more alarming is the overwhelming assumption among a large group of educators is that these culturally diverse students are dropping out because they are failing academically or abusing drugs or alcohol. Such stereotypes are often a conjecture and not based on research (Rehyner & Eder, 2004). Educators of Native American students are aware that the driving forces behind high dropout rates are inappropriate teaching and assessment methods (Hollingworth, 2009). However, there is a change occurring in education that holds potential for not only Native American communities, but for all students outside of the mainstream. One teaching method that is underutilized but holds limitless potential is play-based learning (PBL).

The research theory behind PBL may or may not be effective for all Native American communities, nor do I suggest that they will be effective for every student. The ideas contained in this paper can be utilized for all student cultural groups; however, due to the oral language traditions of Native American communities, PBL has the potential for a greater positive effect in Native American communities.

The Role of Play in Learning

Inequities that exist in education largely stem from educational policies imposed on diverse language and cultural groups. Students exposed to unfamiliar educational contexts struggle with understanding, retention, and application of knowledge. Klenowski (2009) affirms, "To achieve equity the curriculum needs to include valued knowledge and experience, reflective of all groups, not privileging one group to the exclusion of others" (p. 83).

Educators have the responsibility to create a learning environment that allows all students to be successful regardless of context. There are various forms of play, which will be discussed later, through which these goals can be achieved. Students and adults from all cultures at one time in their intellectual and social development have engaged in play in some fashion. Play allows students to express their cognitive faculties in a more relaxed context and fosters growth in the affective domain, which is necessary for the development of creativity (Russ & Kaugars, 2001). This form of creative play often facilitates learning through humor, such as puns, jokes, and various cultural incarnations.

The use of humor can be seen as a building block for literacy skills and the application of humor requires more advanced linguistic and cultural knowledge (Bell, 2005). These forms of knowledge must be present to appropriately use humor in correct ways and is a skill learned through exposure to one's home language and culture. Rarely can this skill be taught in an isolated classroom setting.

Since humor is largely built through unexpected and sometimes sporadic instances, it allows students to draw upon unique linguistic resources that often occur in informal dialogues and playful conversations (Bell, 2005). In doing so, students are able to become more relaxed and take greater risks in their language use. These risks are vital to the success of English Language Learners (ELL), a point I will elaborate on further, by removing language usage from a strict academic pursuit and allowing it to occur in a more natural state. Educators can then provide an opportunity for their students to bridge cultural gaps that may be present in instruction and classroom environments.

In addition to creative play, educators can utilize language play to support language development for both native English speakers and ELL. Language play allows students to experiment, while receiving feedback, through using language in both conversational and academic applications. It should be noted that language play is not always intended to be a fun or creative endeavor, as its counterpart creative play is intended to be, but a means by which learners develop and become familiar with linguistic skills (Bell, 2005). This salient feature is what sets it apart from creative play, which is often viewed as a completely enjoyable pursuit.

Language play is, however, a natural endeavor. It is essential to human thought, culture, learning, and creativity (Antokhin, 2006). It is how children learn the proper use of language during both formal and informal settings. Through experimentation, or play, it allows the learner to use language in a variety of ways and see what works, what is appropriate and not appropriate in various settings.

In a formal classroom setting, language play can take the form of role-play in various literacy activities (Kim & Kellogg, 2008). Though a bit more structured than language play itself, role-play activities allow students to experiment with language in ways that they may not have considered before. With its structure more established, students are able to attempt various forms with guidance and modeling.

Whether play takes the form of creative play, or language play, the element of play is vital to creating a culturally relevant and appropriate learning environment for all students. As mentioned previously, this is due to the presence of play in all cultures. Incorporating this vital element into classroom instruction affords the educator the possibility of influencing all aspects of teaching, not just those found within the literacy domains (Antokhin, 2006). Such examples can be found through role-playing as famous scientists in a science class, or acting out particular amendments of the United States Constitution in a social studies lesson.

Researchers of play are unable to come to a consensus on whether play is a tool for or a result of language learning (Kim & Kellogg, 2008), however, what cannot be refuted are its positive effects on learners of all ability levels. In particular, the use of play for ELL has been well documented though underutilized.

Play for English Language Learners

The role of instruction for ELL students has often been to teach in English using rigid and irrelevant curricula (Nieto, 2010). Success in transitional bilingual education is for students to become fully functional in English (Zuniga-Hill & Barnes, 1995). In doing so, achievement gaps began to widen and ELL students found themselves falling further behind their same-aged peers who were native English speakers.

Though rarely intentional, the attempt to remove a student's culture and language in favor of the mainstream culture and English language is a detrimental act. Zuniga-Hill and Barnes (1995) state, "…the pressure that schools place on students to assimilate is itself an example of educational inequality" (p. 63).

What the ultimate goal of bilingual education should be is a more bidialectal approach, which allows students to comprehend and use features of both Standard English and their home language (Kawakami & Au, 1986). Success in bidialectal uses of language can be viewed as being able to interchange between the two languages to bolster understanding by drawing upon strategies and techniques that are found within each distinct language. An ability to do so fosters success in one or more languages by allowing them to support one another. This type of model is often referred to as the Maintenance Bilingual Education Model that strives to preserve the native language while adding to the second language (Zuniga-Hill & Barnes, 1995). This is no easy task for educators to undertake, however, there are many research-based guiding principles that can be used to model successful bilingual models.

In an effort to create a more equitable learning environment, James Banks (1991, as cited in Zuniga-Hill & Barnes, 1995) developed five dimensions, or components, that educators should employ for their students. These five guiding principles are: content integration, knowledge construction, prejudice reduction, equity pedagogy, and development of an empowering school culture and social structure. Though no educator can be expected to adhere to all five dimensions during every instructional section of the day, they do have direct influence over content integration and equity pedagogy through their attitudes and actions. By incorporating a variety of texts and cultures, students' home languages and cultures are given a place along the mainstream culture. This also allows second language acquisition to occur at a more effective rate, as instruction can occur both in the student's native language, as well as in English. This is most easily accomplished through play, such as creative forms and verbal language play. Verbal interaction is fundamental for all students, but in particular for ELL (Egbert & Simich-Dudgeon, 2001). This flexible interaction will allow students the opportunity to use language in a real-life scenario that models everyday uses.

Instruction in the second language must be flexible in the place of instruction, access, intensity, rhythm, and methodology (Magos & Politi, 2008). This flexibility will allow for more meaningful practices and uses, as previously mentioned. By removing the rigidity of the curricula, students are given the opportunity to interact with language in more relaxed meaningful ways and best achieved through group interactions and variations of role-play.

Researchers who have looked into the effective components of English language lessons have found that the following elements should be evident for success: dramatizing meaning, using hands-on material and manipulatives, and placing language in a physical "here and now" context to the greatest extent possible (Zuniga-Hill & Barnes, 1995). All of these components can be found in activities incorporating language play. In addition, Bell (2005) stresses that language play should not only occur in the second language, but in the first language as well. By playing with one's first language, the student is then able to apply the skills learned to the second language.

Students who do not appear to be interacting in the play activities should not be seen as inactive members of the group. Various levels of participation may occur; students who appear to be complacent must not be treated as if they are not engaged with the activities around them. Marley, Levin, and Glenberg (2010) describe that according to dual-coding theory, "...cognitive representation consists of verbal and nonverbal systems" (p. 397). A student who is not verbally engaged in an activity is not necessarily deficient in their acquisition of the second language, nor an ineffective participant in their native language.

Creative and language play not only are important tools for learning, they can also trigger positive affective responses in the students. In a study of children's emotions in regards to their effects on problem solving, Russ and Kaugars (2001) observed that children who felt either happy or angry produced more original responses on divergent thinking tasks than their peers who reported feeling neutral.

Play allows ELL the opportunity to react emotionally with their instruction that allows the opportunity for deeper, more meaningful interactions. For culturally marginalized groups of learners, such as Native Americans, many of their traditional ways that have been eliminated from classroom instruction mirror language play. In the following sections, I provide a brief understanding of Native American educational policy through a historical perspective, the steps taken to remedy the mistakes of the past, and a glimpse into how incorporating language play for this group of students can benefit both second language acquisition and a strengthening of their tribal languages.

How Play can be Utilized

There is a common misconception among educators that a curriculum is "...a product-in-place and as an unchanging truth that must be passed on unquestioningly" (Nieto, 2010, p. 106). For years, educators had to adhere to a curriculum that was approved, implemented, and monitored by a governing body. However, we now understand that students thrive when teachers implement culturally responsive teaching.

Teachers of Native American students, for example, will find it easier to implement tribal stories and examples into their instructional days, to make learning effective and relevant for their populations. Culturally responsive teaching allows for the students' values, beliefs, histories, and experiences to be represented in a curriculum that is centered on trust and mutual respect between the teacher and the learner (Espinosa, 2005). Everyone, students and teachers alike, have life experiences that should be brought to the process of learning. Utilizing play as an instructional tool for linguistically diverse students allows these experiences to be part of a student's educational environment as well as a tool with which to make meaning of the information presented to them.

The theoretical concepts presented have the opportunity to work for many Native American students, but their effectiveness relies heavily on family background and acceptance. Many tribal stories are sacred texts and have spiritual and religious meanings for those who tell the stories. Therefore, one must first establish criteria for what is appropriate for an educator to use, in particular, if that educator is from an outside culture. The suggestions contained here can be valuable for all students regardless of culture, but must be exercised with caution when considering using stories of value for a particular group. Guidelines must be established between the tribe and the school to ensure proper and respectful implementation.

The Native American Languages Act, Title I of Public Law 101-477 states, "...the statuses of the cultures and languages of Native Americans is unique and the United States has the responsibility to act together with Native Americans to ensure survival of these unique cultures and languages" (Rehyner & Eder, 2004, p. 309). Schools can be a place for strengthening and reinforcing tribal identity and language through respect in an effort to make them a part of the students' everyday lives. Due to the past policies of assimilation, this is a path that educators must be very aware of as schools are still viewed with caution in many communities. To do so, a form of equitable pedagogy must be adopted that focuses on strategies, techniques, methods, and approaches that allow teachers to make learning available and impartial for all students (Zuniga-Hill & Barnes, 1995).

For many Native American tribes or groups, task-based activities should be utilized frequently as it mirrors oral traditions of many tribal dialect (Pomerantz & Bell, 2007). Children will be in a better position to learn the target language by interacting communicatively and purposefully, while still maintaining a child-oriented task. When using a tribal story, the version should remain true to the spirit and content of the original so as to maintain cultural relevancy (Reese, 2007). Some level of adaptation may need to occur to fit within the parameters of the learning goal, but the adaptation should refrain from altering the meaning and understanding of the story.

When choosing to use play as a means for a transmission of education, the educator must first look to the background of the student population and seek an understanding of language development, both in the first language and the intended second. Doing so will allow the educator to gain a snapshot of how the students could benefit from play. Younger children, or students with limited language experience, would benefit from creative play, allowing them to participate in fantasy-type roles using language to convey what is occurring in their session. Older or more proficient students would find success using language play to create dialogues of real-life situations using language to experiment with different forms and function of language, in a more informal setting than dialogue in a social setting.

To most effectively use language play, examples should be drawn from narrative pieces that are relatable for the students. Narration has been the primary means by which humans organize, experience, and justify actions (Coryell et al., 2010). It is the most recognizable and relatable genre for students and therefore would present the least amount of resistance when implemented for student learning.

In Native American narratives, such as the Arizona Tewa, stories generally have a formulaic beginning and ending that almost always includes a song associated with the story's protagonist (Kroskrity, 2009). This formula is very often found within children's literature across various cultural groups, therefore establishing its effective uses in language play. Performances in this style are often utilized as an informal learning style, and exposing students to this type of play may be key to exposing them to language ideologies found within many cultural groups.

In using narration, students are also presented with the opportunity to elicit affective responses from their experiences. Not only would this create an enjoyable experience for students, but according to Russ & Kaugars (2001), it could trigger a broad associative network that may connect to prior knowledge, divergent thinking, and increased comprehension.

Another form of language play that can be utilized is that of talk-story, which is commonplace in Hawai'ian culture and language. In this style, students discuss the salient features of the story and apply their own knowledge, while the narrator tells the events of the story.

Students have more opportunity to discuss text ideas and to use Standard English more than they would in other language-based activities (Kawakami

& Au, 1986). Students "…are able to focus on learning to read rather than on figuring out how to participate appropriately in the discussion" (p. 78). Many Native American cultures also have similar styles of learning and speaking that can be utilized for language play. In using this style, the staff at the Kamehameha Elementary Education Program in Hawai'i was able to reconfigure instructional activities in ways that were familiar to their students. They found this to be a more effective way of increasing students' language acquisition than drastically changing an entire classroom setting and procedure.

Educators who choose to use creative play in their instructional repertoire can adapt stories and narratives into role-play activities such as the ones briefly mentioned in previous sections. These activities represent a real life situation within a particular scenario that is familiar to the students' lived experiences. It aims their understanding of the experience created with a particular situation (Magos & Politi, 2008). The students participating in this particular form of creative play are expected to rehearse their skills and create the appropriate attitudes required to handle a particular situation.

The key to role-play activities is that it reinforces students' active participation in the learning process itself. For language learning to occur, the students cannot be passive recipients of information; they must be engaged in the act so that they may experience the form and function of the activity. This will not only strengthen their skills in the intended second language, but also reinforce skills in their first language.

Whatever the style of play an educator decides to utilize, it should be kept in mind that these events should not occur in isolation, but within social, collaborative groups. Play should allow for interaction and active engagement not only with the intended language targets, but with peers experiencing the activities alongside them (Griva & Semoglou, 2012). The most effective groups and interactions occur when students are placed in flexible groupings with students of varying abilities (Magos & Politi, 2008).

A major indicator of student success using PBL is how effectively students accept and participate in the activities and lessons. Research of motivation in children has found distinct characteristics that can be identified when observing PBL. Challenge, curiosity, fantasy, and control are all found intrinsically within children as they play and interact with the world around them and with languages, both first and second alike (Rieber, 1996). When recognized by educators, play becomes more than just a pleasurable activity, but a tool for learning within a meaningful context.

Above all else, an educator's priority is to make sure that the stories or texts utilized for play are meaningful for the children. The most effective use of a student's cultural background in education can only be achieved when the educator is able to explicitly make the connections between the text and how it applies to their lives, in terms of both lived history and approaching reality.

Implications of Play-Based Learning

There is very little empirical research on how adapting tribal stories and examples can be translated into PBL, and therefore there is a lack of data on its implications in classroom practice. Through careful research of the information that is available on this topic and my own in-classroom implementation, I was able to create a working model of PBL for my classroom through role-play. The students would act out the characters in a morality story, changing the dialogue, setting, and other text to mimic experiences in their lives. Other themes included imagining themselves as an outsider to a story and requiring them to react to a conflict and resolution, provide their own rationale and, if appropriate, alternative choices to the characters' interactions. A popular activity among third graders was what became known as Vocabulary Theater. When presented with academic terminology such as conflict, resolution, and compromise, the students would act out how those would appear in the context of a given story. The success of these and other activities is documented below in the Results section.

For children of various cultural backgrounds, PBL has shown many distinct possibilities and positive results that can be utilized for Native American students. Children's play, regardless of cultural background or history, is a deliberate activity in which they devote great effort and commitment (Rieber, 1996). When engaged in play, Cekaite and Aaronson (2005) found that children exploited several dimensions of language in performing and participating in joking events. Joking can be understood as a form of humor, another type of daily language activity. When students are able to utilize humor in frequent practice, they will process it deeply and therefore, be able to further develop in their language skills (Bell, 2005). By placing learning in a relaxed, comfortable format, students felt more comfortable taking chances and risks when humor was involved in the play-based activities of the classroom. Russ and Kaugars (2001) also found that children who experience more emotion with their learning gave more original responses. Play-based learning has also shown benefits in memory retention and active engagement with learning (Marley et al., 2010). In particular, the authors described at length that when students are involved with activity based learning, they remembered more story content than those students who were only exposed to a rereading activity.

Not only can physical activities contribute to literacy development, it also has a positive impact on psychomotor development, fosters cooperation, enhances problem-solving skills, and develops creative thinking tasks (Griva & Semoglou, 2012), which correlates with the notion that language play is one of the forces behind creativity, and its application in literacy development (Bell, 2005).

It should be reiterated that the successes mentioned above require an understanding of the vocabulary needed and correct implementation (Magos & Politi, 2008). For all of the benefits that come with PBL, students must be familiar and comfortable with the process of the activity itself. As with all aspects of instruction and learning, students cannot be expected to master a skill on initial exposure. The process and procedures must be modeled to ensure effective understanding. This is not to say that spontaneity does not have its place in language play. Instinctive language play has been shown to be vital in the development of linguistic creativity and collaborative pattern variation (Cekaite & Aaronson, 2005). As long as the play initiated by the student or teacher is intended to meet the learning goal, play that develops on a whim can be beneficial to the overall learning of the students.

Due to the diverse nature of this country, educators should infuse their instruction with examples and stories to not only meet the needs of all students, but to also create well-rounded, inclusive curricula. An effective way to do so would be to integrate information across all content areas with examples, information, data, and knowledge from a variety of cultural backgrounds (Zuniga-Hill & Barnes, 1995).

Methods

This research was conducted in part to fulfill the requirements of a comprehensive exam for completion of a Master of Arts in Language,

Literacy, and Sociocultural Studies from the University of New Mexico, but was created and motivated by the need to assist students' performance in various measures. The school, located on a rural reservation in Northern New Mexico, relied heavily on Dynamic Indicators of Basic Early Literacy Skills (DIBELS) assessments and progress monitoring to determine student ability and development towards an established learning goal.

Throughout the 2014-2015 school year, the PBL methods mentioned above were used in various academic settings. These activities occurred over an eight-month period from the beginning of year measure, August 2014, to the end of the year measure, which took place in April 2015. The class consisted of 20 third grade students. Nineteen of the students lived on a reservation and one commuted from a neighboring town. Seventeen students were identified as the area's tribal members, two were from neighboring tribes, and one student self-identified as Hispanic.

The PBL activities occurred three times a week, lasting approximately 60 minutes spread throughout the academic day. The majority of activities occurred during English Language Arts instruction (50 minutes), and 10 minutes in either during math, science, or social studies instruction. After the first nine-week grading period, students were able to fluidly move between traditional curriculum activities and play-based methods. I reasoned that by using a variety of activities in both forms of instruction, the students' words per minute (WPM) would increase from an increase in language comfort.

Results

Table 11.1 shows the average growth from the beginning to end of year measure in DIBELs Oral Reading Fluency:

Table 11.1
Average Growth of Oral Reading Fluency

Average Beginning of Year Score	54 WPM (Goal 70 WPM)
Average End of Year Score	74 WPM (Goal 100 WPM)
Average Increase/Decrease	+20 WPM

To measure WPM, the students were given a passage to read aloud in one minute. An adult staff member of the school, teacher, or reading interventionist followed along on an iPad and noted mispronunciations, and skipped, omitted, or inserted words. At the conclusion of the read, the student responded by summarizing what they had just read.

Although the number of students who were indicated as being on grade level by the End of Year Measure was only a fraction of the class, the gains shown in Table 11.1 were celebrated and the students were recognized for their positive achievements.

Conclusion

In a very restricted and basic definition, learning can be seen as the exposure to and the mastery of skills needed to achieve good grades and high scores (Nieto, 2010). However, learning can be much more than a memorization of rote skills necessary to excel on a standardized test. Learning through playful activities can benefit not only literacy development, but also in all life skills that a student may encounter.

As there is no empirical evidence that supports the idea that high-stakes accountability improves academic skills or close achievement gaps (McCarthy, 2009), educators must find ways to supplement their students' educational experiences beyond the standardized tests. School climates and conditions can either foster success or hinder learning with the attitudes and beliefs of the educators (Nieto, 2010). They must identify cultural and linguistic knowledge that can serve as a tool for success for their students (Coryell et al., 2010).

Teachers of Native American students have a distinct advantage since their students come with a rich cultural and linguistic background to mold PBL around. Researchers have found that learning through play is one of the best ways to learn a language because it creates emotional attachments and focuses on participation and enjoyment in non-threatening and relaxed experiences (Griva & Semoglou, 2012).

The overall effectiveness of PBL is naturally dependent upon the content of the activity in addition to the educator's and students' attitude and role in the activities (Magos & Politi, 2008). Like all academic endeavors, if an educator does not believe in its effectiveness, it will not work. Similarly if the students do not see the value of PBL, they will not fully participate and therefore not reap the benefits of its ability to increase literacy and language development in both their native and second languages.

One step that educators can take to attempt to actively engage their students is to use enjoyable and relaxing teaching techniques to entice excitement (Magos & Politi, 2008), such as PBL. However, as many seasoned educators can attest, the desires and interests of students change very rapidly, so further investigation is needed for each individual group of learners to discover what will work best for them (Antokhin, 2006).

Many Native American students often come to school from an oral language background where history, religion, and entertainment were passed down through storytellers and informed elders for generations. These oral stories were passed on as the storytellers absorbed the tales by hearing others tell the stories and gradually incorporate content and ideals of narrative performance (Kroskrity, 2009). Language play incorporates many of these ideals and therefore would be effective with consistent and thorough implementation.

Despite the long and tragic history of education, many Native American tribes and groups favor schools that teach their children mainstream techniques as long as their own culture and language is maintained (Rehyner & Eder, 2004). In addition, no individual should be denied the right to worship, speak, write, assemble, or learn as they see fit (Tiller, 2000). It is the role of the school and the educators to ensure that there is a balance between a student's home culture and language, and how to succeed using target learning goals.

The greatest benefit for utilizing play for language development comes from the opportunities it presents for students to creatively supplement or subvert the target language system (Pomerantz & Bell, 2007). Unlike native speakers of English, ELL are not often given the opportunity to use the language in a variety of ways that would promote reflection and growth. Play allows for this experimentation and growth. Being able to correctly and collaboratively play with language can ultimately be viewed as a quality of communicative competence (Cekaite & Aaronson, 2005). If students are able to manipulate language, regardless of whether it is their first language or an acquired second, they show competency not only in how to speak the language, but also by understanding the subtle nuances that go with proficient use of language.

The use of PBL is a departure from many traditional and commonly utilized educational methods, but its benefits contain limitless potential for ELL, in particular those students from linguistically diverse cultures such as the many Native American tribes in the United States. For ELL there is no guarantee that speaking English will result in academic success (Nieto, 2010). What must occur is a balanced approach to learning that recognizes and respects all cultures and values, and what they bring to the learning process. As all cultures play, learning conducted in this context gives our students the best chance to succeed.

References
Antokhin, N. (2006). Language play. *Applied Language Learning, 16*(2), 86-90. Retrieved from http://www.dliflc.edu/wp-content/uploads/2014/04/all16two.pdf
Banks, J. A. (1991). The dimensions of multicultural education. *Multicultural Leader, 4*, 5–6.
Bell, N. (2005). Exploring L2 language play as an aid to SLL: A case study of humour in NS-NNS interaction. *Applied Linguistics, 26*(2), 192-218. doi:10.1093/applin/amh043
Brayboy, B. (2005). Toward a tribal critical race theory in education. *The Urban Review, 37*(5), 425-446. doi:10.1007/s11256-005-0018-y
Cekaite, A., & Aronsson, K. (2005). Language play, a collaborative resource in children's L2 learning. *Applied Linguistics, 26*(2), 169-191. doi:10.1093/applin/amh042
Coryell, J., Clark, M., & Pomerantz, A. (2010). Cultural fantasy narratives and heritage language learning: A case study of adult heritage learners of Spanish. *The Modern Language Journal, 94*(3), 453-469. doi:10.1111/j.1540-4781.2010.01055.x
Egbert, J., & Simich-Dudgeon, C. (2001). Providing support for non-native learners of English in the social studies classroom. *The Social Studies, 92*(1), 22-25. http://dx.doi.org/10.1080/00377990109603971
Espinosa, L. (2005). Curriculum and assessment considerations for young children from culturally, linguistically, and economically diverse backgrounds. *Psychology in the Schools, 42*(8), 837-853. doi:10.1002/pits.20115
Griva, E., & Semoglou, K. (2012). Estimating the effectiveness and feasibility of a game-based project for early foreign language learning. *English Language Teaching, 5*(9), 33-44. http://dx.doi.org/10.5539/elt.v5n9p33
Hollingworth, L. (2009). Unintended educational and social consequences of the No Child Left Behind Act. *The Journal of Gender, Race & Justice, 12*, 311-327.
Kawakami, A., & Au, K. (1986). Encouraging reading and language development in cultural minority children. *Topics in Language Disorders, 6*(2), 71-80.

Kim, Y., & Kellogg, D. (2008). Task and play in the words and minds of children. *Journal of Applied Linguistics, 3*(1), 25-47. doi :10.1558/japl.v3i1.25

Klenowski, V. (2009). Australian Indigenous students: Addressing equity issues in assessment. *Teaching Education, 20*(1), 77-93. http://dx.doi.org/10.1080/10476210802681741

Kroskrity, P. (2009). Narrative reproductions: Ideologies of storytelling, authoritative words, and generic regimentation in the village of Tewa. *Journal of Linguistic Anthropology, 19*(1), 40-56. doi:10.1111/j.1548-1395.2009.01018.x

Magos, K., & Politi, F. (2008). The contribution of role-play technique to the teaching of a second language in immigrant classes. *RELC Journal, 39*(1), 96-112. doi:10.1177/0033688208091142

Major, B., & O'Brien, L. (2005). The social psychology of stigma. *Annual Review of Psychology, 56,* 393-421. doi:10.1146/annurev.psych.56.091103.070137

Marley, S. C., Levin, J. R., & Glenberg, A. M. (2010). What cognitive benefits does an activity-based reading strategy afford young Native American readers. *The Journal of Experimental Education, 78,* 395-417. doi:10.1080/002209709032548061.

McCarthy, T. L. (2009). The impact of high-stakes accountability policies on Native American learners: Evidence from research. *Teaching Education, 20*(1), 7-29. http://dx.doi.org/10.1080/10476210802681600

National Center for Education Statistics. (n.d.). Fast facts: Dropout rates. Retrieved from http://nces.ed.gov/fastfacts/display.asp?id=16.

New Mexico Public Education Department. (n.d.). Data and statistics. Retrieved from http://ped.state.nm.us/ped/Graduation_data.html.

New Mexico Voices for Children. (n. d.). New Mexico high school graduation and drop out rates. Retrieved from http://www.nmvoices.org/attachments/nmkc_graduation_rates_10-08.pdf

Nieto, S. (2010). *The light in their eyes.* New York: Teachers College Press.

Pomerantz, A., & Bell, N. (2007). Learning to play, playing to learn: FL learners as multicomponent language users. *Applied Linguistics, 28*(4), 556-578. doi:10.1093/applin/amm044

Reese, D. (2007). Proceed with caution: Using Native American folktales in the classroom. *Language Arts, 84*(3), 245-256.

Reyhner, J., & Eder, J. (2004). *American Indian education.* Norman: University of Oklahoma Press.

Rieber, L. (1996). Seriously considering play: Designing interactive learning environments based on the blending of microworlds, simulations, and games. *Educational Technology Research and Development, 44*(2), 43-58. doi:10.1007/BF02300540

Russ, S., & Kaugars, A. (2001). Emotion in children's play and creative problem solving. *Creativity Research Journal, 13*(2), 211-219. http://dx.doi.org/10.1207/S15326934CRJ1302_8

Sleeter, C. (2001). Preparing teachers for culturally diverse schools: Research and the overwhelming presence of Whiteness. *Journal of Teacher Education, 52*(2), 94-106. doi:10.1177/0022487101052002002

Tiller, V. E. (Ed.). (2000). *The Jicarilla Apache tribe.* Albuquerque, NM: Bow Arrow Publishing Company.

Zuniga-Hill, C., & Barnes, C. (1995). Effective teacher preparation for diverse student populations: What works? In S. Rothstein (Ed.), *Class, culture, and race in American schools* (pp. 163-198). Santa Barbara, CA: Greenwood.

CHAPTER 12

DISCOURSE, GLOBALIZATION, AND THE TRANSLOCALIZATION OF GANGSPEAK:
Evidence from Trinidad

Renée Figuera
Wendell C. Wallace
University of the West Indies, St. Augustine

Studies on the language used among gang members and members of the underworld are usually glossaries from metropolitan locations, which do not include the language used by their Caribbean counterparts (Green, 2011; Knox, 1997; Roman, 2014). In addition, glossaries or dictionaries from these non–Caribbean locations do not usually highlight cultural and linguistic resources from other international contexts as influencing the language use of gang members in their own communities.

In this context, the current study examines the translocalization of lexicon in the gang-related communities of Trinidad as evidence of "the transporting of signs or objects attached to one place into those other places, where they can be reinterpreted otherwise" (Pennycook, 2007, p. 79). As can be expected, the language in use in these gang communities draws its sociocultural and sociolinguistic characteristics from local and global contexts. This results in the transidiomatic practice of creating a combined code of linguistic resources from a range of communicative channels, both local and distant. Given the communities of practice surrounding gang operations and the global spread of hip-hop, rap, and dancehall, this study explores the extent to which the transidiomatic effects from these sources, among others, are similar in more than one gang-community within Trinidad.

Theoretical Framework

Theoretically, this study on "gangsta" discourse occurs within a specific sociocultural context that acknowledges a local and global framework of language use. A few critical constructs are relevant to our analysis of gangspeak within the gang communities of Trinidad, where we draw on both local and global contexts. In the current segment, we explain the relationship between communities of practice, intertextuality, and lexical transidiomatization.

The term "gang" did not always have a drug-related or criminal connotation attached to it in Trinidad and Tobago. As Bissessar (2014) points out, it was originally associated with rival bands of the steel pan in the late 1800s in Trinidad. Contemporary gangs in Trinidad and Tobago are ephemeral, smaller, and not as interconnected as gangs in Latin America (Townsend, 2009, p. 200). They are communities of practice, defined by the co-membership criteria of mutual engagement (coming into physical contact with each other), jointly negotiated enterprise (working towards shared goals), and a shared repertoire (words, jargon, jokes, and slang used over long periods; Meyerhoff, 2006, p. 189).

Hill (2013) shows how gang legislation in Trinidad has given rise to a new definition of gang members by their networks. The Anti-Gang Act No. 10 of 2011 and the Gang (Prevention and Prohibition) Act of 2011 for Trinidad and Tobago define a "gang" as "a combination of two or more persons, whether formally or informally organized which, through its membership or through an agent, engages in a gang-related activity" (Hill, 2013, p. 50). A "gang-related activity" is seen as any criminal activity, enterprise, pursuit or undertaking in relation to any of the offences listed in the Schedule (First Schedule of The Anti-Gang Act No. 10 of 2011 and the Gang [Prevention and Prohibition] Act of 2011 in Trinidad and Tobago) ... acquiesced in, or consented to, or directed, ordered, authorized, or requested or ratified by any gang member, including a gang leader (p. 50). In addition, gang affiliates can be found among minor actors and associated individuals who may not function as active players in gang enterprises. Prouse (2012) views new age gang configurations as having interchangeable players who are analogous to "sports teams whereby individuals are mobilized and see action based on a leader-centered decision maker and elements of skill" (p. 1). Both gang-affiliates and players have access to a common linguistic repertoire.

On the other hand, intertextuality describes the situated indexing of prior situational contexts and their constituent elements, in which tokens of a generic type have been employed (Duranti, 2001, p. 800). In this way, the analysis of Trinidadian gangspeak involves considering lexical entries from prior contexts in published gang dictionaries, and showing how reappropriations in the local context may have occurred, as a result of the dislocation and relocation of some terminology, from prior contexts. In addition, cross-textual analysis links globalization to the outcome of lexical transidiomatization, or the recombination of lexical items from diverse sources and channels, within the local gangsta code. Ultimately, intertextuality presumes the interconnectedness of the local "gangsta slang" of Trinidad and the slang of other international territories.

Intertextuality also gives rise to transidiomatic practices, which are owed to deterritorialized technologies. These technologies inadvertently transmit cultural and linguistic resources into Trinidadian gangspeak from across diverse culturescapes. Transidiomatic practices describe the interaction of transnational groups using languages and communicative codes that are simultaneously present in a range of communicative channels, both local and distant (Jacquemet, 2005, pp. 264-265). Trinidadian gangs can be considered to be transnational groups, in the diasporic, transcultural, and transvarietal sense of appropriating slang terms and discourse styles within their repertoire from other territories and cultures–namely from Britain, the United States, or even Jamaica.

In this way, the local gang code draws on organized forms of cultural capital that are constructed in the interactions of individual members and collective groups (see Appadurai, 1990, pp. 31-36). The transmission of this capital is helped by fast-paced communication technology, which affords homogenizing and heterogenizing linguistic and cultural influences across localities. Ultimately, the local variety of gangspeak consists of recombinant features, which cannot be identified as a single standardizable code. While this code is not equivalent to Trinidadian English Creole (TEC), it is a register within TEC, which is lexicalized mainly by American pop culture, British archaisms, dancehall, hip-hop, and rap speech styles. Due to the illicit drug trade, gangspeak is also associated with the appropriation of lexical items resulting from the geopolitical situation of Trinidad, as a transshipment territory that is susceptible to contact with other language groups such as

Venezuelans. For this reason, a few Spanish terms are known in the repertoire of gang players.

In the following review of the literature, we critically analyze existing research and the sociocultural context for evidence of the nature of gang slang, the status of sociolinguistic research on gang slang in the Caribbean, and the effect of globalization on this code.

The Nature of Gang Slang

Prior studies on gang slang from correctional facilities, and on the language of the underworld, present decontextualized word lists as representative of the language used within gang communities (Green, 2011; Knox, 1997; Roman, 2014). This contrasts with the data collection procedures in this study, which identify gang slang within the natural speech and interactions of gang members from unscripted videos, interviews, and questionnaires. In this way, the features of gang slang in the local context are not compiled as a frozen list of lexical entries. Gangspeak or gang slang arises from direct contact between criminal players, mutual engagement in the common enterprise of criminality, and from a shared repertoire over an extended period (Meyhoff, 2006, p. 189).

The *Longman Dictionary of Applied Linguistics and Language Teaching* equates slang with colloquial speech and "undesirable speech," or a speech variety used in informal situations that often serves as an "in-group" language for a particular set of people (p. 532). As slang has a transient quality and may fall out of fashion, using out-of-date slang has implications for being excluded from a particular in-group. Mattielo (2008) considers slang as a social means of identification and cohesiveness. It varies according to attitude, includes words below the level of stylistically neutral language, and emphasizes novelty, freshness, and innovation (p. 31).

Historical and social factors contribute to a degree of overlap between youth slang and gangsta discourse. Thorne (2014) points out that the idea of slang was only introduced in 1756, in Britain, while "cant" was the term used to describe the compilations by non-linguists regarding the vocabulary in use by beggars, cheats, thieves, and other "undesirable" persona of the society. In a now globalized world, elements of youth language have infiltrated the underworld, as each context no longer feels foreign to the other. According to one informant from a gang community in Morvant, in North Trinidad, youth slang informs contemporary gangspeak (M. M., personal communication, February 23, 2016).

In addition, the fluid structures that define "new–age" gangs result in the use of some terms outside of the structure of gang communities. The popularity of dancehall, hip-hop, and rap music and cultures also accounts for some overlap in language use among residents from gang communities and everyday youth language in Trinidad. Some examples of local and international terms in use, in both youth slang and gang slang, include terms of address like *Dawg*, *Hoss*, and *Soldy-a*, discourse fillers such as *nah boi*, and social greetings and interjections such as *wuz d ceen*, *Ceen*, or *Word*, as opening and closing markers of conversational discourse.

Gangsta codes also confirm the culture and identity of the communities of practice among their players. As a result, the codedness of gangspeak is derived from the shared context of its speakers, while their direct contact, shared goals, and their unique jokes and jargon continue. In other words, the similarities between contemporary youth language and gangsta slang do not account for many polysemous meanings and opaque meanings in the lexicon of gang players, which are characteristically multi–layered. The local repertoires of gang players, within English Creole-speaking communities in Trinidad, also show evidence of adopting performance styles of African-influenced oral discourse, such as "louding" and "signifying" as forms of campaigning for respect and using indirectness in language, respectively. These performance styles are influenced by hip-hop, rap, and dancehall cultures, which are rooted in the resistance cultures of slavery.

As a final point, the features of gang slang are also influenced by Caribbean networks between the United States and the English–speaking Caribbean. *The Economist* records that 16% of cocaine imports into the United States came through the Caribbean islands in 2013, with higher proportions for Europe (Full Circle, 2013). The article attributes these high volumes to the re-opening of old transshipment routes of the 1980s, since counter-narcotics pressures in Honduras have forced in-land transshipments of drugs through Central America, further East, and seawards to the Eastern Caribbean. As the closest transshipment point off the South American mainland, into Caribbean waters, Trinidad is therefore positioned not only as a crossing point for communication among drug gangs, but it is also an active territory for the exchange of drug-gang intelligence, cultures, and heightened gang activities.

Gang Studies and Gang Slang in the Caribbean and Beyond
Traditional research on gangs in the Caribbean has included the political and socio-economic environments, the social and psychological factors for gang growth, and the demographics of gangs in the Caribbean. Much of this work can be found within Seepersad and Bissessar (2013), which include studies on St. Kitts, the Northern Triangle (Honduras, Guatemala, and El Salvador), Jamaica, and Trinidad. However, the current critical language study is possibly the first of its kind in the Caribbean region, as gang language has been overlooked in these Caribbean studies. In fact, Caribbean linguists and criminologists are just beginning to engage in critical language studies in this area of cultural criminology.

Some emergent work in sociolinguistics has examined Jamaican slang and the influence of Jamaican slang on British Cant in *Global Slang*. Within this collection, Farquharson and Jones (2014) have looked at Jamaican slang; in their conclusions, they have called for more lexicographic work on this aspect of Jamaican language use. Although they did not specifically examine gang communities or the role of globalization in spreading linguistic resources to the Caribbean slang context, they identified borrowed Jamaicanisms into Trinidadian slang, such as *chi-chi* man (a male homosexual) and *gallis* (a lady's man), as well as foreign words borrowed into Jamaican slang, like *dude, bro,* and *dawg,* among others.

Two anthologies compiled by American criminologists have taken a glossary approach to gang slang. These are *The Gang Dictionary: A Guide to Gang Slang, Gang Vocabulary, and Gang Socio-linguistic Phrases* (Knox, 1997) and *Introduction to Corrections and Gang Terminology* (Roman, 2014). The former anthology is a compilation of vocabulary from nationwide research projects and interviews with adult and juvenile gang members in the United States in the 1990s. The latter work is an updated compilation, which spans the period of 1972 to 2011, and was gathered from adult male and female inmates and youthful offenders in correctional facilities in California. Finally, *Crooked Talk: Five Hundred Years of the Language of Crime* takes a broader view of the language of crime by including a thematic arrangement and etymological analysis of the slang of diverse criminals, including prostitutes, thieves, gangs, conmen, swindlers, and murders. By its treatment of slang terms from elsewhere, notably Britain, the United States, and Australia, it lends insight into the translocalization of terms in Trinidadian gang culture.

For instance, *bust a cap* was a term used during the American Civil War for firing shots. This term has given rise to Creole calques such as *buss corn, crack corn,* and *fire corn* in contemporary Trinidadian gangspeak, possibly as derivatives of *bus kaan* [bʌs kã:n] or *pap kaan* [pʰap kã:n] in Jamaican gangspeak. The term *one-on-one* (a term for a full-scale gang fight or an encounter between two individuals in the American context) also evolved into *one is one* by folk etymology in Trinidadian gangspeak. The meaning of this lexical phrase has shifted semantically to describe a "tit for tat" reprisal type of gang retaliation.

Globalization and Gangspeak

Research on globalization and gangs has tended to look specifically at the impact of globalization on gang growth but not at the question of the spread of linguistic resources across international borders, where gang territories exist. Consequently, researchers know little about the transmutation of language used in gang communities as a result of globalization. Parker's (2012) article on globalization and gang growth identifies global pillage (ready recruits from impoverished areas), urbanization (an increase in urban populations inhabiting impoverished city spaces), democratization (patterns of consumption that have developed around illegal trade and cultural artifacts), and network enterprise (a shift in the organized structure of gangs towards "swarm structures") as factors facilitating an exchange of language and culture across borders and state boundaries. Democratization and network enterprises outside of the local gang culture have affected the borrowing of Spanish vocabulary among Trinidadian gangstas, who interact directly with Venezuelan seafarers. This can been seen in the adoption of a word *nina*, pronounced [ni:na], a term formerly in use for a 9 mm gun, derived either from Spanish *niña* or a calque of English *niner* [naIna], and known as "a nines" in Caribbean varieties of English.

Critical sociolinguists describe the co-occurrence of the linguistic phenomena in more than one location as the effect of deterritorialization, or "the dislodging of everyday meanings from their anchors in the local environment" (Tomlinson, 1999, p. 29). They describe the relocation of linguistic phenomena in parallel contexts as reterritorialization, or the reappropriation of new meanings, as may occur in the Trinidadian context. This phenomenon is facilitated by the notion of transcultural flows (Appadurai, 1996, pp. 31-34), which explains how the [gangsta] imaginary has been forged into an organized field of shared practices or culturescapes.

On the other hand, cultural theorists ascribe to the adoption and re-appropriation of lexical resources across translocalities "to shifting ethnoscapes," or "the situated imaginations of individuals and groups spread around the globe" (Appadurai, 1996, p. 33). For instance, the adoption of the lexical phrase "a G move," describing gangsta-like behavior circa 2011, showed that migratory patterns have affected language use in Trinidadian gang communities. The borrowing of this phrase in Trinidad was motivated by the spread of "the gangsta culture" of the American G-Unit by slain gang-leader, Jah David, who was an ex-member of the G-Unit, in the United States.

In a similar way, technology continues to move at high speeds across various kinds of previously impervious communication and territorial boundaries or "technoscapes" (Appadurai, 1996). As a result, new technological terms have been introduced into the ammunition trade, which accompanies the drug trade in Trinidad. The most contemporary term for a 9 mm gun, with features for both single shots and rapid fire, is a *selecta*. This term has now replaced the name for a 9 mm gun, formerly known as *nina* or a *nines*. Since trading firearms also accompanies trading in drugs, this is one example of how new age vocabulary in Trinidadian gangspeak can be ascribed to Venezuelan drug traders and their firearm technology across technoscapes.

Financescapes include the circulation of global capital in more mysterious, rapid ways, which have also popularized *dinero* in the contemporary repertoire of gang players who interact with "the Veneez" (Venezuelans). Other terminology for money include *benjamins*, which originally referred to the US president on the American $100 bill, as first coined by P. Diddy in 1997. This term was formerly used in Trinidad, among gang players, although Trinidad and Tobago dollars displayed different iconography. In the contemporary context, "gangstas" brag of spending *sams* or *uncle sams*, which is a nickname for the United States Federal Government. The value of the US dollar in relation to the Trinidad and Tobago dollar in these contexts is underscored by the local reference to *dollar signs, toys,* or *racks* for local currency. The rap song "Racks" exemplifies how *racks*, for "stacks of paper," has become a popular reference for money (Chris, 2011, single). Mediascapes facilitate the distribution and production of gang culture via diverse media. The celebrity status of gangstas as public figures, in particular, has resulted in elements of youth language and gangspeak being owed to the influence of transculturally well-known figures in popular music, namely rap and dancehall in the Caribbean. Penfold-Mounce (2009) observes that "celebrity is ubiquitous and is an all-inclusive term that includes those who earn their well-knownness from working for the advancement of humankind, those on the stage and screen, and the criminal who breaks the rules of society" (p. 7).

Moreover, technology and the media serve to organize a network of images or "ideoscapes," oriented towards global gangsta sub-cultures. Prior to the death of the local G-Unit leader, Jah David, in Trinidad, local gangstas identified with the hairstyles, fashion statements, and tattoos that were representative of this contending gang entity. In the same way, Vybz Kartel, the Jamaica dancehall artist, popularized Clark shoes by his release of the hit dancehall song "Clarks" (Kartel, 2010, single). While the electrocuted afro-hairstyle of Popcaan, another Jamaican dancehall artist, became popular among "ghetto yutes" (ghetto youth) circa 2013 in Trinidad and Tobago, these examples merely serve to underscore the power of global gangsta subculture as influencing language use through ideoscapes.

In a similar way, Grascia (2003) notes that gangster rap has all the information one needs to become a gangsta. In a similar context, he adds that "gangster rap used in the wrong way can teach the youth of today, gang language, different gang colors and that money equals power and power equals respect" (p. 62). The Jamaican dancehall artist, Popcaan, also underscores the role of some dancehall songs in perpetuating gang culture in the refrain "Badnis a di onli ting mi nuo; gi tahnks fi myuuzik. Kaa if mi neva myuuzik mi wuda av mi ting dehm daili a yuuz it" (2014, track 12).

Methodology

Fairclough (2006) notes that "critical analysts of 'discourse' approach language as a facet of social life which is closely interconnected with other facets of social life, and is therefore a significant aspect of all the major issues in social scientific research" (p. 8). Applied Critical Discourse Analysis is essentially a triangulated network of analysis, which brings together the larger societal context (social practices), the community of experts where the language is used (discourse practices), and textual samples of data (textual practice) as an integrated research framework. In the first instance, globalization provides the larger framework for explaining language contact in imaginary spaces or culturescapes, with the end result being transdiomatization. This dimension of the context of language use facilitates our understanding of how global influences on local gangspeak might be formulated and interpreted. Secondly, the discourse context of gang communities in Trinidad highlights the importance of gang communities as locations of situated use of gang slang. Finally, archival data from unscripted videos, filmed within two geographic locations and comparative member data obtained through interviews and questionnaires from three localities in Trinidad, furnish naturalistic data for analysis.

This framework of combined global and local language use is supported by elicitation and verification stages of the data collection process in order to ensure the reliability of the archival data of the unscripted videos. In this way, an applied Critical Discourse Approach uses data systematically by relating prior contexts–global and local–to naturalistic samples of language use.

Sampling
The analysis was initiated through archival data from two suburban territories of Never Dirty and Success Village in the Morvant-Laventille district, which have the second highest number of murders in Trinidad, and Petit Valley in the West End Police District, which showed the fourth highest number of murders within the East–West Corridor of Northern Trinidad (Townsend, 2009). These districts are therefore representative of active gang communities from which to collect purposive data. Townsend also recorded a concentrated amount of murders in the Port of Spain area amounting to 24% of the country's statistics, while 60% of murders occurred in the suburban areas of Laventille, Belmont, and Beetham. Since early 2016, the Enterprise and Chaguanas districts of Central Trinidad have begun to show increased patterns of violent deaths, due to gang activity (Snakie, personal communication, February 25, 2016). Hence, we enlarged the sampling pool to include gang players from the Central district of Trinidad, namely in Enterprise.

Six subjects who participated in this study included gang affiliates, gang members, street soldiers, and drug-pushers between the ages of 19 and 26 years old. They were recruited by snowball sampling, which took advantage of the social networks of identified cultural informants who could provide us with an increasing set of potential contacts, as overcoming problems of access to socially isolated populations (Faugier & Sargeant, 1997, p. 792). Variation in the responses among gang players during these elicitation exercises and member checks was owed to the social and community composition of specific gang entities, their activities, and their ideology.

Data Collection Procedures
In the first phase of data collection, we elicited vocabulary from a gang player from the Enterprise district of Central Trinidad, who provided lexical referents and phrases in response to questions about the activities and social actors in gang enterprises. This interview provided authentic knowledge of "language on the ground" and a means of determining an initial list of familiar terms for further verification and refinement among other consultants. In the second phase, we expanded the list by sourcing high frequency and marked terms within video scripts.

These videos were available for sale in the capital city of Trinidad, Port of Spain, as two movies in separate unscripted ghetto movie series, filmed by members from the communities of Never Dirty in the Morvant-Laventille District, and Petit Valley, in the North Western part of Trinidad and Tobago, via Diego Martin. Selected extracts from the data, based on narrative scenes with parallel story-lines, showed (1) an initiated conflict, (2) betrayal and reprisal, (3) intervention by elders in the community, and (4) block talk preceding a retaliation in response to the situation of conflict. From these common situations, we undertook a cross-sectional analysis of gangspeak in two Northern communities in Trinidad and Tobago. Data from this, the second phase of elicitation, contributed to a more refined vocabulary list of high frequency and marked lexical referents, as representative of Trinidadian gangspeak.

The third phase of data collection consisted of interviews, member checks, and questionnaires among participants from the movies, as well as from gang players and affiliates via snowball sampling. Alim (2004) observed that the "code of the streets" does not look fondly upon someone carrying a tape recorder and asking too many questions, particularly in a cultural environment where people avoid "puttin their business out in the street" at all costs (p. 390). We used these member-checks in Phase Three to verify the meanings of the lexical items and to further refine the list of lexical items accumulated in Phases One and Two. This was made possible by snowball sampling. Participants were gang members and informants from three districts in North and Central Trinidad, namely, Morvant, Laventille, and Enterprise. Figure 12.1 shows the approximate location of these communities on a map of Trinidad.

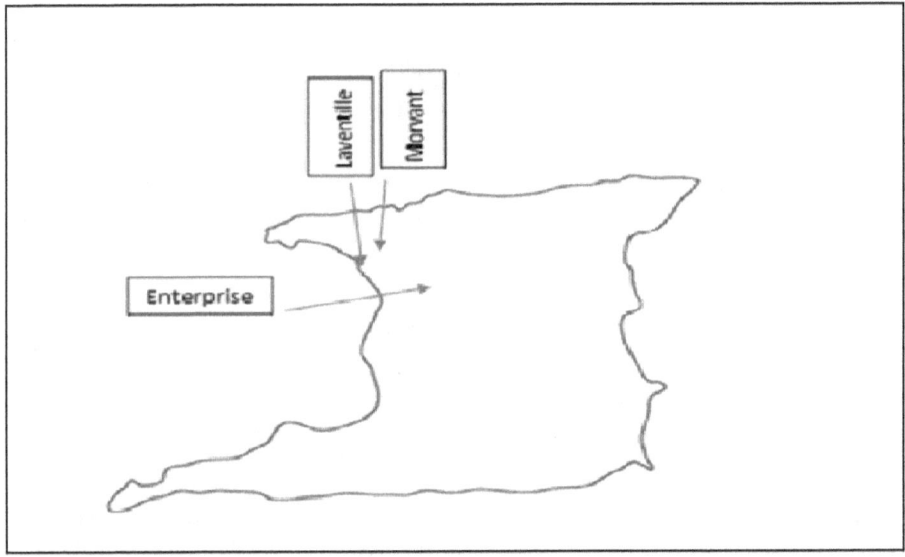

Figure 12.1. Map of Trinidad and Tobago: Approximate Locations of Member Checks

While Mattielo (2008) acknowledges the difficulty of accumulating slang data in naturalistic settings, she recommends the use of dictionaries, corpora, film script excerpts, and questionnaires by native informants for corroborating genuine usage (pp. 27-28). Therefore, we used a combination of instruments for data collection as indicated in Figure 12.2 below. This process of data collection and data analysis entailed elicitation, compilation, and verification phases of research.

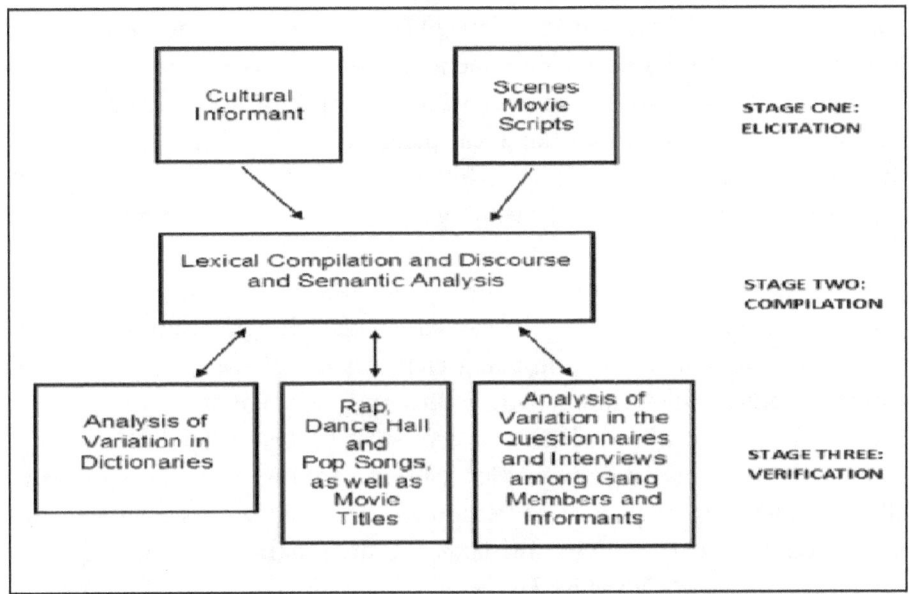

Figure 12.2. Chart of the Research Procedures

Data Analysis

As early as the 1990s, the lyrics "Love Me Browning" by Buju Banton, Jamaican Dancehall artist, commodified the trappings of gangsta identity as performative and concretely associated with violence, status attainment, money, and women. Wilkinson (2001) also observed that "the gangster lifestyle, based on a conspicuous display of masculine symbols of power (women, cars, money) and willingness to use violence to achieve desired ends, [which] has become a model of the good life for thousands of male youths in the ghettos" (p. 11). In "Love Me Browning," Banton (1992) captured the salience of violence and sex to gangsta performativity and identity. He iterated: "Mi louv mi kyaar, mi louv mi baik, mi louv mi moni an ting, bot mos af aal; mi louv mi brounin" (track, B3). In Jamaican slang *browning* is a pun on a desirable brown-skinned girl, as well as a type of gun.

In the same way, we extracted marked functional vocabulary from the movie scripts within the fields of activity suggested by Wilkinson (2001) and Banton (1992). These represented violence, status attainment, women, and money, as well as discourse markers within the repertoire of gang players. These categories yielded specific terms of address, common nouns referring to social actors and women, interjections, and noun and verb categories for objects and activities, which expressed status, social roles, fillers, and vocabulary for activities within local gangsta culture. Later, we checked these selections from the movie scripts in Phase Two of the study against further variation in form and meaning through structured interviews and questionnaires.

The analysis encompassed applying the concept of transidiomacity to "the communicative practices of local players, as belonging to transnational [gang] groups, and interacting using elements of different languages and communicative codes simultaneously present in a range of communicative channels, both local and distant" (Jacquemet, 2005, p. 264). Hence, we compared commonplace linguistic referents in the repertoire of gang affiliates and gang players of contemporary Trinidad with secondary data from metropolitan gang and anti-language dictionaries such as the *Gang Dictionary*, *Crooked Talk: Five Hundred Years of the Language of Crime* and *Corrections and Gang Terminology*. Additionally, we verified local slang usage in dancehall, hip-hop, and rap songs, as well as movies, which were indicative of conventionalized slang usages and meanings. Ultimately, we analyzed the original occurrences and the translocalized re-appropriations of gang slang, as well as local inventions, in context, according to discursive, morphological, and semantic criteria. In the data, the lexicon that fit noun and interjection slots were transcribed differently, using lower case and upper case notation respectively—for instance, *ceen* as noun and *Ceen* as an interjection. We coded terms of address as (N), common nouns as (n), and verbs (v), as well as interjections as (I) and idioms as (id). These categorical terms as identified in Appendix 12 are discussed in further detail in relation to the translocalized nature of gangspeak in the forthcoming sections.

Findings and Discussion

Most terms cited in Appendix 12 were extracted from the movies *Warlock* and *Armed and Dangerous*. Variants also emerged in the course of interviewing informants from the Enterprise, Morvant, and Laventille districts. These words at the primary stage of data collection, along with additional variants, were accumulated in specific semantic fields, consistent with the fields of activity associated with gang members, as suggested by Wilkinson (2001) and Banton (1992). These categories entailed violence, status attainment, women, and money. Moreover, the majority of accumulated words fell into the lexical categories of nouns and verbs. The limited use of idioms and interjections may have been because of the language used by actors in the movies that informed the initial Swadesh list. Later this list was expanded by structured interviews and questionnaires.

Among the accumulated vocabulary, all the terms for firearms, including those which were not confined to the archival data, were well-known across the sampled communities. Even the Spanish term *selecta,* which had become conventionalised within the last year, according to one informant, was a recognized term across gang communities. Noun surrogates[1] such as *gyerls, tools,* and *dawg,* and synonyms such as *burn-a* and *piece,* were also in common use for firearms.

On the other hand, the shortening of "firearm" (n.) to *fire* in local gang slang may have been conventionalized over time. This term seems to be used in Morvant, Petit Valley, and Enterprise communities. The data also indicate that *piece* is the preferred term in the Laventille district, and alternatively, *strap, strap up,* and *strapman* (the person carrying the piece) is preferred among informants in Morvant and Laventille. In the first instance, *strap* is a shortened form, and in the second instance, *strap up* is a Creole calque from the American *strapped up* (Knox, 1997, p. 74; Roman, 2014, p. 127). *Strap* was used only by *eld-as* in *Warlock,* the movie based in Petit Valley, but was more prevalent in *Armed and Dangerous,* which was based in the Morvant district.

Terms for women were even more varied, giving rise to common nouns for women in general, for "good time girls," and for loyal partners. For instance, *birds* or *birdie,* which are considered archaic in Central Trinidad, are still in use somewhat in the Morvant district. They refer to females in the generic sense. The origin of this term dates back to an English term for prostitutes in 1560, as women were associated with game and plumage (Green, 2011, p. 184) or the idea of being hunted. On the other hand, dancehall culture describes a *ball–a* as a female who seeks to be entertained at the expense of others, as is sung about in Beenie Man's "Miss L.A.P." (2002, track 6). In the American context, a *ball-a* denotes a high roller, who makes money from crime, possibly even from gambling. However, the term has come to represent females who live by sex in Trinidadian gangspeak.

More recently, American rap music and hip–hop have introduced *thot* into the repertoire of some gang players, for the same category of female. *Rid-a*, a term used for a "personal companion" in Central Trinidad, was unknown to informants surveyed in Morvant and Laventille, who preferred *loyal*, since *ridin* or *linkin* carry the meaning of "brotherly friendship" among gang members from these districts. *Rid-a* was also less widely used among informants, in contrast with *loyal*, which was more widely understood and used to refer to the girlfriends of gang members, as previously mentioned. *Smallie* (a calque of *shortie* from American hip-hop) and *baby–gyerl* (a reggae/dancehall term) also featured as common nouns for the girlfriends of gang players.

Dawg (N/n) is perhaps the most widely used term for fellow gang members or a close friend (see Roman, 2014, p. 115), as both a common noun and as a term of address. This is potentially a clipping of *road dog* (a type of motorcycle). It is quite possible that Dawg (N/n) became conventionalized globally for a fellow gang player by DMX's American rap song "Ruff Ryders Anthem" (1998, track 2). However, in Trinidadian gang slang, the alternative term *dawg-a* is derived by inflection to distinguish a fellow gang member, who is an even closer associate.

Subtle differences were evident in the use of *dawg* as a coterminous reference to gang associates. In the Laventille district, gang-players favoured *bredrin* or *soldy-a* (n) and justified their non-use of *dawg*, as an animal that is debased and subject to abuse by men. In this context, alternatives *bredrin* or *soldy-a* (n) are transmutations of Dread Talk, as influenced by a Rastafari ideology. Elsewhere, *thug* might be used interchangeably for identifying players in criminal activities; however, fellow gang members are also called [(mih) *hoss*, *dawg*, *bredda*, or *nigga*]. *Hoss* (N/n) is both a shortened address term and a common noun for a fellow gang member, which may have been derived from steel horse, a synonym for a motorcycle, associated with biker outlaws (see Bon Jovi's song, "Dead or Alive," 1986, single).

Informants from Morvant and Laventille suggested that *soldy-a* (N) was a common address term in "hailing" another member of the gang community.

This usage stems from the influence of Dread Talk. Incidentally, the *street soldy-a* for supporting actors in local gangspeak recall Joe Marshall's radio call-in program in the 1980s in California. Over time, this term lost its positive association with leadership and resistance to gang culture, since the modern denotation of *soldy-as*, or players suggests gang-running and drug-dealing. In the local context, a *soldy-a* (n) can refer to a "go-for" or a follower of a gang-member.

Shortened address terms for senior gang members include *G, Boss,* and *Fari*, which seem to be widely used in all communities. Among these titles, *G* can be used as a coterminous address term among gang members for a fellow gang member, while *Boss* (N) may well be a reduction of a word compound, like Crime Boss, or is a direct adaptation from English, referring to a kingpin. On the other hand, *fari* from Rastafari is a respectful address term for an elder or community leader with a Rasta hairstyle. The fore-clipping of this term contrasts with previous examples of shortening. Finally, *eld-a* (n) (from English) refers generically to a community leader or gang player of senior status.

Informants from two of the three gang communities seemed familiar with one of two pseudonyms which refer to internationally notorious personae. *Frank* (N), an address term for a thief, from the pen name of "Frank Hohimer," refers to a notorious cat burglar and the author of *Confessions of a Cat Burglar* by John Allen Seybold. This type of name adoption is called eponomy, which describes how specific address terms are derived from the proper names of persons who were associated historically with criminogenic activity. Gang players in the Morvant and Laventille districts were vaguely familiar with the term *Frank* but less certain of its meaning, unlike informants from the Enterprise community. This might explain the type of criminal activities that are the business of particular gang communities, which might result in some terms of address being less known to some communities.

Another eponym, *Monst-a* (N/n), comes from the nickname of Sanyika Shakur, who was initiated, at age eleven, into the L. A. Crips. In the local gang context, *monst-as* are also gang players who are always willing to *press*, or to kill. *Danz* (n) are turf-level gangstas or drug-lords who command *soldy-as*. *Dan* (N) is also a longstanding address term in the dancehall arena (from the Spanish, *Don*), as a title that was originally ascribed to skilled dancehall DJs. The loan word for the drug supplier or *upline, plug* (n), comes directly from contemporary rap in original releases such as Zuse's "My Plug is Latino" (2015, track 4) and Drake's "I'm the Plug" (2015, track 7).

The field of money had the least shared terms in common across the communities that were sampled. Terms for *cash* ranged from *dollar signs*, *toys*, and *racks* for local currency, and *uncle sams* or *sams*, for foreign currency. This phenomenon might be owed to gang memebers being engaged in a variety of economic/criminal enterprises. Despite the fact that *wetman*, *wettie*, or *wetgal* are terms used within the gang community to describe those "who havin" girls, money, and material possessions, this term is derived from dancehall culture and connotes both sexual and material abundance.

Polysemous Verbs from Dancehall
Other prominent vocabulary included a network of polysemous words, which refer to activities by noun additions and substitutions with transitive verbs. These polysemous verb phrases are idioms with multiple meanings, which have been directly extrapolated from dancehall songs dating back from the 1980s to present. They also highlight the centrality of sex, violence, and status as closely intertwined in a semantic network of meanings across the sampled communities.

For instance, *press* (v) from "Press ganshat inna dehm skin laik steepl" on Kartel, "Sen fi d Magazine," (2008, single) may have popularized the usage of "pressin" as a verb for killing. The idea of moving into killing action is also captured in "leh we press." The meaning of *press* has also been broadened to express the extortion of money and drugs and sexual pursuit embodied in the expression "pressin on ah smallie before somebody else geh she" (Snakie, phone interview, November, 20 2015).

Similarly, *eat ah food* is a calque of West African "nyam" found in Jamaican Creole. However, *food*, as money, has a specific connotation in local gangspeak. An excerpt from the movie *Warlock* refers to "eating a food," or making money, and "eatin up Ratty food," referring to money from drug dealing. *Eat ah food* in Trinidadian gangspeak has maintained the original meaning of *food* in Jamaican gang slang, as money from drug dealing, although the expression has been expanded to other contexts of economic gain in Trinidadadian Creole, as in Jamaican Creole. However, *eat ah food*, as having sex, is more widely used as a reference in the African diaspora for sexual jokes.

Link (v), derived from the dancehall context of use in local gangspeak, fulfils both verb and noun slots, in examples such as *link up wit yuh later* (v), which signifies "contact you later," and *get ah link* (n), which connotes being connected to a drug supplier or wholesaler. The underlying connotation in both cases is "contact" (from English). Underlying the first usage is the conversion of the referent *link* from noun to verb, from English to Creole contexts of usage. However, *touch* (v) is most commonly used in the dancehall arena for physical contact in intimacy. In the local context, *touch* is often used with an intimate connotation of contact with a friend, as seen in "I'll touch yuh later," "I'll link with yuh," or "vibes yuh," in other contexts. This term also retains some traditional connotations of gang activity, such as robbery, as in "touch up somebody and take dey ting," just as in the 17th century Anglo-Saxon euphemistic context of theft. Green (2011) therefore identifies *touch* with swindling and robbery (pp. 16, 85). However, local usage shows a drift in meaning from swindling to smuggling, as in the expressions *touch ah brick ah weed* or *touch ah crate ah guns* and *touch dem up* as a modern euphemism for shooting, or *ah touch up*, a beating.

Buss corn, crack corn, and *fire corn* (v) are Trinidadian Creole calques for *bus kaan* [bʌs kã:n] or *pap kaan* [phap kã:n] in Jamaican gangspeak, also derived from bust a cap, a term used during the American Civil War for firing shots. However, *buss corn* is the most widely known term among gang players. On the other hand, *call ah shot* (v), derived from General Grant's (1992) Trinidadian dancehall song "Shot Call," gave rise to the lexical phrase *call ah shot,* referring to either staging a "hangout" or "big lime" or "ordering a hit." On the other hand, *buss ah shot* refers to bringing a large quantity of drugs into the local territory.

Other polysemous terminology refers to status attainment and relative status negotiation by the different uses of the term *rankin* (adj. v) (from the English "ranking"). In one context, it carries the opposite meaning of the American usage (Roman, 2014, p. 112) as a breach of gang ethics. Rather, as an adjectival verb in *dem fellas rankin*, the connotation is one of "living large." However, *rankin ting* as adjectival predicate following the verb *to be* is equivalent to *playin mad,* or *breaching gang ethics.* In another sense, *Is ah rankin ting* connotes "rank snatching," or an unwillingness to give up sexual favors on the part of a desired female (Snakie, personal communication, November 20, 2015).

Finally, *switch* (v) from Flourgon's (1988) dancehall song "We Nah Get rich and Go Switch" is widely understood in the contexts of "turnin against ah bredrin." *Geh rich an switch* is an idiom for acquiring wealth and then turning against "ah bredrin." Discursive and semantic patterns of language use are addressed further in the following sections.

The Discourse Features of Gangspeak and Gangsta Identity

Beyond the lexical features of gangspeak is a speech style of local gang players that is characteristically performative, showing evidence of discursive and pragmatic features of performativity. Pennycook (2007) suggests that performance acts of identity are an ongoing series of social and cultural performances rather than an expression of a prior identity. These performances include the use of Dread Talk and language expressing the discursive functions of agreement, marking information, greetings, negotiating respect, and speaking in metaphors. In this way, they conjure aspects of gangsta identity, which are context-bound.

Rastafari language. The influence of Dread Talk is a feature of performativity, which points to a Rastafari renaissance, which came to dancehall through dancehall singers and DJs such as Buju Banton, Luciano, and Capleton (Stolzoff, 2000, p. 3). This influence also accounts for elements of Dread Talk that are part of gang speech in the Caribbean. For example, *Ceen* (I) is a longstanding and versatile referent, which was popularized by the Rastafari movement in Jamaica. It was initially an interjection of "overstanding," as a marker of agreement, since the 1970s. The meaning of this interjection is premised on the reversal and rejection of "understanding" in colonial English, which seemed contradictory to the Rastafarian ideology of positivity. In addition to its original meaning, this lexical feature has undergone semantic broadening to perform the role of a multifunctional noun surrogate.

Another example of the lexical influence of Dread Talk on Trinidadian gangspeak can be found in the verb form for connect or link–*vibes* (v), such as in *vibes wit you* or *vibes me* and *ah go vibes yuh*. However, *vibes* as an interjection (I) is synonymous with a friendly parting greeting among gang players. We presume that the origin of this interjection also comes from Dread Talk, and that the noun *vibes* for "feelings" may have undergone conversion from noun to verb in this context. Other variants of *vibes* as a parting greeting are *more love, more life, next rise, after God, Inshallah* (If God wills), and *Mashallah* (God Bless), which reflect both Rastafarian and Muslim speech styles. In Trinidad, these elements are reflective of the influence of Muslim and Rasta worldviews among gang members, which translate into having different greeting and parting rituals.

Finally, although shortened verbs may not necessarily reflect true Dread Talk, they are characteristically a Jamaican dancehall speech style, which was evident in the repertoire of local gangstas. Specific evidence of this feature in data are shortened forms of the verb "allow" and "remember," which were vocalised as *llow* and *memba* in the spoken discourse actors in the movie scripts from the Morvant district. In addition, throughout the interview sessions, these specific elements of a dancehall register, which are Jamaican Creole, were also part of the speech style of all informants. Therefore, we concluded that this was also a performative part of the gangsta speech style, as this feature was isolated only to these verbs.

Diasporic styles of discourse. As gang members are part an "imaginary" network of oral cultures within the African diaspora, gangspeak is also characterised by the ideological and cultural frames of African diasporic speech styles. Therefore, performance features of African diasporic oral language and culture have also been transposed into the local context of Trinidadian gangspeak. Mitchell-Kernan (1972) suggests the following three features as diasporic characteristics of Black English and discourse, which are signifying, loud-talking, and marking. The elements which we deem reflective of local gangspeak, as a form of "street language," are present as the notions of (1) achieving and holding respect (equivalent to louding or gaining status through language), (2) marking (in the sense of discourse markers–a feature that differs from Mitchell-Kernan's marking as mimicry), and (3) signifying (using language to effect indirectness). The following sections explain these elements further.

Terms of address and respect. In Trinidadian gangspeak, the ritualistic performance of respect as a feature of "street language" is evident in use of address terms, as commonplace indicators of relationship and status in the spoken repertoire of gang players. For instance, the ritual deployment of

Monst-a, Hoss, Dawg, or *Dan*, at the beginning and end of conversational turns not only marks the relative status and relationship of the speaker to the addressee, but also denotes a speech style that defers to the status of gang interactants. An example of this feature is found in the proposition: "Dan, Dan. I not on dat ranking ting wit you, you know, Hoss" (excerpt from Warlock, 2014).

Self-imaging and respect. Another marked element of African performance discourse in local gangspeak is "louding" or the verbal predisposition to violence as self-imaging for respect. Anderson (1999) also suggests that the code of the street revolves around the presentation of self as having a violent predisposition as a deterrent to aggression (p. 88). Regarding holding respect by this means, one informant from Morvant underscored that "If you don't stand up for them, somebody go stand up for you" (MM, personal communication, February 23, 2016). Moreover, the need for "loudness" in "gangsta talk" is honed when gang players spend time in the hostile environment of correctional facilities.

The idea of "self-imaging" and "louding" are also tied to the local gangsta speech style that is reminiscent of the "robber talk" among fearsome characters in Caribbean folklore from the colonial past. This legacy was born first among steelband gangs in the 1800s and followed later among urban gangstas who would intimidate their opponents through language. The rhetorical boasts of contemporary gangsta also recall the personae of American gangsters of the 1940s and 1950s who exercised rhetorical power and intimidation over their hearers. Poignant examples of this word play are shown in the following data from Trinidadian gangspeak:

1. "Forgiveness is for God and I arrange d meet" (Excerpt from the What's App status of a gangsta, Snakie, from Central Trinidad, 2015).
2. "When yuh meet yuh maker tell him I sen' yuh" (Excerpt on reprisal killing, from *Armed and Dangerous*).
3. If yuh ketch meh ah dong in hell; if yuh want to see how hell is, come dong and meet meh (Answering service of an anonymous gangsta).
4. "I play yuh, I pay yuh, an' ah take yuh money, Dawg" (Excerpt 1, on gambling, from *Warlock*).

Interjections for marking discourse. Interjections form another category of conventions that is found in the repertoire of local gang players as mostly stand-alone elements of the discourse, fillers and place holders in the gangsta speech style, formulaic words and lexical phrases that mark emotion, quality of information, intention, and agreement. However, the use of interjections as "marking discourse" in local gangspeak differs from Mitchell-Kernan's "marking" as mimicry. For instance, they make liberal use of the discourse markers *boi* and *nah boi* (I) as fillers in discourse to captivate the hearer's attention, to pacify or appeal to the hearer, or to mark new information as important. This is evident in the data in the excerpts: "Boi, hush yuh mout, nah boi" and "Monst-a, ah ceen goin an start for sure here, boi" (*Warlock*). In addition, interjections such as *Ah telling yuh*, or *I tellin' yuh* are features of gangsta discourse, which denotes a pledge of intentions. This function in gang discourse is evident in "Dawg, Dawg, I tellin yuh... dem fellas hatta f#@#-in' go at de en'in' ah d day" (Excerpt from *Warlock*). Finally, the use of *yuh done know* (I) in gangsta discourse also denotes a recognition of an obvious situation, as another type of "marking" of the known quality of information. This usage became conventionalized by Jamaican dancehall artist Beenie Man in "Row like a Boat" (2004). Similar contexts of use in the data were also found in *Warlock*: "Yuh done know I home unplatting meh hair, boi."

On the other hand, stand-alone interjections include *straight* and *word* (I) as examples of parting interjections of agreement (straight or "telling the truth" or "okay" in American gang slang), possibly from African American vernacular speech, hip-hop, and rap cultures. *One* (I) is also used as an opening and departure greeting among gang-players; however, there is the added meaning of unity in an underlying brotherly code of agreement. The meaning of this interjection has most likely shifted from the American gang context of *all is one*, which was originally a full-scale gang fight or an encounter between two individuals. This feature is particular to the Laventille district and not the other districts which were sampled in this study.

"Talking in heights." Gang players in Trinidad also refer to an action called "talking in heights," which is talking above the heads of others, as a type of indirect speech, which is dependent on the interactants sharing a high level context. This feature runs parallel to Gates' (1950) notion of "signifying," as the master trope of rhetoric in the African diaspora, and an umbrella term for assembling together many modes of discourse, which function to turn literal meaning into metaphor (p. 52). Linn (1974) defines a high context as one which suggests a high degree of familiarity with the situation and the speakers in it (p. 7). In the spirit of this speech style, local gang players manipulate specific noun surrogates, verb and noun combinations, allusions, and pseudonyms for law enforcement to create this effect. They also create situationally invented language as indirect speech style for dissuading overhearers.

For instance, informants from Laventille, Morvant, and Enterprise confirmed that the noun surrogate *ceen* (n), such as in *wha iz de ceen* and *wuz your ceen*, can either signal an invitation to an intimate encounter by indirect questioning or an enquiry into the activities of an individual player or gang entity, without naming the activity in question. Alternatives to questioning with a less versatile semantic application include *wey iz d shot* or *wey iz vibes*. Unlike the previous examples, *ceen* can alternate as a noun surrogate in a greeting like *wha iz d ceen*, *wuz d ceen*, or *wey d ceen*, and in *handle ceen*, as a referent to a job, killing, planned activity, or sexual encounter among gang members and prostitutes. This is evidenced in the use of *ceen* in *lock d ceen*, for "policing a territory," as being derived from dancehall by calquing the expression *lok di skihm*. In this case, [skī:m] and [si:n] can easily approximate each other in phonological shape, by an initial consonant cluster reduction [sk] → [si], and word final assimilation where [m] → [n].

Another feature of indirectness within the local gangspeak is the use of allusions, which are "implied, indirect, or passing references to a person or thing, or the action or process of making such a reference" (The Oxford English Dictionary Online). In making allusions to events, future action, and persons indirectly, members of gang communities have drawn on dancehall culture, American movie culture, and references to law enforcement officials from foreign loan terms to confound the context of their speech.

For instance, the phrase "ehniting a ehniting" meaning "by any means necessary" and "by any necessary action" can refer to any context determined by the speaker. Although Jamaican dancehall artists Kartel (2010, track 4) and Kartel and Slim (2012, single) may have made this expression popular within recent times, it has a much older intertextual reach into American cinema of the 1970s whereby Black detectives in movies such as "Shaft," "Uptown, Saturday Night," and "Trouble Man" blurred the lines of law and order to establish law and order. In this context, "anything became anything." In contemporary Trinidadian gangspeak, this same lexical phrase refers to contexts of sexual encounters or violent reprisal, which can denote "whatever yuh for, I for."

Other examples of allusion cover a variety of semantic fields of covert transactions and activity. For instance, *cuttin ah flick* is similar to *handlin ah ceen*, by its indirect meaning. It denotes "going on a ceen" that is exciting enough to be memorable—hence the allusion to a movie episode or "flick." In another example, local gang players have indicated that speaker meaning concerning "havin' ting" is only decipherable by body language and contextual cues, which can refer to drugs, guns, or metaphorical power, as this indefinite idiom has both noun and verb surrogates with varied meanings.

Situational indirectness is another way of safeguarding context against overhearers and intercepted communication among gang players. Hence, the need for situational indirectness leads to two gang players creating "their own heights." In addition, there is also the practice of speaking without the mention of names, since gang players purport that names are only for tombstones. One informant from the Laventille district identified *doan mash dat spot* and *say no more* as examples of cues that can alert to the proximity of a threat from law enforcement or the possibility of an overheard conversation. With these contexts, officers of law enforcement are also referred to as *5-0s*,[2] *Coppers*, *Opps* and *Pigs*, all terms associated with American gang culture that are likely to have been inherited through rap music. Local variants from the local slang include "Look Dem" and "Blue Lights."

Limitations

The limited language samples in this study are the result of concerns for the safety and security of the researchers given the sensitivity of the topic under inquiry. Therefore, this exploratory study is only a beginning point for further research using larger corpora and wider sampling throughout Trinidad and Tobago, in order to capture greater variation in the local gangsta lexicon. Given the shortage of research on gangspeak in the Caribbean, the knowledge gained by this study will facilitate further research into areas such as slang variation in Trinidad and the Caribbean among gang players.

Conclusion

Although gang slang is somewhat elusive, the study of local gang slang or gangspeak is important for identifying the spread of gang culture via language and cultural media. This type of research is relevant to the fields of language contact in sociolinguistics, cultural criminology, and anthropology, as well as to a cross-section of stakeholders who may find it useful to their understanding of gang culture. Among these interested parties are police officers, educators, social workers, criminologists, and lawyers.

The amalgam of resources, which constitutes Trinidadian gangspeak, benefits largely from rap, dancehall, hip–hop, and local coinages and adaptations as the primary lexifiers of the code. The code also shows evidence of transidiomacity by the re-appropriation of rhetorical speech styles of African oral performance discourse. Some lexical referents have also been adopted into local gangspeak from American movies, television programmes on law enforcement, as well as from Rastafari talk. With regard to the morphology of local gang lexicon, clipping and polysemous words supply the largest amount of noun and verb constructs to the repertoire of gang players. Terms of address, common nouns, verbs, idioms, and interjections have been derived from pop culture, dancehall, hip-hop, and rap music. However, global touring by dancehall, rap, and hip–hop singers, Internet networking and telecommunication technology contribute to the rapid distribution of song lyrics, media images, and a worldview and vocabulary, which pertain to the gangsta speech style. Moreover, these cultural modes have diffused elements of British, American, and Jamaican slang terms throughout the ethnoscapes of global gang communities.

Translocalization and transidiomatization are key critical sociolinguistic elements of the discourse, since they introduce novel ways of perceiving the process and results of language contact in the globalized setting of fluid culturescapes, where transnational gang cultures, gang communities, and their language use may seem intangible. In this way they enable the understanding that Trinidadian gangspeak is not one standardizable code.

Even while a global framework affords accessibility and transparency regarding the source cultures of this combined lexicon, opaque elements within Trinidadian gangspeak result from three primary factors. To begin with, Trinidadian gangspeak includes "talking in heights," which is indirect metaphorical language requiring a shared context between interactants, unknown to outsiders. Secondly, the multiplicity of resources that is invested in the local gang code (from Spanish, Muslim, Rastafari, foreign slang terms, dancehall, hip-hop, rap, and American movie culture) has created a complex morpho-semantic relationship, which makes ready-made meaning equivalents unavailable in metropolitan dictionaries. Finally, the polysemous nature of mainly verb elements within the local gang slang covers multiple semantic fields in the arena of criminality, sex, status, and violence, as a closed network of meanings to the outsider.

Overall, the study adds to the limited body of knowledge which has been largely metropolitan in nature, as research on gangspeak has not been based on Caribbean territories, so far. It also confirms that Trinidadian gangspeak is a transmutation of linguistic and cultural resources from local and distant sources and codes, simultaneously.

Notes

1. We use the term noun surrogate to describe a word used in place of a specific noun, but also functioning as a substitute for other nouns in other semantic fields. For instance, *tool* for the male member and a gun, *ceen* for activity, sexual encounter, meeting, among others or *gyerl* for any possession, requiring material investment—gun, car, clothing, including a girlfriend.
2. *Hawaii 5-0* was an American police television show.

References

Alim, H. S. (2004). Hip hop nation language. In E. A. Finegan (Ed.), *Language in the USA: Themes for the 21st century* (pp. 387- 408). Cambridge: Cambridge University Press.

Anderson, E. (1999). *Code of the street*. New York: WW Norton and Company.

Appadurai, A. (1996). *Modernity at large: Cultural dimensions of globalization*. Minneapolis: University of Minnesota Press.

Banton, B. (1992). Love me brownin' On *Mr. Mention* [LP]. Kingston, Jamaica: Penthouse Records Distribution Ltd.

Bissessar, A. (2013). The nexus between structural adjustment and the emergence of gangs: The case of trinidad and tobago. In R. Seepersad & A. M. Bissessar (Eds.), *Gangs in the caribbean* (pp. 131-149). Newcastle on Tyne, UK: Cambridge Scholars Publishing.

Bon Jovi, J. (1998). Wanted dead or alive. On *Slippery when wet* [CD]. St. Louis, MO: Mercury Records.

Chris, Y. (2011). Racks [Featuring Future]. Atlanta, GA: Forever Flexin Entertainment/ Big Play.

Coleman, J. (2014). *Global slang: Methodologies and perspectives*. London: Routledge.

DMX. (1988). Ruff Ryders Anthem On *It's dark and hell is hot*. Capitol Heights, MD: New Horizon Sound Studio.

Drake. (2015). I'm the Plug On *What a time to be alive* [Mixtape] Toronto, CA:OVO Sound.

Drugs trafficking in the Caribbean: An old route regains popularity with drugs gangs. (2014, May 24th). *The Economist*. Retrieved from: http://www.economist.com/news/americas/21602680-old-route-regains-popularity-drugs-gangs-full-circle

Duranti, A. (2001). *Key terms in language and culture*. Boston, MA: Blackwell.

Fairclough, N. (2006). *Language and globalisation*. Oxford: Routledge.

Farquharson, J., & Jones, B. (2014). Jamaican slang. In J. Coleman (Ed.), *Global slang: Methodologies and perspectives* (pp. 116-125). London: Routledge.

Faugier, J., & Sargeant, M. (1997). Sampling hard to reach populations. *Journal of Advanced Nursing*, 26(4), 790-797. doi:10.1046/j.1365-2648.1997.00371.x

Gates, H. L. Jr. (1998). *The signifying monkey: A theory of Afro-American literary criticism*. New York: Oxford University Press.

Grascia, A. M. (2003). Gangster rap: The real words behind the songs. *The Journal of Gang Research*, 11(1), 55-63.

Green, J. (2011). *Crooked talk: Five hundred years of crime*. London: Cornerstone.

Hill, S. (2013). The rise of gang violence in the Caribbean. In R. Seepersad & A. M. Bissessar (Eds.), *Gangs in the Caribbean* (pp. 36-79). Newcastle Upon Tyne, UK: Cambridge Scholars Publishing.

Jacquemet, M. (2005). Transidomatic practices: Language and power in the age of globalization. *Language and Communication*, 25, 257-277. doi:10.1016/j.langcom.2005.05.001

Kartel, V. (2008). Sen Fi D Magazine [Single]. Kingston, Jamaica: Adidjaheim Records.

Kartel, V. (2010). Clarks. [LP] Kingston, JA: Jaheimraheim/Jackrussell/BMI.

Kartel, V. (2010). Gal a weh me duh yuh. *On pon de Gaza* 2.0 [Featuring Shebba, CD]. Kingston, Jamaica: Tad's Record Co.

Kartel, V. (2012). Anyting a anyting [Single]. Kingston, Jamaica: Adidjaheim Records.

Knox, G. W. (1997). Gang dictionary: A guide to gang slang and gang vocabulary and gang socio-lingusitic phrases. *The Journal of Gang Research*, 4(4), 66-75.

Kubrin, C. E. (2005) Gangstas, thugs and hustlas: Identity and the code of the street in rap music. *Social Problems*, 52(3), 360–378.

Linn, M. D. (1974). Black rhetorical patterns and the teaching of composition. Anaheim, CA: Annual Meeting of the Conference on College Composition. Retrieved from the ERIC Database. (ED092966)

Man, B. (2002). Miss LAP. On *Snow storm* [CD]. New York: Virgin Records America Inc.

Mattielo, E. (2008). *An introduction to English slang: A description of its morphology semantics and sociology*. Milano: Polimetrica.

Meyerhoff, M. (2006). *Introducing sociolinguistics.* Oxford: Routledge.
Mitchell-Kernan, C. (1972). Signifying and marking: Two Afro-American speech acts. In J. J. Gumperz & D. Hymes (Eds.), *Directions in sociolinguistics* (pp. 161-79). New York: Holt, Rinehart and Winston.
Oxford English dictionary online (2nd ed.). (2016). Kettering, UK: Oxford University Press.
Parker, M. M. (2012). Globalization and gang growth: The four phenomena effect. *Journal of Gang Research, 19*(2), 33-49.
Penfold-Mounce, R. (2009). *Celebrity culture and crime: The joy of transgression.* Hampshire: Palgrave Macmillan.
Pennycook, A. (2007). *Global Englishes and transcultural flows.* London: Routledge.
Popcaan. (2014). Give thanks. On *Where we come from* [CD] Brooklyn, NY: Dubble Dutch.
Prouse, C. E. (2012). *Defining street gangs in the 21st century: Fluid mobile and transnational networks.* New York: Springer.
Richards, J. C., & Schimdt, R. (2010). *Longman dictionary of language teaching and applied linguistics.* Harlow: Pearson Education Limited.
Roman, M. R. (2014). *Introduction to corrections and gang terminology.* Redding: BVT Publishing.
Seepersad, R. (2013). Crime in the Caribbean. In R. Seepersad & A. M. Bissessar (Eds.), *Gangs in the Caribbean* (pp. 2-35). Newcastle on Tyne, UK: Cambridge Scholars Publishing.
Seepersad, R., & Bissessar, A. M. (2013). *Gangs in the Caribbean.* Newcastle Upon Tyne, UK: Cambridge Scholars Publishing.
Shakur, S. (1993). *Autobiography of an L.A. gang member.* New York: Grove Press.
Stolzoff, N. C. (2000). *Wake the town and tell the people: Dancehall culture in Jamaica.* Durham: Duke University Press.
Thorne, T. (2014). Jamaican slang. In J. Coleman (Ed.), *Global slang: Methodologies and perspectives* (pp. 72-82). London: Routledge.
Tomlinson, J. (1999). *Globalization and culture.* Chicago: The University of Chicago Press.
Townsend, D. (2009). *No other life: Gangs, guns and governance in trinidad and tobago.* Geneva: Graduate Insititute of International Development.
Wilkinson, D. (2001). Violent events and social identity: Specifying the relationship between respect and masculinity in inner-city youth violence. In D. Kinney (Ed.), *Sociological studies of children and youth* (pp. 231– 265). Stamford, CT: Elsevier Science.
Zuse. (2015). My plug is Latino. On *Trap Zuse* [Featuring Young Thug, CD]. Atlanta, GA: Dun Deal.

Appendix 12

Lexical Item	Warlock	Armed and Dangerous	Source	Lexical Variation
Handle a ceen (id)	X	X	Trinidadian slang	Cut ah flick (Am. Movie Culture)
Wey iz d ceen (I)	X	X	Trinidadian slang	Wey iz d shot; Wey iz vibes. (Trini slang)
Wey iz d word (I)	X	O		Wey iz ceen. (Trini slang)
Dawg (N)	X	X	American rap	Dawg-a (Trini slang)
G (N)	X	X	American rap	hoss; dawg (N)
Monst-a (N/n)	X	X	American gang folklore	shoot-a(n); kill-a (n) (Eng)
plug (n)	O	O	American rap	link (n)
Hoss (N)	X	X	American pop culture	Dawg (N) hip–hop/rap
Dan (N)	X	O	Jamaican/Spanish Outlaw	Soldy-a (N) Dread Talk
ball-a (n)	X	X	American rap/ re-assigned meaning in dancehall	thot (n) (Am Rap); rid-a; baby-gyerl; smallie (Trini) loyal (Trini) (Dancehall)
Frank (N)	O	O	American movie culture	N/A
wetman (n)	O	O	dancehall	wettie, wetgal (dancehall)
gyerl (n)	X	O	American rap	piece, smallie
soldy-as (npl)	X	X	American pop culture	thugs (Am Rap)

eld-a (n)	X	X	Trinidadian slang	N/A
say no more (id)	X	O	American Gangs	N/A
Ceen (I)	O	O	Dread Talk	Straight, Word (American Rap)
Straight (I)	X	X	American slang	Word, Ceen, Vibes
Vibes (I)	O	O	dancehall	More Life, Next Rise, After God, More Love (Dread Talk) Inshallah, Mashallah, (Arabic)
touch (v)	X	X	dancehall	vibes, link (v)
Word (I)	X	X	American rap	Ceen, (Dread Talk) Straight (Am. gangs)
rankin ting (id)	X	O	American/Jamaican slang reappropriated as Trinidadian slang	N/A
playin mad (id)	X	X	Trinidadian G. Slang	on rankin ting (Trini slang)
have…ting (v)	X	O	Trinidadian G. Slang	have load; have real ting (Trini Slang)
eat ah food (id)	X	O	Trinidadian G. Slang	eat (Trini slang)
havin (v)	O	O	Trinidadian G. Slang	N/A
press (v)	X	O	dancehall	touch dem up; pepper dem up (Trini slang)
piece (n)	X	O	American slang	burn-a, dawg, tool, gyerl

anyting is anyting (id)	X	X	American/ dancehall	N/A
fire (n)	X	O	Trinidadian slang	burn-a, dawg, tool, gyerl
selecta (n)	O	O	Venezuelan Spanish American	N/A
cash (n)	O	O		sams; uncle sams racks (rap); dollar signs (Trini slang)
strap (n)	X	X	American Gangs	strap up; strapman
memba (v)	O	X	Dancehall	N/A
Llow (v)	O	X	Dancehall	N/A
switch (v)	X	O	Dancehall	N/A

CHAPTER 13

REACHING OUTSIDE THE CLASSROOM:
A Qualitative Look at the Effects of Community on the Heritage Language Development of University Students[1]

N. Ariana Mrak
University of North Carolina, Wilmington

Introduction

Researchers are in agreement on the connection that needs to exist between heritage language education (HLE) and the community in which the heritage language (HL) resides. First and foremost, while instructors may be concerned with increasing the academic skills of their students, the latter have a long-term need to interact in and with their communities. A survey of post-secondary HL learners (HLLs) confirmed that the most important need students have for their HL is to connect with their communities (Beaudrie, Ducar, & Relaño-Pastor, 2009). It is for this reason, if no other, that curriculum design for HL courses needs to involve knowledge about the communities to which the learners belong (Carreira & Kagan, 2011). Interestingly, because speakers do not always initiate interaction on their own, the connection made through the classroom becomes even more significant (Schwarzer & Petrón, 2005). Moreover, there is strong evidence that development and maintenance of the HL requires more than just interaction with family; exposure to different linguistic domains is needed in order to develop vocabulary outside of the traditional areas of home and church in which speakers use their HL. In order to extend the use of the HL, there must be additional forms of comprehensible input such as those provided by watching television, reading, and traveling to the country where the HL is spoken (Cho & Krashen, 2000; Fishman, 2004). The impact group membership has on language proficiency and performance has been demonstrated by several studies (Oriyama, 2012; Tse, 2001; Zentella, 1997). Furthermore, investigators agree on how crucial it is to develop curricula for HLE that incorporate community connections as these reinforce learners' cultural identity. Beaudrie et al. (2009) specifically proposed interviews with relatives and friends, descriptions of social gatherings, and cultural projects in the community; Rodríguez-Pino (1994) suggested ethnographic studies; Roca and Alonso (2006) developed the *Abuelos Project* in order to get students to interview elderly family members (as cited in Carreira & Kagan, 2011), and Carreira and Kagan (2011) recommended interviews with family and community members, recording oral histories, and researching the history of the country of immigration. Martínez and Schwartz (2012) took students into medical settings as interpreters, taking into account Aparicio's (2000) suggestion of the need to show students the usefulness of their HL. Unfortunately, in spite of all of the above work being done, most HL programs at the post-secondary level have a lot of improvement to make in order to forge ties with their respective communities (Villa, 2010; Wiley, 2005).

Work conducted by Showstack (2010) on Texas Spanish described a curricular design that included student interviews with local Spanish speakers and subsequent student reflections designed to encourage critical language awareness. This is part of a larger project intended to bring local varieties of Spanish into the L2 classroom as well as to create a space in the HL classroom for discussions on language, power, and linguicism.[2] This type of approach to the curriculum falls within the parameters of place-based learning, a culturally responsive and relevant pedagogy that allows HLLs to develop their own critical views of social inequalities through their very own experiences (Helmer, 2010). Furthermore, allowing students to see that these varieties are worthy of study breaks away from the dichotomy that continues to exist in HL classes between what is spoken in the community and what is taught in the classroom. Even though Spanish is everywhere in the United States, the varieties of HLLs rarely, if ever, are a part of what is taught in the L2 classroom or even what is used in the HL classroom (Wiley, 2005). Another aspect that deserves attention is student motivation. Helmer (2010) showed community building between the instructor and the students as well as between the students is needed before learning can occur. Further research by this investigator on the lack of interest and motivation she found in some of her HL subjects indicated that the cause for this disengagement with the subject matter was a negative opinion of the instructor—when they perceived a lack of understanding or respect of their culture—or due to subject matter that students did not feel was relevant to them (Helmer, 2013). A facet of HL development that highlights the importance of helping students connect with their HL is that speakers at the post-secondary level are most likely in the ethnic emergence stage of the ethnic identity development model proposed by Tse (1998). They are moving away from ethnic ambivalence and are reaching the stage in which they are receptive to learning about their heritage culture and language; thus, it is crucial to take advantage of the timing.

It is with all of this research in mind that we decided to create an activity for our class for Spanish for HLLs that would: (1) present students with an opportunity to study the varieties spoken by community members, (2) demonstrate to students that these varieties are worthy of study, (3) validate all the varieties, both the ones in the community and those in the classroom, (4) provide opportunities for interaction with members of the Hispanic community, since students report this as the primary reason for studying the HL (Beaudrie et al., 2009; Carreira & Kagan, 2011), and (5) give HLLs ownership of their language, as oftentimes HLLs feel the language belongs to native speakers, not to them (Chamberlin-Quinlisk & Senyshyn, 2012). A description of the entire project in which the students participated is presented, followed by an assessment of the outcomes and suggestions for continued development that can be applied to other heritage language classrooms.

The Study

Given the investigations that have shown that connecting Spanish HLLs to the Hispanic community creates a classroom environment where the principles of critical pedagogy can be applied and where students get a voice in analyzing and determining the value of language varieties, the intent is to reach out to the community to initiate discussions on the local varieties of Spanish, on how the language is being used in the community every day by its speakers. In other words, the goal is to show students that the focus of study is the Spanish that surrounds them.

The Subjects

The focus of analysis is one Spanish for heritage speakers' class at the intermediate level in a public university in the Southeastern United States. This class is the first of two courses that make up the Spanish for Bilingual Speakers track and it is the first Spanish course at the post-secondary level for all of the students included in the sample. They all fall within Valdés' (2000) definition of heritage language learners, as they were all raised in Spanish-speaking homes and they are bilingual in English and Spanish. This class took place in Fall 2014. The HLLs in this study live in one of the states that belong to the New Latino Diaspora (Harklau, 2009), one that has seen an increase of 111% in its Hispanic population in the ten-year period between 2000 and 2010 to a total of 8.4% (CensusViewer, 2014a). The city in which the university is located experienced even more dramatic Hispanic growth: 196.5% in the same time period to a total of 6.1% (CensusViewer, 2014b), a percentage that is also reflected in the institution (6%) (CollegeData, 2014). These new locations of Hispanic immigration present the need to apply some of the pedagogical approaches that advocates of Spanish education for heritage speakers have long suggested. It is with this intent that the present study was conducted.

Procedures

Two class assignments directed students to work with community members. Each was comprised of three parts. The first asked students to interview a Spanish speaker from the community who shares the same geographic language variety as the student, to present the results of the interview to the class, and to write an essay reflecting on the interview experience. The second assignment includes the same three tasks, but this time, the speaker must be from a different variety of Spanish than the student. Ethnographic interviews have long been a part of the HL classroom (Carreira, 2012; Roca & Alonso, 2006, as cited in Carreira & Kagan, 2011; Rodríguez-Pino, 1994). These two assignments are designed to allow for an emic as well as an etic perspective on the HL by having the students work within their language variety in the first task and then reflecting from the outside for the second one (Whitehead, 2004).

In order to prepare students for the interviews, class discussions included the topic of geographic variation, both between and within countries. For the first part of the assignment, students could reach out to a family member or acquaintance from their parents' country of origin. For the second part, they approached an acquaintance or friend or they contacted members of the university's Hispanic student center in order to find a subject from a different Hispanic country. For the interview, the instructions gave students some sample questions but also indicated that the purpose was to obtain the person's opinion on the Spanish s/he speaks as well as other varieties of Spanish including the one spoken in the U.S. and that the questions were intended merely as a guide. They were asked to conduct a twenty-to-thirty-minute interview and to record it, excluding any identifying information on the interviewee. Classmates could not be interviewed. Another consideration that went into the instructions had to do with demonstrating to students the instructor's knowledge of and membership in the community for the purpose of providing students a sense of connection between themselves, the instructor, and the community; and thus, increasing student motivation and interest. Instructor's assistance with possible locations to find subjects generated discussions on the layout of the community, the different businesses and their owners as well as possible contacts. These insights into the local community helped those students not familiar with the Hispanic areas in the city. The analyses of different varieties spoken in the class and in the community added relevance to the learning experience and made sure that students did not feel any of the varieties spoken in the classroom or in the community were stigmatized, as such a perception would affect the HLL's motivation to learn (Wiley, 2005). Because the student population in this particular class was composed of individuals from a variety of Spanish-speaking regions—eleven the semester this study was conducted—and the majority of the Hispanic community is Mexican, it seemed important to have students interact with individuals with whom they may not otherwise come in contact. The oral presentation gave the entire class the opportunity to hear everyone's experience conducting the interview as well as the results from a broad variety of speakers. The essay part of the assignments is the focus of this study.

Data Analysis and Results

This work falls within what Norton Peirce (1995) termed "classroom-based social research" where "learners become ethnographers in their local communities" (p. 26). This type of analysis is conducted by the learners in their communities and it encompasses the following objectives: (1) interact with other heritage language speakers, (2) reflect on the interactions and observations in a written format, (3) note and record unusual events, and (4) compare data with fellow students/researchers. Even though Norton Peirce originally proposed this framework for second language learners, it has been applied to heritage language learners (Wong & Xiao, 2010; Wu, Lee, & Leung, 2014).

For the first essay, the prompt asks: *¿Qué aprendí de la primera entrevista? / What did I learn from the first interview?* What follows is an analysis of students' reflections as they relate to their HL development. The comments on example (1) are from a student born in the U.S. who grew up in a home with a Spanish-speaking mother and an English-speaking father. The interview provided her with an example of language variation and new insights into Spanish.

1. Este proyecto fue la primera vez que yo he dado cuenta en las formas distintas que hay para hablar el español. Y fue la primera vez que yo pude oír la diferencia.[3]
This project was the first time that I have realized the different ways there are to speak Spanish. And it was the first time that I could hear the difference.[3]

The second example is from a student that was born in the U.S. to Hispanic parents and spent six years of his life in a Spanish-speaking country. He interviews his grandmother, who does not live in the U.S. As he interviews her, he starts to detect differences between her Spanish and his. He becomes aware of dialect leveling, how his exposure to other varieties of Spanish has changed his own. At the same time, he welcomes it as an interesting feature of the language.

2. Lo último que aprendí en mi entrevista fue que mi español ha cambiado un poco desde que me mude a EE.UU. Al hablar con mi abuela, escuche el español [argentino][4] y sonaba raro. Algunas palabras tenían un tono diferente pero familiar al mismo tiempo. La mayoría de mis amigos hispanos son centroamericanos. Entonces, comprendí que al hablar con ellos, mi español ha cambiado un poquito. Pero a mí me da lo mismo porque el español es una lengua hermosa y las variedades en esta lengua son lo que la hace tan interesante.

> The last thing I learned from my interview was that my Spanish has changed some since I moved to the U.S. While speaking with my grandmother, I heard [Argentine][4] Spanish and it sounded strange. Some words have a different tone but familiar all at the same time. The majority of my Hispanic friends are Central Americans. So, I understood that by speaking with them, my Spanish has changed a little. But I don't care because Spanish is a beautiful language and the varieties of this language are what make it so interesting.

Clearly the interviewee in the above example is not a local community member; yet, there was value added for this student due to this experience and to the classmates with whom he shared it. Example (3) is from a student born in the U.S. to Hispanic parents. It presents a case of HL development. The student realizes how her Spanish writing skills are coming back as she now finds herself willingly writing in Spanish.

3. …aprendí que necesito paciencia cuando escribo para evitar errores. Todavía quiero mejorar mi español pero no es el mismo como antes. Antes de la composición no me di la gana a escribir en español a menos que necesitaba, por ejemplo escribiendo esta y la primera composición. Ahora escribo mensajes de texto para mi mamá en español. Así, de la primera composición aprendí que si practico más puedo aumentar mi confianza y mejorar mi español como lo era cuando yo era pequeña.
    …I learned that I need patience when I write to avoid errors. I still want to improve my Spanish but it is not the same as before. Before the composition I did not feel like writing in Spanish unless I needed to, for example writing this and the first composition. Now I write text messages to my mom in Spanish. So, from the first composition I learned that if I practice more I can increase my confidence and improve my Spanish as it was when I was little.

Example (4) comes from a student that arrived in the U.S. at the age of three. The first part of the example demonstrates one of the limitations students might encounter when setting out to conduct their interviews. There could be a lack of technical equipment or familiarity with the technology needed on the part of an elderly family member. Having stricter guidelines that limit the students to only local community members may solve this problem. However, this student does succeed in his second attempt, when he interviews his mother. The interview format created a situation in which he was able to practice his language skills. The fact that the conversation went outside familiar domains exposed him to vocabulary that was most likely new to him. Also, he describes how they engaged in conversation in Spanish for a sustained period of time, which had not happened since he was a child.

> 4. Cuando pensé en personas para entrevistar para este proyecto, al principio pensé ah mi abuela. Siempre ha querido la oportunidad para aprender mas de ella y tambien preguntarle cosas de [Paraguay][5] además de las comidas que ella puede cocinar de halla. El problema con entrevistar mi abuela era que ella no sabia como usar Skype entonces no podía gravar la entrevista. Al final entreviste a mi mama y la entrevista resulto perfecto y exacto como lo que necesitaba. Esta conversación con mi mama en español creo que era lo mas largo tiempo que pase hablando con mi mama desde cuando era bien pequeño y ella me hablaba en español mucho mas frecuente que ahora. Era una experiencia muy interesante aprendiendo cosas de la vida de mi mama que no sabia antes.
> *When I thought about people to interview for this project, at first I thought of my grandmother. I have always wanted the opportunity to learn more about her and also ask her things about [Paraguay][5] besides the food that she can cook from there. The problem with interviewing my grandmother is that she did not know how to use Skype so I could not tape the interview. At the end I interviewed my mom and the interview turned out perfect and exactly as I needed it. This conversation with my mom in Spanish I believe that it was the longest time I spent speaking with my mom since I was very little and she would speak to me in Spanish much more frequently than now. It was a very interesting experience learning things about my mom's life that I did not know before.*

The essay prompt for the second interview asked to compare the results from both interviews. In (5)—from a student born in the U.S. to Hispanic parents—we find someone who, after both interviews are completed, gets the opportunity to deepen her knowledge of her family and its variety of Spanish as well as her husband's.

> 5. Estoy muy contenta, que llegué a conocer más acerca de mis antecedentes de dialectos y el dialecto de la familia de mi esposo. He aprendido mucho y era una buena práctica para hablar en español.
> *I am very happy, that I was able to know more about my ancestor's dialects and my husband's family's dialect. I have learned much and it was good practice for speaking in Spanish.*

A very insightful reflection on language is provided by the student in (6) as she compares both interviews. She is also U.S.-born with Hispanic parents.

While she goes into the first interview with the very common perception held by Spanish heritage speakers in the United States that there is something deficient about their Spanish because they incorporate words from English, she comes out of the second interview with a completely different perspective. She recognizes that languages change, that change is not a flaw found in Spanish or in Spanish speakers in the United States. This is all the more amazing because this type of analysis does not usually happen unprompted. HLLs often come to class carrying very negative feelings about their HL. For example, most of them have had to defend why they enroll in Spanish classes, not knowing how to explain why they are taking Spanish courses when they already speak the language. They also feel that borrowings from English into Spanish and code-switching represent a lack of knowledge of their HL thus reflecting negatively on their language abilities or even on the HL itself. Yet, after just two interviews, her viewpoint has dramatically changed.

6. Antes pensaba que inventar nuevas palabras era malo pero con esta entrevista, vi que no es tan... Con la primera entrevista vi que solamente algo negativo sale de inventar palabras cortas que inventan los hispanos de los Estados Unidos. Ahora con esta entrevista vi otro perspectivo. Ahora veo que todo, incluyendo los lenguajes, cambia. Todo se tiene que evolucionar y adaptar a lo nuevo. No se significa que no estamos haciendo flojos con inventar nuevas palabras, simplemente adaptarnos a una nueva sociedad y generación así como en inglés, ya no escribimos como Shakespeare.
Before I used to think that making up new words was bad but with this interview, I saw that it is not so. With the first interview I saw that only something negative comes out of making up short words that Hispanics in the United States make up. Now with this interview I saw another perspective. Now I see that everything, including languages, changes. Everything has to evolve and adapt to new things. It does not mean that we are becoming lazy by inventing new words, simply adapting to a new society and generation just like in English, we do not write like Shakespeare.

The data for example (7) comes from a student born in the U.S. to parents who have a Meso-American language as their L1. She has both her parents' language and Spanish as L1s. In the first interview, she discovers that variety exists even within the same country. In the second interview, she gets to observe geographic variation. In addition, she notices the effects of language contact and how they operate not just in her but in the person she interviewed.

7. Cuando entreviste a la persona que habla el mismo español que yo, aprendí que aunque dos personas son de la misma parte no hablan el español igual. Siempre hay alguna diferencia en el español que habla cada uno. .. En la segunda entrevista, entreviste a una persona que es de [Guatemala].[5] Aprendí que los [guatemaltecos][6] usan "usted" y "vos" cuando hablan. Este fue interesante porque los [peruanos][6] no usan las palabras diariamente. También aprendí como cambia el español de alguien cuando llegan a los Estados Unidos. Fue interesante escuchar cómo ha cambiado el español de la segunda entrevista porque es casi igual como el mío. Eso me sorprendió mucho porque su dialecto es muy diferente pero nosotros tenemos problemas cuando hablamos el español. Los dos tenemos que parar y pensar en cómo vamos a decir algo.

When I interviewed the person that speaks the same Spanish as I, I learned that even though two people are from the same place they do not speak Spanish the same. There is always some difference in the Spanish each one speaks... On the second interview, I interviewed a person that is from [Guatemala].[5] I learned that [Guatemalans][6] use "usted" (formal you) and "vos" (a variety of informal you) when they speak. This was interesting because [Peruvians][6] don't use the words daily. I also learned how someone's Spanish changes when they arrive in the United States. It was interesting to listen to how the Spanish of the second interview has changed because it is almost the same as mine. That surprised me a lot because his/her dialect is very different but we have problems when we speak Spanish. The two of us have to stop and think how we are going to say something.

The student in (8) was born in the U.S. to Hispanic parents and spent fifteen years during elementary and secondary school living in his parents' country of origin. He had a theory on lexical borrowings that he had developed before he ever came into the HLL class, one he had shared in class. His father worked in farming and cattle-raising before moving to the United States. Once here, he started to work in landscaping. The son realizes that the father never had or needed any of the tools for this new trade before immigrating and thus, did not know their names. Now, he incorporates the names from English into his Spanish lexicon out of necessity. One of these lexical borrowings is given in the example, a *weed eater* becomes a *wira* in Spanish.

8. También pude ver y presenciar como el spanglish se forma. Mi familia por ejemplo, era una familia dedicada al ganado y a la siembra pero cuando llegaron a Estados Unidos se vieron con la necesidad de expandir sus conocimientos laborales así que comenzaron a trabajar en la jardinería cuyas

> herramientas de trabajo estaban por encima de la tecnología [hondureña].[6] El caso mas interesante es el de la herramienta llamada "weed eater" en Inglés cuya traducción fue hecha a "wira" en ves de orilladoras. Y es esta palabra la cual predomina el vocabulario de los jardineros hispanos en carolina del norte.
> *I was also able to see and witness how Spanglish is formed. My family for example, was a family dedicated to cattle and agriculture but when they arrived in the United States they found the need to expand their work knowledge so they started to work in gardening whose work tools were above [Honduran][6] technology. The most interesting case is the one of the tool named "weed eater" in English whose translation was made to "wira" instead of orilladoras. And it is this word that prevails in the vocabulary of Hispanic gardeners in North Carolina.*

Example (9) is the second interview for the student in (8), and it is the one that allows him to confirm his theory. The interviewee is a speaker of [Ecuadorian][6] Spanish whose father started working on cars upon arrival in this country; therefore, he did not know the terminology in a mechanic's shop and he had to operate in the same manner as the interviewer's father: adopt and adapt the English terminology into his Spanish vocabulary, as we can see from the analysis below. As Otheguy (1993) has pointed out, these are cases of cultural contact, artifacts from the new culture that require a name in the speaker's L1 lexicon.

9. En la entrevista como tal reafirme mi teoría sobre el spanglish y aprendí algo nuevo. Reafirme que si hay palabras extrañas cuando uno entra a un nuevo país con un nuevo idioma esas palabras pueden entrar y establecerse como palabras plurilengüísticas. Al igual que en el caso de mi padre y las herramientas de jardinería, el papá de la entrevistada tuvo una experiencia similar con las partes de los carros.
In the interview itself I confirmed my theory about Spanglish and I learned something new. I confirmed that yes there are strange words when one enters a new country with a new language those words can enter and establish themselves as plurilinguistic words. The same as in the case of my father and the gardening tools, the interviewee's dad had a similar experience with car parts.

Pedagogical Considerations and Limitations

The two assignments discussed above make up a small part of the curriculum for this course; students have other sources of input that could help develop their linguistic and metalinguistic knowledge of their HL. As an intermediate level language course, it focuses on the development of all four skills as well as culture. As a HL course premised on the principles of critical pedagogy, it introduces students to sociolinguistic concepts of language variation, linguistic prestige and subordination, and linguicism. It also provides students some grammatical explanations to which most of them have not being exposed. Grammar is presented via examples and classroom practice; assessment of learning is conducted via homework, exams, and essays. At the beginning of the semester, the first composition asks students to think about what they would like to learn in the class. The prompt given, *¿Qué quiero poder hacer con mi español que no puedo ahora? / What do I want to be able to do with my Spanish that I can't now?*, attempts to get students to think about their plans for their HL but also to give the instructor an idea of what the student wants to get from the class. There is a reading component that allows students to self-select the material. Journals produced from the readings are awarded a minor grade in order to promote fulfillment of the activity even though it is intended as free voluntary reading to promote HL development, as discussed in McQuillan (1998). In addition to the cultural component provided by the readings, the textbook includes narratives with pre- and post-reading activities that delve into cultural themes for Hispanics living in the United States. These schema-prompting and discussion activities help introduce vocabulary on domains that may not be familiar to the students. The stories in the textbook and the interviews conducted by the students work as launching points for class discussions on sociolinguistic issues regarding language contact and change. These, in turn, reinforce the discoveries students are making through their interviews and the reflections provided in the compositions.

    Based on students' reactions to the interviews presented here—as well as others from the larger group—more assignments that engage them with the community seem to be in order. A community language map—as explained in Smith, Sánchez, Ek, and Machado-Casas (2011)—had been the community-related assignment in a previous semester. Students shared pictures of signs they found in Hispanic businesses. A larger project along the lines described by Helmer (2010)—a photographic map of the community—may produce even more student involvement. For this project, photos would not be limited to signs but would include any artifact found in the community that the student found descriptive. In the case of HL programs with more than one course, an appropriate, more in depth, follow-up project could be added. Helmer (2010) has suggested *museums of place*, exhibits that include photographs, maps, interviews, poetry, artifacts, or history.

Quantifying the results of this type of study is not straightforward. For future iterations, a pre- and post-survey of students' opinions would help determine with greater precision the effects of the interviews. Separating the other components of the curriculum in order to determine what each one brings to students' perceptions about their HL would assist with pedagogical development. Also, in this instance, the choice of interviewee was left up to the student and as discussed above, some reached outside the speech community. From the comments received, restricting students' selection may end up being counter-productive as, in spite of their choice of interlocutor, they all formulated in-depth insights into issues of language and power. However, a comparison of data from interviews within the immediate community and those from students' extended social networks may shed new light on this line of inquiry. Clearly, for those of us working on HLE, much work remains to be done.

Conclusion

The work described here is an initial attempt at bridging the gap between HLLs and the HL community. Even though space only allowed for the examination of a few students' comments, overall, the responses of the entire class point in the same direction. This activity not only opened the door for class discussions on topics relevant to the critical pedagogies advocated in HLE, they also allowed HLLs to discover many sociolinguistic aspects of their HL on their own. Taking into account Tse's (1998) model of ethnic development and the research cited earlier pointing to the need to create connections between HLLs and HL communities, university-level HL classes are the perfect environment to promote HL development.

Notes
1. I would like to thank Erin Mikulec for her insightful comments. All errors remain my own.
2. The entire project can be found at: spanishintexas.org
3. The narratives from the students are reproduced exactly as written by them.
4. Name of Spanish variety has been changed for anonymity.

5. Name of country has been changed for anonymity.
6. Nationality has been changed for anonymity.

References

Aparicio, F. (2000). Of Spanish dispossessed. In R. D. González (Ed.), *Language ideologies: Critical perspectives on the official English movement (Volume 1: Education and the social implications of official language*, pp. 248-275). Urbana, IL: National Council of Teachers of English.

Beaudrie, S., Ducar, C., & Relaño-Pastor, A. M. (2009). Curricular perspectives in the heritage language context: Assessing culture and identity. *Language, Culture and Curriculum, 22*(2), 157-174. doi:10.1080/07908310903067628

Carreira, M. M. (2012) Meeting the needs of heritage language learners: Approaches, strategies, and research. In S. M. Beaudrie & M. Fairclough (Eds.), *Spanish as a heritage language in the United States: The state of the field* (pp. 223-240). Washington, DC: Georgetown UP.

Carreira, M., & Kagan, O. (2011). The results of the national heritage language survey: Implications for teaching, curriculum design, and professional development. *Foreign Language Annals, 44*(1), 40-64. doi:10.1111/j.1944-9720.2010.01118.x

CensusViewer. (2014a). *Population of North Carolina: Census 2010 and 2000 interactive map, demographics, statistics, quick facts*. Retrieved from http://censusviewer.com/state/NC

CensusViewer. (2014b). *Wilmington, North Carolina Population: Census 2010 and 2000 interactive map, demographics, statistics, quick facts*. Retrieved from http://censusviewer.com/city/NC/Wilmington

Chamberlin-Quinlisk, C., & Senyshyn, R. M. (2012). Language teaching and intercultural education: Making critical connections. *Intercultural Education, 23*(1), 15-23. doi:10.1080/14675986.2012.664750

Cho, G., & Krashen, S. (2000). The role of voluntary factors in heritage language development: How speakers can develop the heritage language on their own. *ITL: Review of Applied Linguistics, 127/128*, 127-140.

CollegeData. (2014). *College profile University of North Carolina at Wilmington*. Retrieved from http://www.collegedata.com/cs/data/college/college_pg01_tmpl.jhtml?schoolId=1603

Fishman, J. A. (2004). Language maintenance, language shift, and reversing language shift. In T. K. Bhatia & W. C. Ritchie (Eds.), *The handbook of bilingualism* (pp. 406-436). Malden, MA: Blackwell.

Harklau, L. (2009). Heritage speakers' experiences in new Latino diaspora Spanish classrooms. *Critical Inquiry in Language Studies, 6*(4), 211-242. http://dx.doi.org/10.1080/15427580903118689

Helmer, K. A. (2010). "'Proper Spanish' is a waste of time": Mexican-origin student resistance to learning Spanish as a heritage language. In L. Scherff & K. Spector

(Eds.), *Culturally relevant pedagogy: Clashes and confrontations* (pp. 135–163). New York: Rowman & Littlefield Publishers.

Helmer, K. A. (2013). A twice-told tale: Voices of resistance in a borderlands Spanish heritage language class. *Anthropology & Education Quarterly, 44*(3), 269-285. doi:10.1111/aeq.12025

Martínez, G., & Schwartz, A. (2012). Elevating "low" language for high stakes: A case for critical, community-based learning in a medical Spanish for heritage learners program. *Heritage Language Journal, 9*(2), 175-187.

Norton Peirce, B. (1995). Social identity, investment, and language learning. *TESOL Quarterly, 29*(1), 9-31. doi:10.1111/aeq.12025

Oriyama, K. (2012). What role can community contact play in heritage language literacy development? Japanese-English bilingual children in Sydney. *Journal of Multilingual and Multicultural Development, 33*(2), 167-186.

Otheguy, R. (1993). A reconsideration of the notion of loan translation in the analysis of U.S. Spanish. In A. Roca & J. Lipski (Eds.), *Spanish in the U.S.: Linguistic contact anddiversity* (pp. 21-45). Berlin: Mouton de Gruyter.

Roca, A., & Alonso, H. (2006). *The abuelos project: A multi-discplinary, multitask unit for hertiage and advanced second-language learners of Spanish*. Paper presented at the annual meeting of the American Association of Teachers of Spanish, Salamanca, June 28-July 2.

Rodríguez-Pino, C. (1994). Ethnographic studies in the SNS program. *Teaching Spanish to Native Speakers, 1*, 1–4.

Schwarzer, D., & Petrón, M. (2005). Heritage language instruction at the college level: Reality and possibilities. *Foreign Language Annals, 38*(4), 568-578. doi:10.1111/j.1944-9720.2005.tb02523.x

Showstack, R. (2010). Going beyond 'appropriateness': Foreign and heritage language students explore language use in society. *Proceedings of Intercultural Competence Conference, 1*, 358-377. Retrieved from http://cercll.arizona.edu/ICConference2010

Smith, H. L., Sánchez, P., Ek, L. D., & Machado-Casas, M. (2011). From linguistic imperialism to linguistic concientización: Learning from heritage language speakers. In D. Schwarzer, M. Petrón, & C. Luke (Eds.), *Research informing practice-practice informing research: Innovative teaching methodologies for world language teachers* (pp. 177-199). Greenwich, CT: Information Age Publishing.

Tse, L. (1998). Ethnic identity formation and its implications for heritage language development. In S. Krashen, L. Tse, & J. McQuillan (Eds.), *Heritage language development* (pp. 15-29). Culver City, CA: Language Education Associates.

Tse, L. (2001). Heritage language literacy: A study of US biliterates. *Language, Culture and Curriculum, 14*(3), 256-268.

Valdés, G. (2000). Introduction. In *Spanish for native speakers. AATSP professional development series handbook for teachers K-16* (Volume 1, pp. 1-20). New York: Harcourt College.

Villa, D. J. (2010). ¿¡Cómo que Spanglish!? Creating a service-learning component in a Spanish heritage language program. In S. Rivera-Mills & J. A. Trujillo (Eds.), *Building communities and making connections* (pp. 120-35). Newcastle, UK: Cambridge Scholars.

Whitehead, T. L. (2004). What is ethnography? Methodological, ontological, and epistemological attributes. *Cultural ecology of health and change: Ethnographically informed community and cultural assessment research systems working paper series*. Retrieved from: http://www.cusag.umd.edu/documents/workingpapers/epiontattrib.pdf

Wiley, T. G. (2005). The reemergence of heritage and community language policy in the U.S. national spotlight. *Modern Language Journal, 89*(4), 594-601. doi:10.1111/j.1540-4781.2005.00331.x

Wong, K. F., & Xiao, Y. (2010). Diversity and difference: Identity issues of Chinese heritage language learners from dialect backgrounds. *Heritage Language Journal, 7*(2), 153-187.

Wu, M.-H., Lee, K., & Leung, G. (2014). Heritage language education and investment among Asian American middle schoolers: Insights from a charter school. *Language and Education, 28*(1), 19-33. http://dx.doi.org/10.1080/09500782.2013.763818

Zentella, A. C. (1997). *Growing up bilingual: Puerto Rican children in New York.* Oxford: Blackwell.

CHAPTER 14

LITERACY PRACTICES AND IDENTITY CONSTRUCT:
A Critical Discourse Analysis with an SFL Perspective

Leonor Juárez García
Benemérita Universidad Autónoma de Puebla

Literacy practices are a key feature in formal-educational contexts. These practices intricately enfold general knowledge, social understanding, and cultural issues, especially of the communities in which we live, experience, and grow. Needless to say, literacy is an essential tool in formal-institutional contexts. However, what are the reasons high levels of illiteracy continue to be present in many communities in Mexico? In order to better understand this phenomenon we must examine formal institutional education from a critical-social approach, where "human societies create particular arrangements and groups to function, [and] within those features of structuring some dysfunctions are generated too, such as; suffering, discrimination, inequity, and lack of self-confidence" (Wodak, Fairclough, Graham, & Lemke, 2004, p. 1). I would add that illiteracy may well be seen as one of these dysfunctions.

Since literacy is generally learned in formal educational practices, government policies, institutions, and educators play a paramount role in the acquisition, development, and practice of it. In educational contexts, "authority and power are manifested and perpetuated by the ways language is used and the purposes for which it is used" (Auerbach, 1994, p. 10). Literacy practices then may be seen as a tool to perpetuate or change existing power relations and social roles (Freire, 2006). This investigation aims to shed some light on this issue. The general purpose of this study is twofold. On the one hand, it seeks to explore literacy from a critical-social approach

(Wodak et al., 2004), from the perspective of ten kindergarten educators from public schools in several rural communities in the south of Mexico, where high levels of illiteracy continue to be present. On the other hand, it aims to examine participants' discursive resources from an Appraisal System perspective (Martin & White, 2005), which is derived from Systemic Functional Linguistics (SFL; Halliday, 1994).

In the light of these perspectives, this study addresses the following research questions:

1. What advantages and disadvantages about literacy do participants perceive between rural and urban communities?
2. What resources of the Appraisal System do participants utilize to express their views toward literacy actors in their specific contexts?
3. How may these markers explain illiteracy as a social dysfunction in these contexts?

Literature Review

Despite the variety of information and investigations about equity in education (Cassany, 1998; Clark, 2006; Freire, 2006; Gee, 2008; Seth, 2002; Tannen, 1996) we might say that the causes of illiteracy have been underinvestigated, compared to other types of social inequalities. Furthermore, based on an empirical exploration, we can recognize that educational differences and literacy practices between urban and rural communities in Mexico are abysmal. Some of the reason for these inequalities may be rooted in educators' perceptions, attitudes, and beliefs. To address this issue, I would argue that kindergarten educators, as well as parents, may influence and permeate children's viewpoints on what literacy is and how it must be approached.

As basic formal education develops literacy, it also nurtures and cultivates the understanding and learning of values, social norms, hierarchical relations, and power issues (Clark, 2006; Freire, 2006). Tannen (1996) claims that "the consequences...work to the disadvantage of members of groups that are stigmatized in our society and to the advantage of those who have the power to enforce their interpretations" (p. 10). She argues that "dominance" should not be the starting point of an analysis of such disadvantages, but the cultural differences. In other words, cultural differences as a framework may provide a model for explaining how dominance is created (p. 10).

Thus, institutional and socio-cultural patterns frame and organize beliefs, values, and behaviors but also enfold formative expectations that may establish differentiated opportunities (Cain & Oakhill, 2007; Cummins, 2000). Educational contexts teach and develop discourses that shape the construction of our identity. It is worth noting that identity and personality are both closely related to our discursive communities (Alliende & Condemarín, 2000; Fabretti, 2012; Ferreiro, 1984; Freire, 2006; Pahl & Rowsell, 2006).

Undoubtedly, identity construction is a lifelong process; however, according to Fabretti (2012) this process has a paramount importance during childhood. Fabretti argues that children, until the age of six, predominantly observe and absorb information from the people and environment they are surrounded by. He also affirms that children act based on their observations and follow the behavioral and attitudinal models and patterns provided to them. This means that the time children spend in kindergarten schools becomes crucial in their identity construction. Among other issues, what kindergarten educators think about educational topics and how they address them becomes relevant.

Regarding identity, Kroskrity (2000) affirms that this may be constructed on two different levels of linguistic use. The first level is through the use of language and linguistic forms associated with specific social groups and the second level is through communicative practices that guide affiliation to a particular social group. It thus may be inferred that language and/or discourse at school and the specific linguistic resources used in any form do not simply work as a medium of communication but as a social practice, a way of doing things. As Wood and Kroger (2000) observed,

> talk is action, and discourse analyses involve talk; therefore, it is a form of action. Discourse analysis can contribute to change in the way that people talk. And again, because talk is action, change in talk is important not as something that is associated with change in practice; it is change in practice. (p. 3)

The interrelatedness of talk and action is represented in the present discourse study. It examines discourse as a form of practice that has perpetuated dysfunctions and biased social relations regarding literacy in communities where diverse indigenous languages are spoken. In order to explore literacy as a social shaped dysfunction, this study aims at analyzing discourse critically and with an SFL lens (Halliday, 1994). SFL has been chosen as an analytical tool because its approach provides an account of how people use the language in social contexts. This approach considers cognitive structures, processing constraints, and social factors as the precepts of functionalism in the linguistic system (Butler, 2005). Although this study is discourse-oriented and the concept of structure is probed, the social aspect of language is highlighted.

The specific framework to examine discourse in this analysis is an extension of SFL, the Appraisal System (Martin & Rose, 2003). The Appraisal System proposes an interpersonal model closely related to the social context and/or situational context (Poynton, 1985). This model identifies three dimensions to organize social relations: power/status, contact, and affection. The Appraisal System analyzes the linguistic items by which speakers naturalize their ideological position (Martin & White, 2005). This naturalization is particularly expressed by speakers positioning themselves toward their propositions/proposals. The system divides appraisal (evaluation) resources into three semantic domains: attitude, engagement, and graduation.

The analysis of discourse in this study is centered on the attitude semantic domain and focuses on the Judgment sub-system. The Judgment sub-system evaluates the lexico-grammatical resources used to evaluate positively or negatively social behavior in relation to institutional rules. The resources used to judge these behaviors depend significantly on the social/cultural/ideological standpoint of the speaker/writer (Martin & Rose, 2003). Table 14.1 shows the judgment categories to be used as a tool to analyze part of participants' discursive markers; they have been marked in bold.

According to Martin and Rose (2003) judgments may be of social sanction or social esteem. Social sanction judgments involve rules in a culture that are at issue to praise or condemn (legally or morally). On the other hand, judgments of social esteem involve evaluations of admiration and criticism that will enhance or reduce the good opinion of a community toward someone. Martin and White (2005) clarify:

> Thus, negative values of social esteem will be seen as dysfunctional or inappropriate or to be discouraged but they will no be assessed as sins or crimes. If you breach social sanction you may well need a lawyer or a confessor but if you breach social esteem you may just need to try harder or to practice more or to consult a therapist or possibly a self-help book. (p. 23)

Table 14.1
The Appraisal System (Martin & Rose, 2003)

A.	**Attitude**	1. Affect (positive or negative)
		2. Judgment (Social esteem: normality, capacity, tenacity; and Social Sanction: veracity, propriety)
		3. Appreciation
B.	**Engagement**	Interpersonal space
C.	**Graduation**	Force and focus

Methodology

This study uses a qualitative method (Denzin & Lincoln, 2003) with a critical-social perspective (Wodak et al., 2004), where participants' discourse was explored to provide an interpretation of the issue (i.e., literacy). As previously mentioned, the analysis of the linguistic data was carried out using the Appraisal System (Martin & Rose, 2003). The analysis followed an axial coding in a constant comparative analysis (Strauss & Corbin, 1990) based on the Appraisal System framework.

The context of the research was an English as a Foreign Language (EFL) classroom in Puebla City in central Mexico. The participants were ten female kindergarten educators who worked in Huaquexchula, Chila de las Flores, Tezonteopan, Atlixco, and some other rural communities in the south of Puebla. These are considered rural communities because most people have farms, barns, and work in crop growing. There is no variety of means of transportation, hospitals, communication technologies, and amusement or leisure places. According to The Mexican National Institute of Statistics and Geography (INEGI) these communities have between 2400 and 2500 inhabitants and most men emigrate to the U.S., leaving mostly women inhabitants in these communities. Illiteracy percentages vary from 12 to 15 percent of the population; and from 29 to 35 percent of the people speak an indigenous language.

At the time of the investigation, the participants were enrolled in a Basic English course at a private institution, for which they paid tuition out of their own pockets, and I, the researcher, was their teacher. This course was held every Saturday for three hours, and there were a total of ten sessions. The data were collected in session number five.

The means to collect the data was a focus group (Flick, 2006). There were five pre-structured questions initially; however, because of the richness and interaction during the focus group, only three questions were asked (the actual questions are in Appendix 14). The day of the interview the students were asked to participate in a study about literacy and they all accepted. They sat around a table and then I asked the questions. A camera was put in the middle of the table to audio-record the whole interview. The interview took about 21 minutes. Questions were asked in Spanish and then transcribed and translated into English by the researcher for the purpose of this study. The obtained data were utilized to accomplish a larger project about literacy.

Table 14.2
Participants' Information

Name of participant	Age and how long they have been in these communities
Grace	30/10
Vanessa	45/25
Lola	36/14
Emma	45/23
Emilia	31/5
Sophy	47/22
Anna	34/5
Cathy	52/12
Ruth	32/5
Ally	50/25

Note. Participants' names have been changed to protect their privacy.

Participants' ages ranged from 30 to 52 years old. They had all been working in these communities from 5 to 25 years. They all hold a certification from the Secretaría de Educación Pública (SEP) in Mexico as kindergarten educators. However, because teacher-training policies have changed over time, the oldest ones obtained this certification at the same time they finished high school, whereas the youngest ones had to complete a Bachelor's degree after high school. There is only one participant (Anna) who has a Master's degree in basic education. This is illustrated in Table 14.2.

As previously mentioned, the data were transcribed, then categorized and analyzed following the sub-system of Judgement within the Appraisal Framework.

Findings and Discussion

The present paper deals with the relation between educators' perceptions about literacy and a model of construction of identity that might explain illiteracy as a social dysfunction. A general assumption has been that one of the vital means for identity construction, especially during the first years of life, may be kindergarten educators' perceptions and beliefs about literacy issues to the extent that, at some point, children's beliefs and perceptions about literacy and literacy actors may align with those of their teachers.

In this section I present the analysis of participants' discourse with the aim of answering the questions posed in the introduction. Regarding the first research question about the advantages and disadvantages participants perceived between rural and urban communities, discourse has been categorized based on the general topics and expressions participants referred to as exemplified in Table 14.3.

Beyond the amount of discursive resources to express the advantages and disadvantages, it is interesting to note how the themes they refer to as advantageous in one type of community are perceived as a disadvantage in the other type of community (e.g., parents, context). Also, it is worth mentioning that sometimes participants perceive conflicting points of view. For example, there is a marked contradictory perception between the ones who have spent more time in the rural community and the one who has just been in the rural community for five years (i.e., Anna). Ally and Sophy, who have been in the rural community for 25 and 22 years respectively, seem to defend parents and express positively about them. Conversely, Anna seems to have a more critical view and express negative views about them.

Table 14.3

Participants' Discourse on Advantages and Disadvantages

	Advantages	Disadvantages
Rural Community	**Parents** *Ally*: "In the rural community parents may not have enough knowledge but they care for their children and are willing to learn and help." *Sophy*: "This lady told me she couldn't read or write but she was so committed to help her child." **Kindergarten reading program:** *Lola*: "Our kindergarten reading program requires a reading partner, not necessarily the parents… It's motivating for children." **Ex-students:** *Sophy*: "Some of my ex-pupils are now high school students and they have little brothers who want to follow their model."	**Parents** *Anna*: "Children who have illiterate parents do not even care for learning." **Financial situation/poverty:** *Lili*: "In a rural community it's hard for parents to buy or have books at home." *Anna*: "I have worked in high economic contexts and here… and here parents do not even care, and they are the model for children to follow." **Context:** *Emma*: "In the rural community family context is culturally poor." *Anna*: "Children who have illiterate parents never do homework…they don't care for learning. It's like the model they receive."
Urban Community	**Context:** *Ruth*: "In the urban community there may not be parents but children read and write just by imitating others." *Ally*: "Books in the city are very inexpensive."	**Parents:** *Ally*: "Children have everything but they do not have their parents´ attention and care." **Context:** *Ally*: "In the city there are lots of libraries with comfortable spaces and there are no children."

A salient point that may not be so evident in this table is parents' participation in the rural communities, according to most participants' views. They affirm that parents in rural communities actively participate and get involved in the social and educational context. They "read tales," "care for their children," and "solve situations," participants argue. Sophy even describes a situation of one of her students whose mother did not know how to read and write and she told her, "Miss, write down my daughters' homework for me, I'll later see who…I can't write, I can't read but I'll find someone to help me to help her."

On the other hand, the advantages mentioned about urban communities are based on imitation and reproduction of behaviors. As Emilia mentions, "My daughter is four and she just did a book, nobody taught her…she just observes that (at home) we are all reading or writing and she just did it." Ruth noted "in the urban community children may not have parents' time and willingness but they do it (reading and writing) just by imitation because they know they'll use it."

A further unexpected, but not surprising, finding was the one regarding parents' perceived behavior in urban communities. Participants argue that these parents do not have the time due to work and that they do not pay attention to their children. When the following comments were made most participants nodded showing agreement to these excerpts. Ally commented that "in the urban community parents work and that is a disadvantage, children have everything but not attention." Additionally, Ruth admitted that "in the urban community children may not have parents' time and willingness."

Because parents' roles in literacy were particularly noteworthy in these findings, a more detailed analysis was implemented to illustrate participants' ideological and socio-cultural perceptions toward parents and their roles in literacy development. The second research question is answered based on this analysis. As Table 14.4 illustrates, clauses and discourse resources have been categorized using the parameters of the Judgment sub-system of the Attitude domain: Social Esteem and Social Sanction. Clauses have been classified into positive and/or negative judgments.

Table 14.4
Participants' Appraisal System Resources

Social Esteem	Positive [admire]	Negative [criticize]
Normality	*Lili*: "(School) is an opportunity to be in touch with books a very important one."	*Emma*: "They [in the rural communities] have very few possibilities to reach a cultural level."
Capacity		*Grace*: "…creations from the others"
		Anna: "Children with illiterate parents are the hardest ones to convince."
		Ana: "There are many, well several moms who can't read and write."
		Emma: "Family context is culturally limited [in] places where mothers only have high school… Where moms have university degrees children are richer culturally."
Tenacity	*Ally*: "Parents have responded well to reading programs."	*Anna*: "Illiterate parents aren't minimally interested [in learning to read and write]."
	Sophy: "She said she'd solve it."	*Emma*: "In places where mothers are illiterate, children will have limited possibilities."
Social Sanction	**Positive [praise]**	**Negative [condemn]**
Veracity	*Anna*: "I have worked in super-high economic level and here and I see it and I've proved it."	*Emilia*: "In an urban context the child observes, gets interest and, motivation (but just by imitation)."
	Ally: "I disagree because I also work in this community."	*Ruth*: "In the urban context children do it by imitation."

Propriety	*Ally:* "In the rural community at least parents are here."	*Ally:* "In the urban community parents work, children don't have parents' attention."
	Ally: "Here in the rural community parents have responded well to literacy collaborative practices."	*Ally:* "In the urban communities there are libraries and there are no children, they don't take advantage of them."
	Sophy: "The mother told me, 'I can't write, I can't read but I'll find someone to help me.' There are people who are willing to help. They just find a way to solve it."	*Anna:* "Illiterate mothers tell me they don't want to learn to read and write, they claim they are too old for that."
	Ally: "And that is parents' commitment… in the rural community the collaboration between parents and educators motivates children."	*Anna:* "I have worked in super-high economic level and here… Here they don't care."
	Sophy: "In the rural communities nowadays people have a different attitude, they do want to read and write."	

As we can see, the resources to positively or negatively judge the behaviors of actors are based on social norms, created contextually by what may be acceptable or sanctionable. Most judgments in Table 14.4 are in the Propriety sub-category, which means that participants evaluate acceptable behaviors and sanction the social norms parents seem not to follow. A significant issue found here was that most of this positively-judged behavior refers to advantages in the rural communities. Judgments regarding parents' commitment and their responsibility are mentioned as an advantage. Some examples include comments such as, "in the rural community at least parents are here;" "here in the rural community parents have responded well to literacy collaborative programs;" "I can't read, I can't write but I'll find someone to help [I'll solve it];" and "this is in fact parents' commitment."

Conversely, in the Social Esteem category, some specific judged behavior is expressed specifically about "mothers." In this sense, discursive resources, such as "illiterate," "culturally poor," and "uninterested" are seen as Capacity and Tenacity markers of negative judgments. It is interesting to note that participants mention parents in general as potential actors of the literacy process and mothers only to refer to the "illiterate" ones. This may also be a mirror of the absence of fathers in these communities. This is illustrated in Anna, who noted that "there are many people, well, many illiterate mothers."

Conclusion

The last question in this study was meant to provide an account of the manner in which discursive markers might explain illiteracy as a social dysfunction in these contexts. As shown in Table 14.4, social judgments of behaviors suggest that institutional-formal education and the concept of literacy are perceived as an idealization opposed to the stigmatized identity (Foucault, 1995) of the illiterate. In fact, discursive resources regarding literacy suggest an attempt to implement an idealization of literacy that could be leading to stereotypes and the denigration of the Other (Clark, 2006), the illiterate, such as "illiterate mothers," " a culturally limited context," and "culturally poor." It may seem that the only fact of becoming literate in these communities might automatically provide a higher status and "culture."

A vital issue in this analysis is that an illiterate person may seem to have no "culture" or as being "culturally poor." In terms of culture, none of the participants mentioned anything about bilingual parents and/or children who speak indigenous languages. As previously mentioned, about 29 to 35 percent of the population in these communities speaks an indigenous language and none of the communities where participants worked had bilingual schools. In the view of some participants, parents' illiteracy plays an important role in children's literacy development, but parents' culture, background knowledge, individualities, ideologies, and traditions do not seem to be significant. Perhaps these matters may be some of the reasons that illiteracy is seen as a social dysfunction.

The fact that participants expressed negative and positive Tenacity markers to refer to parents and no Capacity linguistic resources on the positive side may also be an explanation for the contextual perception of literacy as a dysfunction. Thus, findings in this study display a challenge for educators and for public education in general. The task to generate effective practices to deal with literacy in a more contextualized form seems appropriate.

Programs that appreciate and value indigenous languages seem to be pertinent, too, as well as programs that take into account parents' "cultural richness" and bilingualism to be incorporated to the understanding of literacy as a social function. As Kayi-Aydar (2014) argues, "Goals of multicultural social justice education are achieved only when diverse (cultural) identities are recognized, accepted and appreciated" (p. 150).

This study is limited in scope in terms of the specific linguistic framework utilized and the selected fragments for interpretation, as well as the number of participants. I hope that the present article motivates a deeper focus on literacy practices as a social dysfunction that may be alleviated through thoughtful contextual and situational practices interwoven with identity construction.

References

Alliende, F., & Condemarin, M. (2000). *La lectura: teoría, evaluación y desarrollo* [Reading: Theory, evaluation and development]. Santiago, Chile: Andrés Bello P.

Auerbach, E. (1994). Participatory action research. *TESOL Quarterly, 28*(4), 693-697. doi:10.2307/3587555

Butler, C. (2005). Functional approaches to language. In C. S. Butler, M. G. González, & S. M. Doval-Suárez (Eds.), *The dynamics of language use* (pp. 221-242). Amsterdam: John Benjamins.

Cain, K., & Oakhill, J. V. (2007). Reading comprehension difficulties: correlates, causes, and consequences. In K. Cain & J. V. Oakhill (Eds.), *Children's comprehension problems in oral and written language: A cognitive perspective* (pp. 41-76). New York: Guilford Press.

Cassany, D. (1998). *Enseñar lengua* [Teaching language]. Barcelona: Graó.

Clark, T. (2006). Language as social capital. *Applied Semiotics, 8*(18), 29-41. http://vuir.vu.edu.au/id/eprint/772

Cummins, J. (2000). *Language, power and pedagogy: Bilingual children in the crossfire*. Aberystwyth, UK: Cambrian Printers Ltd.

Denzin, N., & Lincoln, Y. (2003). *Handbook of qualitative research*. Thousand Oaks, CA: Sage.

Ferreiro, E. (1984). *Nuevas perspectivas sobre los procesos de lectura y escritura* [New perspectives on the reading and writing process]. San Ángel, Mexico: Siglo XXI.

Foucault, M. (1995). *Madness and civilization: A history of insanity in the age of reason*. London: Routledge.

Frabetti, C. (2012). *La lectura y la construcción de la identidad* [Reading and the construction of identity]. Retrieved from: http://www.kaosenlared.net/component/k2/item/20527-la-lectura-y-la-construcción-de-la-identidad.html.

Freire, P. (2006). *Pedagogía de la indignación* [Pedagogy of the oppressed]. España: Morata.
Gee, G. P. (2008). *Social linguistics and literacies: Ideology in discourse* (3rd ed.). New York: Routledge.
Halliday, M. A. K. (1994). *An introduction to functional grammar.* London: Edward Arnold.
Halliday, M. A. K., & Matthiessen, C. M. I. M. (2004). *An introduction to functional grammar* (3rd ed.). London: Arnold.
Kayi-Aydar, H. (2014). Multicultural social justice education through the lens of positioning: English language learners in K-12 contexts. In M. Mantero, J. L. Watzke, & P. C. Miller (Eds.), *Readings in language studies: Language and social justice* (Vol. 4, pp. 147-160). Grandville, MI: ISLS Publishing.
Kroskrity, P. (2000). Identity. *Journal of Linguistic Anthropology, 9*, 11-114.
Martin, J., & Rose, D. (2003). *Working with discourse.* London: Bloomsbury.
Martin, J., & White, P. (2005). *The language of evaluation: Appraisal in English.* London: Palgrave.
Pahl, K., & Rowsell, J. (2006). *Literacy and education.* London: Paul Chapman Publishing.
Poynton, C. (1985). *Language and gender: Making the difference.* Victoria, Australia: Deakin University Press.
Seth, M. J. (2002). *Education fever: Society, politics, and pursuit of schooling in South Korea.* Honolulu: University of Hawai'i Press.
Strauss, A., & Corbin, J. (1990). *Basics of grounded theory methods.* Beverly Hills, CA: Sage.
Tannen, D. (1996). Researching gender related patterns in classroom discourse. *TESOL Quarterly, 30*(2), 341-344. doi:10.2307/3588149
Wodak, R. (2006). Discourse-analytic and socio-linguistic approaches to the study of nation(alism). In G. Delanty & K. Kumar (Eds.), *The Sage handbook of nations and nationalism* (pp. 104-117). London: Sage.
Wodak, R., Fairclough, N., Graham, P., & Lemke, J. (2004). Introduction. *Critical Discourse Studies, 1*(1), 1-7.
Wood, L., & Kroger, R. (2000). *Doing discourse analysis. Methods for studying action in talk and text.* London: Sage.

Appendix 14

1. How would you define reading comprehension?
2. What skills and/or competences do you believe are necessary in children at preschool in order to reach an efficient literacy in the future?
3. What advantages and disadvantages do you see in rural communities compared to urban communities about literacy acquisition and development?

INDEX

B

belonging 125, 186, 246
bilingualism x, 12, 185-186, 188, 191, 278, 293

C

college xii, 18, 20, 21, 24, 26, 28, 31, 34, 68, 125, 127-130, 133, 135, 137, 143-144, 149, 156, 170-179, 181-183, 185-190, 278-279
commodification xi, 83-85, 87-88, 90, 96-97, 99
community x-xv, 9, 17-18, 20, 26, 29, 31-34, 40, 42, 53, 59-60, 63, 68, 75, 96, 125, 128-137, 141, 144, 167, 170-172, 176-177, 179-181, 183-194, 197, 200, 204, 206-207, 211, 233, 236, 242-243, 248-250, 265-269, 271, 276-277, 279-280, 284, 287-291
critical analysis xi, 58-61, 63, 65, 69-70, 74-75

critical discourse analysis 200-201, 206, 211, 214
critical literacy xi, 58, 74
cross-cultural xii, 37, 145, 150, 157-158, 162

D

discourse xiii-xiv, 4, 34, 47, 100, 121, 123-124, 152-154, 166, 197, 200-201, 204-206, 208-214, 234-237, 241-242, 246, 253-256, 258, 283-285, 287, 289, 294
discrimination x, 2-3, 10, 69-70, 177, 179-180, 192, 200, 281

E

education ix, xi-xiv, 15, 17, 35-37, 48, 51, 59, 61, 76, 84, 86-87, 90, 96, 100, 103, 129, 137, 139, 143-144, 148-149, 161, 166, 170-176, 179, 181-184, 186-187, 189-192, 194, 203, 214-217, 219, 223, 225, 229-231, 265, 268, 278, 280-282, 287, 292-294

educator xiii-xiv, 148, 182, 215-216, 218-226, 228-229, 258, 281-283, 285-287, 291-292
English as a Foreign Language xi, 35, 37, 83, 90, 121, 285

G

gang xiii-xiv, 233-244, 246-262
globalization 194, 235-236, 238-239, 242, 259-260

H

hegemony xi, 146, 198
heritage language xiv, 168, 185-192, 194, 230, 265, 267-268, 270, 278-280

I

identity ix-x, xiii, 9-10, 12, 15, 17-18, 20, 29, 31, 35-37, 60, 77, 153, 165, 191, 198, 200, 203-204, 206, 208, 222, 237, 245, 252, 261, 266-267, 278-279, 283, 287, 292-293
ideology xi, xiii, 15, 18, 32, 34, 39, 41-43, 49, 53, 59, 62, 77, 197-201, 203-204, 208, 211, 243, 248, 252

L

language classroom 103, 109, 120
language development 218, 223, 229-230, 278-279
language rights 11-12
literacy xi, xiv, 16, 58-62, 74-77, 145, 157, 165-166, 205, 217-219, 226, 228-229, 279, 281-283, 285-289, 291-293, 295

M

maintenance xiii, 188, 190,-191, 194, 198, 201, 203-204, 211, 265, 278

minorities x, xiii, 1, 9, 29, 31, 137, 143-144, 167, 194, 198, 200, 202-203, 211-212, 214, 230
minority language x
misunderstanding xi, 103, 105-106, 109-110, 113-114, 116-117, 120, 122, 201
multicultural xi, xv, 57-58, 64-65, 76, 165, 230, 293
multilingualism 127, 143, 145, 147-149, 154, 184

N

narrative inquiry x, 21, 34, 37
nation-building xiii, 197, 201, 203, 211
Native American xiii, 71, 79, 215-217, 221-225, 228-230
network xiii, 5, 68, 137, 168, 170, 173-174, 176, 179, 184-186, 188-191, 223, 229, 234, 237, 241-242, 250, 253, 258-259, 261, 277

P

play xiii, 31, 47, 57-59, 61, 63, 65-74, 77, 78, 81-82, 170, 177, 217-231, 254, 279, 281

R

refugees xiii, 198, 200, 202, 209, 211
rural xiii, xiv, 20, 32, 41, 167-170, 172-181, 183-184, 187-194, 227, 282, 285, 287-291, 295

S

settlement xiii, 3, 167-173, 184-185, 188-193
social control xi, 46
sociolinguistics xii, 83, 85, 87, 104, 144, 201, 213, 238, 258, 261

Spanish xiii, xiv, 1, 3-11, 13, 48, 84, 89, 105, 130, 140, 168, 170-171, 173-174, 176, 179, 184-194, 230, 236, 239, 247, 249, 259, 264, 266-280, 286

T

teacher x-xii, xiv, 1, 8, 13, 15-18, 20-27, 29-37, 62-64, 67, 77, 85, 103-104, 106-107, 111-112, 117-118, 120-122, 126, 141, 143-145, 151, 154-155, 165-166, 182, 185, 187, 215-216, 221-222, 226, 228, 232, 279, 285-287
teaching abroad x, 17-18, 29, 31, 33, 34, 38
transformation 15, 20-21, 29-31, 37

W

writing xii, 27, 32, 62, 76, 86, 88, 89, 95, 99, 102, 115-116, 119, 122, 127, 129, 143-146, 148-155, 157-159, 162, 164-166, 175, 271, 289, 293

ABOUT THE EDITORS

Paul Chamness Miller, Ph.D., is currently Professor of English for Academic Purposes in the Faculty of International Liberal Arts at Akita International University in Akita, Japan, where he teaches writing and teacher preparation courses. His research focuses on instructional methods of teaching languages, critical pedagogy and the issues of under-represented youth and teachers in the K-12 setting. He has published many books and peer-reviewed articles in such journals as *Queer Studies in Media and Popular Culture, Teaching and Teacher Education, Journal of Thought, Multicultural Perspectives*, and *Journal of Second Language Teaching and Research*, and was guest editor for a special LGBT issue of the *International Journal of Critical Pedagogy*. He recently completed a term as President of the International Society for Language Studies, and is co-chair of the upcoming ISLS conference in Honolulu in June, 2017. He is also editor of *Critical Inquiry in Language Studies*, an international journal published by Taylor & Francis and co-editor of *Research in Queer Studies*, a book series published by Information Age in the U.S.

Brian G. Rubrecht, Ph.D., received his Master's degree in TESOL and Bilingual Education from Georgetown University and his doctoral degree in Foreign Language Education from The University of Texas at Austin. He is currently Professor in the English Department of the School of Commerce at Meiji University in Tokyo, Japan, where he is Head Coordinator for the School's English Concentration program and one of the editors of the university's bulletin of arts and sciences, the Meiji University *Kyōyō Ronshū*. In his university courses he instructs students on test preparation, phonetics and phonology, translation and interpretation, English academic writing, and the history of Western philosophy. His research interests include language learning motivation, identity, language learning strategies, pronunciation, and second language writing. He is currently researching the perceptions Japanese university EFL learners have of peace and violence in foreign entertainment media. He is also working as head proofreader for the *Smile* English textbook series used by Japanese elementary school students.

Erin A. Mikulec, Ph.D., is Associate Professor in the School of Teaching and Learning at Illinois State University. Dr. Mikulec received her Ph.D. in curriculum and instruction with an emphasis in second language acquisition, foreign language education, and TESOL from Purdue University. In spring 2014, Dr. Mikulec was a Fulbright Scholar at the University of Helsinki in Finland, where she studied teacher education and taught English at schools throughout the area. Her research interests include teacher education, international education, and second language studies. She is currently serving as the Interim Director of the English Language Institute. She is also a member of the Board of Directors of the International Society for Language Studies, and has served as co-chair of several ISLS conferences.

Cu-Hullan Tsuyoshi McGivern, M.S., is Lecturer of Health and Physical Education at Akita International University in Japan, where he teaches sport, exercise, and health education courses. He is an active member of the Japan Society for the Study of Obesity with his main expertise is in exercise science and weight management. His research interests also include LGBT discrimination in amateur and professional sports, and multiracial identity and equality. He has published in the peer-reviewed journal, *Queer Studies in Media and Popular Culture*, and is co-editor of a new edited volume entitled *Queer Voices from the Locker Room*, published by Information Age. He is currently a member of the Board of Directors of the International Society for Language Studies and co-chair of the 2017 ISLS conference in Honolulu.

ABOUT THE CONTRIBUTORS

John Eliason, Ph.D., is a Professor of English and the Director of the Composition Program and the Writing Center at Gonzaga University in Spokane, Washington, USA.

Eduardo D. Faingold, Ph.D., is Professor of Spanish and Linguistics in the Department of Languages at The University of Tulsa in Tulsa, Oklahoma, USA.

Renée Figuera, Ph.D, is Lecturer of English Linguistics and Coordinator of TESOL Programmes in the Faculty of Humanities and Education, at the University of the West Indies, St. Augustine, Trinidad and Tobago.

Leonor Juárez García, is an English teacher educator in the Faculty of Languages at Benemérita Universidad Autónoma de Puebla, in Puebla, México.

Thomas M. Hill, Jr. is a Doctoral Candidate in Language, Literacy, and Culture at the University of Pittsburgh in Pittsburgh, Pennsylvania, USA.

Mary Jeannot, Ed.D., is Associate Professor of TESOL Programs and ESL, Center for Global Engagement, Gonzaga University, Spokane, Washington, USA.

Keiko Kitade, Ph.D., is Professor of Japanese Language Teacher Education in the faculty of Letters and Education Language and Information Science at Ritsumeikan University in Kyoto, Japan.

Priscila Leal is a Ph.D. Candidate of the Department of Second Language Studies at the University of Hawai'i at Mānoa in Hawai'i, USA.

Ho Hon Leung, Ph.D., is Professor of Sociology at the State University of New York College at Oneonta in Oneonta, New York, USA.

María Cristina Montoya, Ph.D., is Professor of Spanish Linguistics in the Department of **Foreign** Languages and Literatures at the State University Of New York College at Oneonta in Oneonta, New York, USA.

N. Ariana Mrak, Ph.D., is Associate Professor of Spanish Linguistics in the Department of World Languages and Cultures at the University of North Carolina Wilmington in Wilmington, North Carolina, USA.

Gerrard Mugford, Ph.D., is Lecturer in pragmatics, discourse analysis and sociolinguistics in the Modern Languages Department at la Universidad de Guadalajara in Guadalajara, Mexico.

Bettina P. Murray, Ph.D., is Assistant Professor in the Department of Communication and Theatre Arts at John Jay College of Criminal Justice, City University of New York (CUNY), New York, USA.

Paulo Andreas Oemig, M.A., is a Doctoral Candidate in the Department of Curriculum and Instruction, in the Language, Literacy and Culture Program at New Mexico State University in Las Cruces, New Mexico, USA.

Timothy G. Reagan, Ph.D., is Dean of the College of Education and Human Development at the University of Maine in Orono, Maine, USA, where he is also Professor of Education.

Anton Vegel holds an B.A. and M.A. in Foreign Language Education from Kent State University, Kent, Ohio, USA, and is currently an independent researcher investigating nation-building and maintenance, literacy, discourse, and language policy.

Wendell C. Wallace, Ph.D., is Lecturer of Criminology and Criminal Justice in the Faculty of Social Sciences at The University of the West Indies, St. Augustine, Trinidad and Tobago.

Also Available from ISLS!

READINGS IN LANGUAGE STUDIES
VOLUME 1
Language Across Disciplinary Boundaries

Edited by
Miguel Mantero, University of Alabama
Paul Chamness Miller, Akita International University
John L. Watzke, University of Portland

Available at all bookstores and online vendors:
ISBN-10: 0977911411
ISBN-13: 9780977911400
Publisher: International Society for Language Studies, Inc.
Publication Date: 2008
Paperback: 652 pages; 35 Chapters
Average price: $39.00 paperback; $55.00 hardcover

READINGS IN LANGUAGE STUDIES
VOLUME 2
Language and Power

Edited by
John L. Watzke, University of Portland
Paul Chamness Miller, Akita International University
Miguel Mantero, University of Alabama

Available at all bookstores and online vendors:
ISBN-10: 097791142X
ISBN-13: 9789780977911424
Publisher: International Society for Language Studies, Inc.
Publication Date: 2010
Paperback: 466 pages; 23 Chapters
Average price: $45.00 paperback; $60.00 hardcover

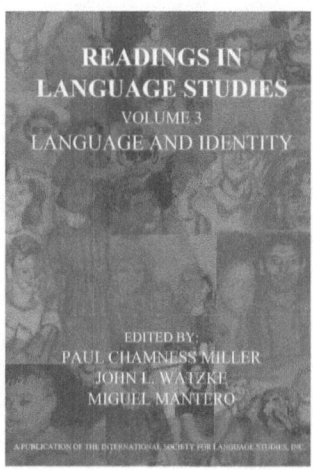

READINGS IN LANGUAGE STUDIES
VOLUME 3
Language and Identity

Edited by
Paul Chamness Miller, Akita International University
John L. Watzke, University of Portland
Miguel Mantero, University of Alabama

Available at all bookstores and online vendors:
ISBN-10: 0977911446
ISBN-13: 9780977911448
Publisher: International Society for Language Studies, Inc.
Publication Date: 2012
Paperback: 467 pages; 32 Chapters
Average price: $50.00 paperback; $63.00 hardcover

READINGS IN LANGUAGE STUDIES
VOLUME 4
Language and Social Justice

Edited by
Miguel Mantero, University of Alabama
John L. Watzke, University of Portland
Paul Chamness Miller, Akita International University

Available at all bookstores and online vendors:
ISBN-10: 0977911462
ISBN-13: 9780977911462
Publisher: International Society for Language Studies, Inc.
Publication Date: 2014
Paperback: 348 pages; 18 Chapters
Average price: $30.00 paperback; $60.00 hardcover

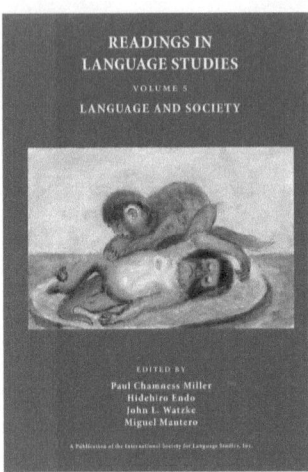

READINGS IN LANGUAGE STUDIES
VOLUME 5
Language and Society

Edited by
Paul Chamness Miller, Akita International University
Hidehiro Endo, Akita International University
John L. Watzke, University of Portland
Miguel Mantero, University of Alabama

Available at all bookstores and online vendors:
ISBN-10: 0977911497
ISBN-13: 9780977911493
Publisher: International Society for Language Studies, Inc.
Publication Date: 2015
Paperback: 316 pages; 14 Chapters
Average price: $30.00 paperback; $45.00 hardcover

Publications of the International Society for Language Studies, Inc.
To learn more about ISLS and its mission, visit their website:

www.isls.co

ISLS retains a low membership fee that includes:
a quarterly journal, monthly newsletter, and a reduced conference rate.

www.ingramcontent.com/pod-product-compliance
Lightning Source LLC
Chambersburg PA
CBHW030434300426
44112CB00009B/998